The Art of

OFFICIATING SPORTS

The Art of
OFFICIATING SPORTS

John W. Bunn
Professor of Physical Education and Director of Athletics, Springfield College, Springfield, Massachusetts

and

OTHERS

PRENTICE-HALL, INC.

NEW YORK 1950

PRENTICE-HALL, INC.
70 FIFTH AVENUE, NEW YORK

PRINTED IN THE UNITED STATES OF AMERICA

Collaborators

SWIMMING and DIVING — CHARLES E. SILVIA
Professor of Physical Education and Coach of Swimming, Springfield College, Springfield, Mass.

VOLLEYBALL and HANDBALL . . . . MARSHALL L. WALTERS
Associate Professor of Physical Education, Springfield College, Springfield, Mass. Editor, Annual Volleyball Guide and Rule Book.

SOCCER . . . . LAWRENCE E. BRIGGS
Coach of Soccer, University of Massachusetts, Amherst, Mass.

WRESTLING . . . . . ERASTUS W. PENNOCK
Chairman, New England District Committee for Approved Wrestling Officials, Springfield College, Springfield, Mass.

SKIING . . . . ROBERT ROCK
Section of National Ski Patrol System, Springfield College, Springfield, Mass.

Introduction

OFFICIATING IS AN IMPORTANT PHASE OF ATHLETICS that has been very much neglected until recently. Because poor officiating detracts so much from the enjoyment of spectators and players, and results in dissatisfaction and bitterness, efforts to improve it have increased in recent years.

To produce better officials, amateur and professional sports organizations have studied and conducted research in the officiating of the various sports and have organized schools and clinics for officials. These efforts have done much to improve officiating. However, until recently, an additional, definite need in the field of sports was an authoritative and up-to-date book on sports officiating. Such a textbook, experts agreed, should bring together all of the data that had been developed on officiating the different sports. Material on the techniques and mechanics of officiating was also needed in this volume, since this very important aspect of officiating had never been adequately stressed.

Fortunately for everyone concerned, such a volume on officiating has been prepared by John W. Bunn, with the assistance of a group of authorities in different sports. THE ART OF OFFICIATING SPORTS is an outstanding contribution to physical education literature and will be welcomed by officials in the various sports as well as by the instructors of professional courses in officiating at teacher education institutions.

ARTHUR A. ESSLINGER
Department of Health and Physical Education
Springfield College

Preface

THIS BOOK HAS BEEN PLANNED PRIMARILY FOR USE IN courses on officiating. However, it is also written to serve as a handbook on officiating for those who are engaged in administering sports programs. It brings together the best information available for the administration of a large variety of sports. The material in each sport has been compiled by experts in coaching and officiating that sport. For many years such a treatment has been needed to fill the gap in a field that has been growing in importance with each season. Students, teachers, coaches, and officials will find this information indispensable in their work.

The book is divided into three logical parts. Part I lays a foundation for the job of officiating in general. It states a point of view, it discusses the qualifications for an official, and it lists some general principles that are necessary for the efficient and successful administration of a sport. This part is designed to cover all sports and proposes to build a pattern by which the greatest uniformity may be attained. Parts II and III apply the theses developed in Part I to specific sports.

The activities covered in this book have been divided into two groups according to the nature and type of officiating required by each. Some sports, for the most part, require a decision on every single action that takes place. The officiating required in this type of sport may be likened to a true-false test. Baseball, track, and tennis are typical of this group of activities. In baseball, for example, a decision must be made on every pitch. It is a strike or a ball. The ball, when hit, is fair or foul. The base runner is either safe or out. The umpire must make a declaration on every action that takes place. The official is usually stationary in such a game. He must, however, be alert every minute. He is under constant tension. For convenience, the sports that fit into this category are grouped together in Part II.

The sports that generally require discriminating judgments by the official—sports in which his decision depends upon the effect created by the players and the rules that permit him to exercise discretion—are grouped together in Part III. Football, basketball, wrestling, soccer, and lacrosse are typical of this group. The officiating techniques for each of these are treated in exactly the same fashion as those for sports in Part II.

Each sport is treated separately and the techniques required of the official in each are explained in detail. In addition, those play situations that cause the official the greatest concern, those that are likely to create a divergence of judgments, or those that need the special attention of officials are given particular treatment.

By this comprehensive coverage of many sports the necessity for a large and expensive library of the many pamphlets and guides in various sports has been eliminated. And, much valuable material that has not been recorded previously is also presented.

No attempt has been made to present the rules *in toto*. These change too often to justify their inclusion in a volume of this kind. The reader has been provided, however, with the foundations necessary for the proper interpretation and administration of rules in general.

The unique feature of the book is the emphasis on the guiding philosophy that forms the basis for the judgment and decisions by the official in each sport. This philosophy helps the official to orient himself with respect to his activity. The reader should acquaint himself thoroughly with this phase of the book (Part I) before proceeding to the study of the techniques of each of the individual sports.

The author if deeply indebted to those who have so willingly and generously contributed to, and assisted in the preparation of, that part of the manuscript which deals with the individual sports, and to those who have permitted the use of materials from other publications. Without their co-operation and expert knowledge in the field of their specialties, this book would not have been possible. To all of them, my warmest thanks.

JOHN W. BUNN

Contents

Part I

Part II

Part III

Figures

Diagrams

Forms

The Art of

OFFICIATING SPORTS

Part I

FUNDAMENTAL PRINCIPLES

I

The Job

THE PRIMARY JOB OF AN OFFICIAL IS TO CAUSE THE game or contest to progress with as little interference as possible on his part. Officiating is an art. The individual who can develop this art from his potentialities can become a successful official.

The first sentence connotes some definite practices and attitudes on the part of the official. It relates the official to the game and to the contestants in a specific role. The following are considered essential if the official is successfully to perform his duties.

THE POTENTIAL OF PRESENCE

The official who through the influence of his presence causes players to avoid rule violations has attained the perfect relationship to the game. His influence is felt, but he himself is not noticed. Probably no single rule or set of personal characteristics can be listed which each official must have in order to approach this relationship. Neither is there necessarily a set pattern. Men are individuals and many reach the same goal, but usually by entirely different and devious routes. Likewise, no two games or situations are the same.

The successful official, by some combination of characteristics and through some pattern which may vary from game to game, creates an influence which causes the players

Be felt, not heard, as much as possible

to avoid rule infractions. Confidence and co-operation are established. The players somehow seem to sense that here is a man who is on the job; he is in the right place at the right time; he is fair; he is consistent; he has understanding; and he senses the significance of each situation.

Time or several experiences with the same official are not primarily necessary to establish this relationship. It may happen the very first time an official works a particular game. Recently, the author had occasion to recommend an official for a very important basketball game. The man recommended was in no way known to any of the parties concerned. He was chosen as the official for the game.

The game was a hard fought one. However, it was not five minutes old until it was evident that the players had complete confidence in the official. The game—bitterly contested—was played in the smoothest fashion. Seldom have more complimentary remarks been heard concerning the work of an official. Somehow or other, this man made his influence felt at the outset. He could have almost literally retired from the floor after the first quarter and the game would have progressed satisfactorily.

The opposite results have been attained at times by the same official. On occasions, it seems that in spite of the efforts of the arbiter, the game goes badly. Much whistle blowing is necessitated. The play is not smooth. It may be the players, the official, the particular game that evening, or a combination of factors. Somehow the official never seems to gain control. He has not hit upon the right formula or sensed the situation.

The author's basketball teams have traveled throughout the country and have experienced many kinds of officiating and many types of officials. It has been interesting to note that the officials either established their influence, or failed to establish it, right at the beginning of the game. The initial reaction is seldom changed. The players invariably reflect in their play the influence of the officials

Win friends but don't violate principles

on the game. The same may be said for officials in other sports.

OFFICIAL–PLAYER RAPPORT

A personal relationship which breeds friendliness and trust and not antagonism is essential to successful game control.

Several years ago, a friend presented my wife with a dog, a registered schnauzer. The pup felt strange, looked sad, and remained aloof when it was put into our automobile to be taken away. However, as soon as the car was out of sight of the dog's former home and she was cut off from the other pups and her mother, she accepted her new mistress with complete devotion. She crawled close and laid her head in my wife's lap and looked trustingly up into her face. From that moment, there was complete understanding. The dog would have given her life henceforth for her new mistress.

What brought about this relationship? One can speculate endlessly. All that is definitely known is that perfect rapport was established between dog and mistress. Likewise, one sees a harmonious relationship between players and officials without knowing exactly how it is brought about.

Some officials have attained it by extra-strict tactics at the beginning of a game. Others, by a stern, firm, but courteous, attitude. And still others by a warm, pleasant, friendly, and helpful approach. Some officials have used an authoritative approach, while others have been more humble yet sincere. Some have put fear into the hearts of players, but with it have won their respect.

Here again it must be said that right approaches must be used to fit the occasion. Also, each individual must follow that tack which seems to fit best his own personality. No one method will fit all situations or all officials. The art of being one's self and being able to sense the correct ap-

Use your strong points to win respect

proach to each situation is the secret of establishing the correct rapport.

When one sees a game in which the players are in conflict with the official, one may know that the official is either incompetent from the standpoint of rules and mechanics or that he lacks those personal qualities which help create mutuality between himself and the players. Sometimes he is lacking both essentials.

GOOD PUBLIC RELATIONS

An official may make his influence felt effectively by the players and develop the finest relationships with them, but be an anathema to the spectators. The mannerisms of the official may arouse the antagonism of the public. If an official gives the audience the impression that he is arrogant, if he is dramatic to the extent that he becomes the center of attraction and detracts from the game itself, if he is overly officious, if he gives the impression of being antagonistic, then he is likely to draw the condemnation of the spectators. Such a relationship unfortunately creates an undesirable crowd behavior and thus reflects on the contest. Likewise, the official who seems excitable or who reacts slowly or who seems indecisive or who does not interpret his decisions or make them clear for the spectators, will have difficulty in establishing good public relations.

Specific personal qualifications of a good official will be discussed in the next chapter. The attempt here is to impress upon the individual that he should be the strong, silent man; that he should dominate the play, but be noticed as little as possible. He should remember that the sport was created for the players and not for the official; that his success can be measured by the degree to which he keeps the game going within the rules, with as little interference as possible on his part. If the players comport themselves as if no official were present and yet accept his decisions without question; if he controls or wins the crowd to the extent

Be pleasant, but firm and fearless

that when the whistle blows or he pauses to announce a decision, it waits eagerly to get the official action and then agrees with the decision—that official can be assured that he has arrived. He'll be in constant demand and he'll find himself amply repaid for his efforts. He'll reap tremendous satisfaction out of the realization that he is contributing immeasurably to the greatest of our American institutions—sports.

Officiating is one of the most difficult jobs related to sports. By many it is considered a thankless task. On the other hand, it produces a dynamic challenge. For the individual who has inherited the necessary attributes which go to make up a high-class official and who has developed these traits to the point where he has gained the acclaim of players and spectators for his performance, there is tremendous personal satisfaction.

Larry Newman [1] attested to the difficulty of officiating when he wrote his parody on Joyce Kilmer's lovely "Trees."

Referees

I think that I shall never see
A satisfactory referee
About whose head a halo shines
Whose merits rate reporter's lines
One who calls them as they are
And not as I should wish, by far.

A gent who leans not either way
But lets the boys decide the play
A guy who'll sting the coach who yaps
From Siwash Hi or old Millsaps
Poems are made by fools like me
But only God could referee.

[1] Larry Newman, *Referees* (Springfield Union, March 29, 1948).

2

Qualifications of An Official

THE ART OF OFFICIATING IS LARGELY DEPENDENT UPON human variables. It is good or bad in accordance with the degree to which each individual has a favorable combination of these variables together with an intelligent understanding of the application of the rules. The more important personal qualities which most authorities agree are necessary in a good official will be discussed in this chapter. These are the factors which will help provide "the potential of presence," "official–player rapport," and "good public relations" if developed and applied artfully.

At the outset, the young official should be advised that he be himself in all cases. He may have an older and more experienced official as an example, but unless he has all the characteristics of his model, he should not try to mimic him. The tyro can gain much valuable information by watching the techniques of his idol, but they should be adopted only to the extent that they fit his own personality.

The following qualities are listed in the order of their importance and in the reverse order of the control which the individual has over each quality. These qualities may be used as factors in a rating scale, so that one may give himself a self-test of his personal qualities. By use of a point system in which 5 is excellent; 4, above average; 3, average; 2, below average; and 1, inferior, he may get a

Be yourself

quantitative estimate of where he stands in relation to his fellow officials. The qualified officials average 4 or better.

REACTION TIME

This quality is placed first on the list because one either has quick reaction time or one does not have it. Likewise, by a little practice, one reaches the maximum of one's potentialities in this quality. Additional practice does not change the results materially. A person who does not possess above-average reaction time has little chance of becoming a top-grade official.

> Split second decisions must be made. The tempo of games is such that unless the official can react quickly enough to make his decision at the moment the action occurs, subsequent play will have confused the situation. A deliberate, slow-reacting official will let play get out of hand. The best method of gaining the confidence of players is to make decisions at the time a player is going through his maneuver. A player is often unconscious of the fact that he is committing a foul or violation. If, for instance, a player is pushing or holding illegally and the act is called to his attention while he is pushing or holding, he is likely to have the greatest respect for and confidence in the official in the future. In addition, he is often surprised to find that he has developed a habit which is contrary to the rules. By good officiating with respect to reaction time in this instance, the official is making a player conscious of mistakes and thus helping him to correct them.

If, after considerable experience in officiating, the aspirant finds that he is always late in making decisions, he has rather conclusive evidence that he is not likely to become a successful official. Without this first essential—fast reaction time—he has little favorable prospect.

During the war, the author was refereeing a basketball game in which the great St. Mary's preflight team was

React quickly

participating. One of the outstanding players on that team, a former college star, had unconsciously developed the habit of pushing an opponent who was in front of him and jumping to rebound the ball. In quick succession, three personal fouls, all for this type of pushing, were called on the player while he was still in the act of pushing. He was embarrassed when he was made conscious of his foul and realized that he had his hands on the small of the back of his opponent.

As a result, every time thereafter, when he was in a rebound position, he deliberately restrained himself. He did not commit another foul during the game and corrected a habit which he had developed without being aware of it.

CONFIDENCE

There are many factors which reflect the confidence of an official and which gain the confidence of competitors, coaches, and spectators. Probably the most effective characteristic is the manner in which he comports himself in carrying out his duties. A movement which denotes sureness—even a degree of cockiness, when not carried to the stage where it causes resentment—transmits a feeling of confidence to others.

Decisive action which is not hasty but which has no element of hesitation is highly desirable. It leaves no question of doubt in the minds of others. It portrays positiveness which wins acceptance. For example, balls or strikes in a baseball game should be called instantly and with conviction. To be apologetic or hesitant conveys the idea of uncertainty. It even leaves the suspicion that the umpire by his delay is being influenced by the catcher or other players. Certainly the time to make the decision is the moment when the ball passes the plate. The after-image may be distorted.

A resonant, strong voice is a great asset to an official in

Spread confidence—not distrust

those sports in which vocal announcement of decisions is necessary. By means of a clear, strong voice, the official is able to convey to all, particularly the participants, the exact decisions which he has made. His voice properly pitched, carrying conviction, displaying firmness, can do more to breed confidence and give poise than any other factor. A baritone quality is probably best; a high-pitched voice is poorest. Tennis is an example of a sport in which the voice is all important. Not only the decisions on play but a running account of the game and match must be given repeatedly. It is the only means whereby both players and spectators can be kept informed of the progress of the play. In this sport the voice becomes of primary significance.

The use of the voice supplemented by pantomime for the purpose of clarity in signaling decisions is desirable. Only a few of our officials have mastered the acting stage of their art. Most of our officials have not developed the techniques of using their voices and motions effectively.

Officials tend to be too timid in this phase of officiating. They display indistinctness and indefiniteness in conveying their decisions to the players and spectators. As a result, they sometimes create a lack of confidence toward themselves.

On the other hand, it should be emphasized that dramatics carried to the extreme of putting on a show or of entertaining are definitely frowned upon. Such tactics take attention from the game and the players and focus it upon the official.

If a whistle is used, it can do much to give a feeling of certainty. The whistle should be blown to produce a sharp, staccato sound—not a slow, feeble, extended wheeze.

CALMNESS

The excitable official contributes more than the players to a raggedly played game. As a matter of fact, a highly

Make decisions clearly

nervous official usually upsets the equilibrium of a team and even induces jumpiness among the players.

Players, particularly the younger and more immature ones, are usually nervous, and they play under considerable tension. Consequently, any actions which will produce calmness and emotional control should be employed. The better official will inject sufficient pauses and quieting maneuvers to create a steadying effect upon the contestants. He will do this throughout the game and particularly toward the end, when a closely contested affair might otherwise become disorganized and players become so overwrought that pleasing performance would be impossible.

There are many play situations in which the official's quiet influence can be a saving grace. The official may employ several tactics to relieve the tension. They are actions which are seldom noticed and yet are tremendously effective.

As an example, a warm friendly attitude on the part of the official has a disarming and relaxing effect upon players; yes, even upon spectators. An official who makes his decisions with a show of belligerency or intensity or with a "there, I caught you that time" expression often arouses the animosity of the players (and the spectators) and thus heightens tension. On the other hand, the official who makes his decisions just as firmly, but with a smile and a friendly manner which says, "I'm sorry, but unfortunately you made a mistake and I have no alternative," tends not only to inject a bit of relief into an otherwise hectic scene but also to create a cheerful atmosphere between opponents, which makes for a better game—certainly one that is easier to officiate. The oft quoted expression, "A soft answer turneth away wrath," applies perfectly.

It seems that the best officials are those who remain human and approachable. It is observed that they are always most warmly received; usually they are accepted even when they are wrong. At least, everyone is more

Be calm at all times

charitable toward them when there is disagreement with their judgments. The players invariably react favorably toward such an official. They respect him and co-operate with him. On the other hand, the official with a chip on his shoulder is disliked and quite often distrusted. It is surprising how frequently he engenders the ill will of everyone at a game. He may be feared by the players, but he is seldom rated above average by them. It often appears that he is presenting a brusque exterior as a cloak behind which to hide inferior ability. It is surprising that an official who has developed unfortunate mannerisms or who presents negative personality traits does not realize that they reflect adversely upon his effectiveness, so that he may, therefore, seriously work to change them.

Deliberate moves are sometimes indicated in the progress of a game. In basketball, for instance, when handling the ball out of bounds, the official can restore poise by even, unhurried action rather than hasty, impatient motions. Likewise, hesitation on free throws, to permit adjustments at the free-throw lines and to give clear, complete information on the number of shots, tends to ease the situation considerably. It may even steady the nerves of the free thrower.

Quietly reporting a penalty to the referee in football, oblivious to the mounting fury that one senses on the part of the guilty player, usually avoids a heated scene. Holding one's gaze on a play in baseball, after a decision is made, seems to reduce the pressure that appears to be developing in opposition to the decision.

A pause before announcing a decision, after blowing the whistle to stop play, is effective in keeping play under control. It also causes the players and spectators to hesitate and turn expectantly to the official to get his decision. Timing the announcement of decisions in this way tends to carry the crowd along in a more co-operative fashion. If the voice is also steady, the result is doubly effective.

Do you excite or soothe?

As has been stated, the subtleness of tactics of this kind hides the intent, but nevertheless produces the desired results.

CONSISTENCY

Consistency is the greatest virtue which an official can possess. He may have a warped interpretation of a rule; he may practice techniques contrary to those to which a team is accustomed; his judgment on some play situations may vary from the commonly accepted pattern—but with it all, if the official's practice and decision are exactly the same under the same or similar circumstances, players can readily adjust their play to fit the official. They may be surprised and confused momentarily, but when they discover that the official is unwavering in his procedures, they can reorganize their play and continue the game with confidence.

On the other hand, if an official is vacillating in his methods and decisions, he will disrupt the play of a team. He will keep the players in a dither and upset them emotionally, so that their effectiveness is lost entirely. Situations have occurred in which players have become so wrought up that they had to be removed from the game.

A few examples of these two situations will more clearly point up the importance of consistency and the disaster which accompanies the absence of it.

In baseball, some umpires have the habit of giving the batter the benefit of the doubt on all low balls. When pitchers learn this and find that the umpire is consistent, no difficulty arises. But if one time the call is a ball, and the next time a similar pitch is a strike, then both the pitcher and the batter become disturbed and much bickering results.

The football linesman who becomes hypertechnical on offside play at one time, and extremely lenient the next, can throw the timing of both lines into a frenzy.

Be consistent

Some years ago, teams which traveled to New York to play basketball found a great difference in officiating practices. But they also found that there was the greatest consistency in these practices. For example, guarding from the rear was permitted so long as a player in the rear could get his hands on the ball. It seemed not to matter if such a player was clamping down on the arms of his opponent or if he had him in a tight embrace so long as he had his hand or hands on the ball.

At the other extreme, there was the strictest practice with respect to blocking, or picking off as it was called. In this connection, if an offensive player so much as moved in a manner that made it appear that he was intending to interfere with the free movement of his opponent, he was guilty of blocking, though there was no contact whatever.

The reverse of these situations was at the same time prevalent in the northern section of the Pacific Coast. There, a slight brush from the rear drew a whistle with the announcement of a foul. Screening was permitted to the extent of actually rolling into an opponent so that contact occurred without penalty.

The fact that two extremes existed in the same locality and that the opposite practice was in vogue at the other side of the continent would seem to augur for chaos when teams from the two sections met. However, this was not the case. The officials' decisions were so consistent that players after an initial surprise quickly adjusted themselves to the strange conditions and played with little or no handicap.

In basketball, probably the greatest inconsistencies occur in judgments on charging and blocking and with respect to personal fouls. If, one time, a dribbler is penalized for charging and the next time the opponent is penalized for blocking under identical circumstances, players are very much at sea. Likewise, when a highly technical decision is made and then a flagrant act is passed unnoticed, players are finally forced to resign themselves to the hopelessness of the situation. It is not always the novice in the official's job who commits these errors. Some of the most experienced are guilty.

As justification for his decision, the official will hide behind the screen of creating a different situation in his mind. Officials have been known to say, "I have been calling them that way for twenty years." The rejoinder to that one is, "You don't want to make the same mistake for the next twenty years, do you?"

But when the preponderance of evidence is against the official from unbiased sources, one is forced to conclude that the official either has poor judgment or has no sound foundation upon which to base his decisions. More often the latter condition is the reason for the great variation in an official's decision on relatively the same situations.

Of course, some officials may never be able to attain a high degree of consistency. They should be eliminated from games, just as the incapable players are gradually weeded out of the squad and do not get a chance to play with the first team. However, much can be done to point the way and set guides by which all officials may arrive at uniformity and consistency. The presentations in later chapters are intended for this purpose.

JUDGMENT

Judgment and consistency go hand in hand. They are Siamese twins. If basic principles are established which will be the guide for determining the legality of play and the responsibility for acts committed, the foundation upon which to develop judgment has been laid. If these basic principles are thoroughly understood, then sound judgment will be built up through experience in handling contests. One needs to practice the art of officiating in order to become proficient, in the same way that a player must practice the technique of the game in order to develop his skill. It is not absolutely necessary to have played a game in order to qualify as an official. To have been a player, however, gives one an understanding of and a background for officiating which is invaluable.

The young official is likely at first to feel lost and incapable of discriminating between legal play and violations and fouls. Play may even appear as a blur of movement out of which he is unable to distinguish any pattern whatever. Under such circumstances, he will probably be hesitant to act. Such a state of confusion need not deter him in the least. With continued practice, the picture will gradually clear. Good judgment will develop with experience. If the official possesses the qualities already mentioned, he should not be discouraged by any difficulties which present themselves during his early training period.

CO-OPERATION

In contests which require more than one official, the ability to team with fellow officials is absolutely essential to a well-handled game. The men should gauge their decisions so that they are as uniform as possible. If they diverge to any great extent, the game will be conducted in a very erratic fashion.

Each must have faith in the other, and there must exist the greatest harmony. Any tendency for one official to attempt to dominate the game may cause a poorly administered game. Likewise, if one official is so sensitive that he resents the other for making decisions on plays which he feels are his responsibility, harmonious relationship between them may be destroyed. Rather, each should welcome the support of the other. Each should realize that he is not always in an advantageous position to see all the action, even though he is close to the play. Each should be ready to cover play for the other when one is momentarily caught out of position.

Assist, don't resist fellow officials

There are occasions when the personalities of officials clash. Their temperaments, mannerisms, tactics, seem to conflict rather than blend. Their general analyses of play are often antithetic. When these differences become evident and seem to be fundamentally difficult to resolve, then these officials should not work in the same game. Each may otherwise be an excellent official in his own right.

There must be a spirit of mutuality and of team play for effective game administration. Without this complete cooperation, there is not likely to be good game administration, even though the officials have all the other essential qualities.

KNOWLEDGE OF THE RULES

Knowledge of the rules, the mechanics of movement, and the duties of the officials prior to and during a game are listed near the end of this chapter on qualifications of an official because any individual with even average intelligence can learn the rules and duties and can practice the mechanics of officiating. The development of these qualities is one of the functions of the officials' organizations.

It is desirable that an official know the rules perfectly. He should review the rules many times before each season begins. But this alone is not enough. A perfect knowledge of the rules would not in itself guarantee good officiating.

It is essential also that the official know the relationship of one rule to another. Further, it is most important that he have a background for the rules: if the reason why a rule has been inserted into the official guide is understood, if the history of the evolution and development of the rule in connection with the progress of the game is known, and if the official interpretation of the rule in its application to play situations is clear and properly related to the literal wording of the rule, he is most likely to administer the rules intelligently during a game. It is the job of the

Know—don't guess

officials' associations and athletic conferences and leagues to furnish this information to officials. Through their delegated officers these organizations should continually work at the job of indoctrinating officials with the above information.

Many sports, such as football, soccer, and basketball, do not permit a literal interpretation of the rules. Rather, the official must make his decisions largely on the effect a violation of the rules has upon the play in a particular situation. An official who would insist on a literal construction would ruin the play in such games. In these sports the official must make judgments and decisions within his discretion.

In football, many instances of violations of the rules in the use of the arms in blocking have no effect whatever on the play. Consequently, the violations are ignored or the violator is quietly warned of his practice before he commits an offense which really places his opponent at a disadvantage.

In basketball, essentially a noncontact game, there are no end of instances of contact. However, only that contact which materially affects the play is recognized.

On the other hand, baseball, track, tennis, and swimming require exactness in practically all decisions. In addition, a decision must be made on each play. The official, while largely stationary, must be constantly alert and poised, ready for every single play.

In baseball, every ball thrown to the plate by the pitcher when in position, must be called a ball or a strike. Every hit ball is fair or foul. The baserunner is either safe or out.

In tennis, the serve is in or out of the service court. The ball hit was in the court or was outside. A decision must be made.

Likewise, in track or swimming, one competitor finishes first, another second, and so on. A choice must be exercised. There is not the opportunity to make decisions about the action as a whole; each situation is separate and distinct and should be ruled literally.

It is an understanding of these differentiations which discriminates between the competent official and the incompetent one. Knowledge of the rules is not complete without this understanding.

Various play situations and background for interpretations of rules are presented in Parts II and III.

DUTIES OF OFFICIALS, MECHANICS OF OFFICIATING

Rules vary in the completeness of the instructions concerning the duties of officials. For the most part, only general directions are given for the administration of the rules. For example, the Basketball Guide, with the exception of describing the relation between the scorers and timers and referee, presents only two specific directions for the guidance of the officials in controlling the actions of the players during the progress of the game. In only one instance is there any mention of officials in the tennis rules. In contrast to this, the Track Guide has developed a pattern in great detail for the officials in both the track and field events.

To implement the rules, manuals for officiating have been created by various groups under the auspices of authorized conferences and associations. These manuals present complete patterns of action for all the officials for all situations prior to, during, and at the conclusion of actual play. Some of them go so far as to designate which official should provide for transportation for the other officials.

It is the duty of every official to know exactly where he should be, what he should look for, and how to support and co-operate with his fellow officials on every play situation which may occur during a contest. These are the mechanics of officiating. An official who is in the right place

At least look efficient

at the right time will, at least, look efficient. He will be where he can make decisions when necessary.

The techniques which are contained in these manuals represent a development which has evolved through years of experience in handling athletic activities. There is great uniformity throughout the country. A few differences in practice do appear, so that it is the job of the official to acquaint himself with the fashion in the locality where he operates.

Not only will the essential features of the various habits in officiating be presented in this text, but in addition, a background to justify the practice will be discussed. It is hoped that by such a logical and reasoned development, the official will have a more intelligent understanding of his duties.

APPEARANCE AND CONDITION

No man has any right to pose as an official, who is not willing to dress the part and to get into good physical condition. Almost every sport has a distinct uniform for the official. Some sections of the country adhere to special fashions. Each official should secure the proper uniform and should be sure that it fits. He should at all times present a neat, clean appearance. Figures 1 and 2 show two sets of officials properly attired. The men in figure 1 are dressed for basketball and those in figure 2 for baseball. Their neat, tailored, athletic appearance is evident. It will be noticed that one official is wearing glasses. The fact that an official wears glasses should not disqualify him. If he needs glasses for perfect sight under normal circumstances, he should wear them when he officiates.

Officiating requires the best physical condition. It will not be possible for a man to be alert and to perform successfully at a high standard throughout a game unless he is in top condition. He should, therefore, start strenuous

Figure 1. Basketball officials in official uniform. Note neat, athletic appearance.

training before his first assignment. Leg strength and endurance (heart power) should receive his attention. Some practice officiating before the season opens is just as essential to the official as play practice is to the athlete. Even those sports, such as baseball, in which the official is comparatively stationary, demand an alertness and a con-

FIGURE 2. BASEBALL OFFICIALS IN OFFICIAL UNIFORMS. MAN ON THE RIGHT IS WEARING CHIN GUARDS AND CHEST PROTECTOR UNDER UNIFORM; NOTE INDICATOR IN RIGHT HAND. MAN ON THE LEFT IS PROPERLY EQUIPPED FOR DUTIES AS FIELD UMPIRE.

centration which necessitate top physical condition for the best performance.

It is surprising how neatness of dress and a conditioned athletic appearance will make a favorable impression on the spectators and players.

The foregoing emphases on qualifications are worth the most serious attention by officials. Since, to a certain extent, officiating is a profitable business, it is not too much to expect each official to come to a game fully qualified and prepared to measure up to the highest standards. Many officials earn as much as $1,500 during a season in one sport; scores of them will pick up $250 to $500. This money represents extra earnings, since most officials hold regular jobs. Officiating is their side line.

3

A Basic Philosophy

EACH OFFICIAL SHOULD HAVE A DEFINITE AND CLEAR conception of his over-all responsibility, when he reports for duty. If all officials possessed the same conception, then there would be the greatest uniformity in administration of all contests.

Some years ago, Mr. Oswald Tower expressed an opinion on the application of the basketball rules to the game by the official. No other individual is better qualified to speak on this subject. He has been a member of the Basketball Rules Committee since 1910. As editor and official interpreter of the basketball guide since 1914, he has watched the game develop and the rules evolve. He has been able to view the work of officials from a detached, objective vantage point, since he is neither coaching nor administering athletics. His opinions bear the weight of a sage. They are entitled to serious consideration and evaluation by coaches and officials.

Mr. Tower is a modest and retiring man. Consequently, his opinion on the application of the rules by the official has never been presented in written form before as a basic philosophy upon which the whole officiating structure should be built.

The essence of his utterance is: *It is the purpose of the rules to penalize a player who by reason of an illegal act has placed his opponent at a disadvantage.*

It is not only what happens, but also what effect it has on the play

Here is the most realistic approach by which a common but intelligent understanding of the rules may be reached. It puts a tool into the hands of the official for his use in implementing the rules during the game. Tower's statement was applied to basketball, but it represents the underlying principles which guide the judgment of officials in making decisions on all situations where the effect upon the play is the factor in determining whether or not a rule violation has occurred.

The following examples chosen from the football, soccer, and basketball rules are presented to illustrate and substantiate the application of this philosophy. In football, at least seven players of the team in possession of the ball, must be on the line of scrimmage when the ball is snapped (Rule 7, section 2). The same rule states that no player of either team may be ahead of his line of scrimmage when the ball is snapped. Yet, anyone who has ever acted as a head lineman knows that, on many occasions, one or more of the players of the team in possession of the ball may be behind the line of scrimmage, and the fact is ignored. Immature linemen seem to form a "V" with the ball as the apex, so that all the linemen except the center and guards are not legally on the line. Such a situation operates to the detriment of the team violating the rule and, therefore, seldom if ever, draws a penalty. Similarly, players may line up slightly off side with only a warning from the official. In such cases no real advantage is gained by using these innocent tactics, and, likewise, the opponents are not placed at any disadvantage.

Rule 10, section 2, of the football rules states that each player of the team in possession of the ball, except the runner or passer, must have his hand or hands in contact with the body when contacting an opponent with said hand, hands, or arms. The purpose of the rule is, of course, to prevent a player from reaching out with the hands to interfere for a teammate with the ball. It is also to prevent striking with the hands or fists. Blocking is supposed to take place with the body, and only the arms under the limitations mentioned above are allowed.

If one were to apply the rule literally, a foul would have occurred if a space could be detected between the player's body and his hand when he was blocking with that hand or arm. However, no capable official will administer the rule in this fashion. Instead, he judges the act in terms of the total situation and the effect any deviation from the exact rule may have on the play.

Rule 10, section 7, of the basketball rules says in part: "A player shall not contact an opponent with his hand unless such contact is only with the opponent's hand while it is on the ball. . . ." If one were to administer this part of the rule literally, the game would be one of continual fouls. Even the most technical officials do not go to that extreme in their whistle blowing. The more outstanding officials realize that contact not only in this instance but in other phases as well must be viewed in the light of the effect it creates. If there is no apparent disadvantage to the opponent, then, in reality, no rule violation has occurred. The official must use discretion in applying the rule.

In soccer, a player may be off side, but if in the opinion of the official such player is not interfering with the play (that is, the opponents are not placed at a disadvantage), a violation need not be called. The decision is within the discretion of the official.

These examples (and there are others) taken from the rules themselves, should furnish sufficient evidence to establish the logic of our basic philosophy. They should convince even the most skeptical that here is the only realistic solution to the hue and cry about too much whistle blowing.

Weigh the effect of all acts

In essence, this philosophy states:

> It is not the intent that the rules shall be interpreted literally. Rather, they should be applied in relation to the effect which the action of players has upon their opponents. If they are unfairly affected as a result of a violation of the rules, then the transgressor should be penalized. If there has been no appreciable effect upon the progress of the game, then the game should not be interrupted. The act should be ignored. It is incidental and not vital. Realistically and practically, no violation has occurred.

This whole philosophy presupposes that the official has a thorough understanding of the game. It further assumes that he has been employed to officiate the game because he has sport intelligence. It expects him to exercise mature judgment in evaluating each play situation in the light of this basic philosophy.

Some officials will be confused by an officiating procedure of this kind. They are the ones who are looking for a mechanical device which may be used for making decisions. They are the literal-minded individuals, the strict constructionists. They have no faith in their judgment. Consequently, they feel insecure when presented with this kind of responsibility. They are inveterate whistle blowers, who are ruining our games. They want a rule for every little detail to replace judgment. They are the robots of sports who should be weeded out and replaced by human beings.

Officials and coaches are too concerned over minor unimportant details about play situations. Much time is wasted in digging up technicalities which are of little or no significance. Unfortunately, officials' meetings, rules clinics, and interpretation sessions get sidetracked too often by heated discussions over many of these nonessentials. Some situations might happen once in a lifetime. If they did, and no ready solution was at hand, no great harm

Are you realistic or hypertechnical?

would be done. From the officials' standpoint, it would be better to have overlooked the situation than to have worried unnecessarily beforehand. More profit can be gained by concentrating on the basic, fundamental issues. These should not be lost sight of by letting the technicalities cloud the picture.

This basic philosophy is the starting point from which a set of general principles have been developed and guides to specific play situations have been established. These are intended to supplement the primary tool and to give the official some handy devices by which he may implement the basic philosophy. They should also help him to develop a pattern by which he can be consistent in all his judgments.

The general principles follow in Chapter 4, and the guides to specific play situations appear in Parts II and III, where the techniques of officiating the various sports are discussed.

4

General Principles of Officiating

A BASIC PHILOSOPHY HAS BEEN STATED. ITS VALIDITY HAS been established from evidence and precedents which have been taken from the official rules. The logic of this philosophy has been developed in the interest of greater uniformity and consistency in officiating. The need for the elimination of excessive whistle blowing and for the reduction in the number of game interruptions has been clearly demonstrated.

To accomplish these goals, the following basic principles are presented. These are *six* principles chosen from a long list which might have been presented, because it was felt that these six were primary. They are given emphasis because they are the ones most often neglected. Failure to employ them gives rise to many of the wrong decisions which are made and to many of the unfair situations which develop during a game.

1. *The primary responsibility for good officiating and for uniform interpretation of the rules rests with the coaches whose teams create the officiating problems.*

Unless the coaches can agree on a uniform interpretation of the rules, and coach their players accordingly, the official has little chance to work satisfactorily for both teams. Whatever pattern he may follow in his work is likely to be in conflict with one of the teams.

The coaches in many sports have recognized this responsibility. The wrestling coaches have conducted training programs for officials for many years. Their procedure has been to discuss rules, to instruct officials in the techniques of officiating, and to conduct tryouts for qualifying officials. As a result, a mutual understanding exists between the officials and the coaches, and there is great harmony and confidence during the progress of their contests.

The soccer coaches have been carrying on similar programs, although not on quite so extensive a basis. In those sports which have become more commercialized, there has been a tendency for the coaches to divorce themselves from the officials. This does not augur for a mutual understanding, but the most serious fact is that the coaches themselves have not always had a common understanding.

The basketball coaches, for example, have not been entirely in harmony with respect to their understanding of the rules. However, there are at present fewer differences than there were ten years ago. Intersectional games and the national tournaments have helped to weld uniformity. The coaches themselves, alerted to their problems, are actively working to correct the situation.

2. *The officials have the responsibility of carrying out the policies adopted by the coaches or the organization which the coaches represent.*

The officials are employed by the organization which they represent. Consequently, they have no alternative but to work in accordance with the desires of their employers.

This obligation on the part of the officials further emphasizes the necessity for a uniform, nationwide interpretation of the rules by the coaches. It also assumes that this interpretation shall conform to that of the official

A necessity—close collaboration between coaches and officials

interpreter for the national rules committees of the various sports.

This principle connotes the necessity for a mutual association between the coaches and the officials' associations. If there is complete understanding between those who coach the teams and those who officiate the games, the most satisfactory results can be obtained.

Unfortunately, there has been a lack of co-operation, at least of common relationship, in this respect in too many of our sports. The fault has been largely that of the coaches. Usually, the officials have been eager to reach a meeting of the minds, but they have been left to operate alone.

Unless the coaches are willing to give the time and effort to this most essential undertaking, they have no justification for criticism of the type of arbitrating which they receive, and officials will be absolutely correct in passing the blame for their inability to satisfy right over to the coaches.

3. *The official must observe play from close quarters in order to make accurate judgments.*

In spite of the fact that the spectators at games do considerable second guessing, it is not possible to make correct judgments on most play situations without being within a few feet of the action. It is necessary to be close enough to determine the effect of maneuvers of all kinds. From a distance, the picture presented may have all the earmarks of foul play, while at close quarters little or no effect upon the play or on the movement or freedom of players has taken place.

In wrestling, for example, when a fall appears about to occur, the official must get his face close to the mat and sometimes use his hand to measure the situation in order to be able to rule correctly. It would be impossible for anyone from a distance to render a just decision. Holding in close line play in football requires that the umpire be within two or three yards of the total scene in order to give a fair ruling. Unless the umpire in baseball is right

Keep close to the play

on top of a close play when a runner slides into a base, he cannot be sure whether the runner is safe or out.

Because of the underwater touch at the finish of a swimming race, the judges must be next to the scene in a tight race to be able to pick the winner correctly.

4. *The official must see the total scene in order to be able to make a just decision.*

Three situations will clearly illustrate this principle. A player is dribbling a basketball with his back to an official. An opponent comes up from the rear, thrusts at the ball, and either knocks it away from the dribbler or misses it. The view of the official who is directly behind the dribbler is partly obscured so that he cannot see the arm of the defensive player as he reaches in front of the dribbler for the ball. There is no apparent charging or contact from the side. Since the official in the rear is unable to determine whether or not an illegal act has occurred, he is unable to make any decision. If he rules on suspicion, he may be doing an injustice to the defensive player, who may have performed a clever legal maneuver.

Unless an overt act is committed and is seen in its entirety by the official, he should refrain from acting. In this case, he should defer a decision to his colleague who is in front of the play. It is better to do nothing when all the facts are not available.

Jockeying for position on the center pivot play in basketball usually causes contact. Quite often the end court official, who is primarily responsible for this play, does not see the preliminary movement before the contact occurs. He must, of necessity, divide his attention between the ball and the action of players around the basket. Therefore, when he is attracted to the center pivot situation, he finds two opponents in a pushing contest; one is exerting pressure to maintain his position and the other is attempting to move him so that an advantage may be gained.

Since the official did not see the initial action, how can

Don't imagine or suspect—you must see it happen

he differentiate between the aggressor and defender of the position? Both are pushing for dear life. It is obvious that he cannot make a just decision. He can call a double foul, but if one of the players was wholly responsible for the original contact, then the other would be penalized unfairly. The official should see the action at its inception; otherwise, he should not make a decision. This particular type of play is not at all difficult to handle if the official will watch it develop. The players will quickly become aware of the fact that an official is on the job in this instance and they will eliminate the problem of their own accord. Here is an instance where the "potential of presence" eliminates illegal play.

The football rules specifically charge the officials with the responsibility of seeing the beginning, as well as the completed act, of clipping. If, when an official first sees the situation, a blocker is lying across the back of the legs of an opponent he shall not call a clipping penalty. The official must see the initial contact.

No criticism of officials is intended in this discussion. It is the duty of the official to see all and to know all. However, it must be realized that there are human limitations. Something may happen right in front of an official and entirely miss his attention because at that moment he was concentrating on another phase of play or he had his vision blocked by players. He did not encompass that which occurred in the periphery of his vision.

Coaches, players, spectators, need to recognize this fact. An official should be commended for his refusal to render a decision when he does not see the complete act. He should not be accused of partiality or lack of courage. It is remarkable that officials are able to see as much as they do. These particular situations can be kept at a minimum by techniques which will be discussed in Parts II and III.

5. *Officials must rule on acts completed—not on anticipation.*

Don't blow if you don't see

It is a common fault among officials to anticipate play to the extent that they make decisions too hastily. In basketball, two players go for a loose ball. Two players rebound the ball and both get their hands on it. A player sees an opportunity to steal the ball from an opponent. The official sees the action. He senses the possibility of a held ball or concludes that a held ball is inevitable. Consequently, he blows his whistle for a jump ball before the conditions for a held ball have been met. He may act to prevent rough play. In either case, he is wrong. His move has been too hasty. As a result, he deprives a clever player of capitalizing on his skill. Here is a situation where it is better to hesitate than to be too quick. Be sure the conditions which justify calling for a held ball are complied with, before making a decision. This is not the time to imagine what may occur and to act on supposition.

Again, a player, moving rapidly, receives the ball, stops, and then lifts his pivot foot. He may do this at the end of the dribble. The official is watching the play intently. The moment the pivot foot is raised from the floor he anticipates a violation of the running rule. As a result, he blows his whistle before the violation occurs. The player shoots or passes and very often a score results. He is penalized for a legal play.

Or, the football referee blows his whistle before the forward progress of the ball is stopped. The ball carrier breaks away for a touchdown. Because of hasty action, a team is deprived of a score. There is no such thing as a quick whistle. The play has or has not been completed. No whistle should be blown until the play is completed.

In tennis a lineman judges that a ball will be out and calls the play before the ball hits the surface. Even though his judgment was subsequently correct, he should not announce his decision until the play is completed.

Of course, officials should be alert. They should be anticipatory to the extent that they instantly size up

Don't blow on anticipation

possible situations. They should be poised in readiness to act instantly, but they should make no decision until a violation or a foul has become an accomplished fact.

6. *Except in situations where specific jurisdiction is given by the rules to one official, all officials should make decisions on any play which they see anywhere.*

There should be no division of authority. It is true that by reason of many of the mechanics which have been developed for the efficient administration of games, one official will tend to focus his attention on specific phases of play or on definite areas under certain play situations. Because of this fact, one of the officials would be more likely to see the movements of players more closely in a certain area.

While these are the areas of special concentration, it does not mean that any official should be oblivious to what the other players are doing. Although particular assignments are laid out for the co-operation of the officials and for the co-ordination of their work, they should so far as is humanly possible keep the total field of play within their vision. They should make decisions on any situation that comes to their attention and that requires their official action. In many of the rule books, under the section on the duties of officials, statements authorize all the officials to make decisions on all plays that come to their attention. The basketball and football rules are typical examples. There are limitations, as will be found in the baseball and tennis rules. Thus, each official must be conversant with his prerogatives in each sport and conduct himself accordingly.

Call what you see anywhere

Part II

The Fundamental Principles of officiating which have been presented and developed in Part I are applied in Part II to those sports which require a decision on every action that takes place. Baseball, Softball, Track, Swimming, Tennis, Volleyball, Badminton, and Handball are included in this section and in this order.

5

Baseball

EVERY FAN THINKS THAT HE IS AN AUTHORITY ON THE baseball rules and on the art of baseball officiating. Yet there is probably more misinformation at large about baseball than any other sport. Consequently, more opportunities for argument arise about play situations in baseball.

These statements prevail no doubt because baseball is our national pastime and is a common subject for conversation summer and winter, and because most of the decisions which must be made are surprisingly simple. Balls and strikes, fair and foul balls, safe or out decisions, are for the most part obvious and childlike in their simplicity. Because these are so simple, the erroneous analogy is made with respect to all situations, many of which become quite involved.

The rules of baseball are most precise and carefully codified. There are, however, many conditional factors upon which correct decisions depend. A sufficient number of problems of this type arise during a game, so that only a very astute individual may qualify as a capable umpire.

The fact that an umpire must make repeat decisions inning after inning requires a consistency of judgment unequaled in the other sports. Few games are played where less than 100 decisions on balls and strikes are made. There are fifty-one to fifty-four out decisions in each nine inning game and at least as many more decisions in which

Baseball requires a decision on every play

the player may be declared safe. Many fair and foul ball decisions are required. Any one of these called incorrectly may be the deciding factor in a ball game. Any evidence of vacillating judgment produces an erratic ball game.

Emphasis is placed on the above points in order to demonstrate the necessity for the presence of the highest qualities of good officiating in baseball. The umpire must be constantly alert lest he slip up on one tiny bit of his duty. While his job appears to be a passive one, he is, on the contrary, under tremendous pressure and tension every moment the contest is under way. He must make a decision on every single play.

The further fact that the very nature of baseball seems to invite and sanction protest, argument, and disagreement on the part of players, coaches, managers, and captains, does not make the task of the umpire any easier. He is challenged continually. Unless he has great endurance, fortitude, and mental and emotional poise, he is likely to falter.

The comments which follow are applied to games which are administered by one or two officials. Our amateur games seldom have more than two officials, and most of them have only one.

INCLUDE THIS

PREGAME PREPARATION

The uniform for the baseball official is the only one that has remained comparatively unchanged through the years. His dark-blue outfit with the ample pockets for balls is historic. He is very much in the limelight because he is looked to for every decision. Consequently, he should be sure to keep his clothes well pressed and his shoes shined. He needs a special protector, a mask, shin guards, and special capped shoes to protect the feet. This is equipment for the umpire-in-chief. Figure 2 shows the umpires in proper dress and with full regalia.

He should without question have an indicator for recording balls and strikes. It is rather easy to lose count of balls and strikes. An intervening play or game interruptions which require the attention of the umpire, may cause him to forget the ball and strike count. The indicator, therefore, is his only safe protection from embarrassment.

PREGAME DUTIES

1. When two umpires are involved, they should review their plans for co-operation during the game. For example, they must team together on balk movements, on covering bases when more than one runner is on base, and on some fair or foul ball situations. One may assist the other upon request in clearing up questionable plays such as whether a ball was trapped or caught on the fly, whether a runner missed a base, whether or not a player dropped a ball in catching it or throwing it.

Some of these problems are specifically covered by the rules, but all should be discussed for the purpose of review and also for the distinct purpose of establishing a harmonious and understanding relationship between the umpires. Each should remember that there is no overruling of judgment of one official by the other, but that either may ask for the opinion of the other on a decision which he has made. There are certain duties which are the sole responsibility of the umpire-in-chief.

2. Probably the most important pregame duty of the umpires is to get a clear understanding before the game starts concerning ground rules. They should also state, repeat, and discuss these with both coaches and captains so that there is a mutual understanding. Failure to follow this pattern is likely to invite trouble during the game. After the game starts, the full responsibility rests with the umpires. The ground rules may be perfectly clear to the home team which makes them, but the visitors and the umpires must have the same interpretation.

3. The umpires, before the game, should survey the field and appurtenances. By following this practice, they

Planned pre-game cooperation assures efficient support

will assure themselves concerning all matters which violate the rules and which need special ground rules to cover them.

4. Get a supply of balls from the home team. As a general rule, the supply of balls for amateur games will not be so generous as in the case of professional games. Often, only two new balls are available. Seldom will there be more than a dozen. As a consequence, the umpire must use greater discretion before throwing balls out of the game than would be the case in a professional game.

5. The umpire-in-chief should secure the starting line-ups from each captain before the game begins. Following the receipt of the line-ups and after ground rules discussions, the batteries should be announced. It is customary and courteous to announce the visitors first. The pitcher is announced first and then the catcher.

6. Begin games exactly on the scheduled time.

POSITION AND DUTIES ON BALLS AND STRIKES

When there are two or more umpires, the umpire-in-chief is always behind the plate, where he calls all balls and strikes. His position is slightly to the side of the catcher, so that he may look over the catcher's shoulder. Most catchers crouch, so that the umpire can maintain a semi-crouched position from which he can get a full view of the ball, the plate, and the batter.

If the batter is right-handed, the umpire will usually be able to see better by looking over the left shoulder of the catcher. If the batter is a left-handed batter, the umpire should look over the right shoulder of the catcher. There is no hard and fast rule for this procedure, but experience has demonstrated that better results accrue from these practices. Figure 3 shows the umpire in position to call balls and strikes on a right-handed batter.

Low balls are the most difficult to judge. The umpire should, therefore, get as low as possible on low balls in

Neglect ground rules and invite trouble

order to better judge their position with respect to the batter's knees. Inside balls are next in difficulty. The fact that the umpire's position is toward the inside of the plate places him in a strategic position for judging inside balls. Batters are more cautious about inside balls. They may dodge a ball that cuts the inside edge or corner of the

FIGURE 3. UMPIRE-IN-CHIEF IN PROPER POSITION TO CALL BALLS AND STRIKES ON A RIGHT-HANDED BATTER. NOTE THAT HIS POSITION IS SLIGHTLY TO THE LEFT OF THE CATCHER SO THAT HE CAN LOOK OVER THE CATCHER'S LEFT SHOULDER.

plate. Because of this fact, the umpire must be particularly alert to judge inside balls correctly. Looking over the inside shoulder of the catcher gives him a direct line from the pitcher to the plate.

Curve balls can be very deceiving and misleading. A pitch is a strike if it goes over the plate at the right height. The position of the ball when it hits the catcher's glove is of no consequence whatever.

This latter leads to the admonition that the umpire should announce his judgment on balls and strikes without hesita-

Remember the low ball bogey

tion. It is never reliable to attempt to retrace the imaginary path of the ball. Neither should the umpire be persuaded by jerking actions or other attempts by the catcher to influence his judgment. It is not bad practice to assume that the pitch was a ball if the catcher by his action has attempted to alter the actual direction of the pitch by his attempts to deceive.

The field umpire should take his position about twenty feet behind first base and on, or just outside, the right-field foul line. Many umpires stand at the back edge of the skinned area.

Diagram 1 shows the position of the two umpires at the start of the game and at any time when the bases are unoccupied.

If the game is being officiated by one umpire, he should take his position behind the plate whenever possible. Decisions on balls and strikes are by far the most difficult to make. To be able to make accurate and consistent judgments, it is necessary to be as close as possible to the plate.

The umpire should, therefore, be stationed behind the plate:

a. When no runners are on bases.
b. When the bases are full.
c. When third base only is occupied.
d. When second and third bases are occupied.

On all other occasions it will be necessary for the umpire to take a position behind the pitcher. These occasions would include:

a. Runner on first base.
b. Runners on first and third bases.
c. Runner on second base.
d. Runners on first and second bases.

Under these conditions, the umpire must not only call balls and strikes, but he must be able to make decisions on plays that may occur at first, second, or third base. For

Decide promptly. The ball doesn't leave a tracer

this reason, he places himself in a middle position. Certainly, he could not make accurate decisions on pick-off plays at second base or at first base from his position behind the plate.

His position behind the pitcher should be just off the mound. If the pitcher is right-handed, the umpire will have a more uninterrupted view of the flight of the ball if he stands behind the right arm of the pitcher. If the pitcher is left-handed, he should get to the left side.

The foregoing procedure for a single umpire is recommended so that he will be close to the plate. Here is where the majority and the most difficult of his decisions must be made. In most ball games he will be able to work from behind the plate from two-thirds to three-quarters of the time.

There is, however, a school of thought which feels that when there is only one umpire for a game, he should make all decisions from behind the pitcher. The reasoning for this is that there will be more consistency throughout the game because all decisions are made from the same spot. Further, that any mistakes on close pitches where depth perception is involved would be equal for each team. Thus, the team which was unable to get men on bases would receive the same treatment as the team which, because of base running situations, was forcing the umpire to rule from behind the pitcher.

One must recognize a certain validity in this line of reasoning. Since there is no rule or objective evidence which dictates that either technique be followed, the practice which one should adopt becomes a matter of personal preference. The author has tried both procedures on many occasions and feels that he can do a much more efficient and accurate job by the method which he recommends.

The umpire should keep the edges of the plate clear at all times. When it is necessary for him to work from be-

Work behind the plate as much as possible in a one-umpire game

hind the pitcher, he should be doubly sure that the edges of the plate stand out sharply.

To declare a strike, the umpire swings his right arm in a chopping movement. At the same time he announces "Strike!" Some dramatics are desirable for the purpose of making the decision crystal clear. Figure 4(a) shows the action of the umpire in announcing a strike. No motion at all denotes a ball. The umpire should, however, call "Ball!"

POSITION AND DUTIES ON FAIR AND FOUL BALLS

Any time the ball is hit, the umpire-in-chief should move so that he may sight along the foul line in the direction of the ball. In this way, he is able to judge more accurately those hits which fall beyond the base or roll along the foul line before reaching the base.

If the base umpire is on the foul line behind first base, he may assist the umpire-in-chief with difficult decisions on balls that are hit sharply along the right-field foul line. The arm raised horizontally and pointing toward foul territory indicates a foul ball. When pointing toward fair territory or no signal at all, a fair ball is called.

Figure 4(d) shows the umpire-in-chief in a position to rule on balls hit along the right-field foul line. He is indicating a foul ball. For balls hit along the left-field foul line, he should stand so that he can sight along the left-field foul line.

The umpire has six possible situations upon which he may be required to rule in connection with batted balls:

a. Balls which settle or are touched by a fielder before reaching first or third base.

b. Balls which when bounding to the outfield may or may not go over first or third base. (The field umpire may assist on this situation.)

c. Balls which hit first or third base.

d. Fly balls which first hit the ground beyond first or third base.

Sight the foul—avoid the howl

(a) Strike. (b) Out. (c) Safe.

(d) Foul ball.

(e) Count of strikes (right hand) and balls (left hand).

(f) Runner or batter awarded a base.

(g) Time.

Figure 4. Signals commonly used by umpires to convey decisions.

e. Fly balls which are touched by a fielder.
f. Fly balls which are knocked out of the park.

In all cases of balls which are touched, the position of the ball at the time it is touched and not the position of the fielder who touches it determines whether it is fair or foul.

POSITION AND DUTIES OF FIELD UMPIRE IN COVERING BASES

With no one on base, the field umpire is back of first base and on the foul line. When the batsman hits the ball, the field umpire moves to a position where he can see the ball (after it is fielded and thrown) hit the first baseman's glove, see the first baseman's feet with respect to the base, and at the same time have a clear view of the runner and the base. The preferred position is to crouch in foul territory either back of first base or in front of it. Such a position will permit him to see whether or not the ball is caught

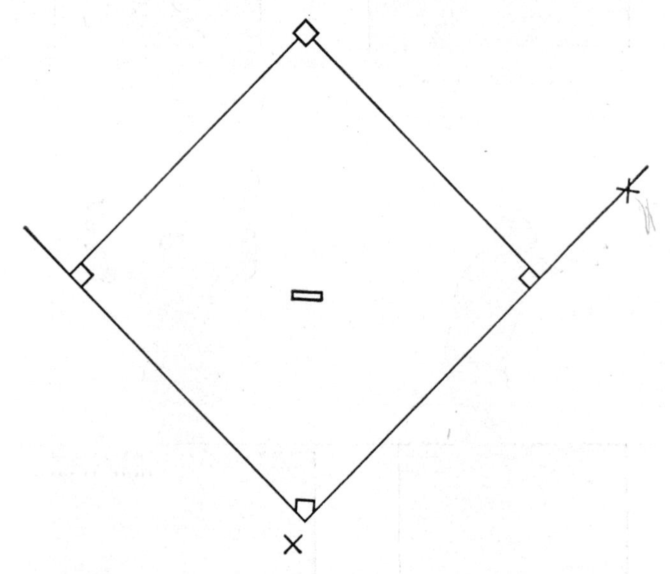

DIAGRAM 1. POSITION OF UMPIRES AT START OF INNING OR WITH NO ONE ON BASE.

For play at first—"see the ball, the base, the baseman, the runner"

before the runner touches the base, and, at the same time, whether or not the baseman is touching the base after or at the time he catches the ball. If the runner and the ball reach the base at the same time, the runner is, of course, safe. In no case should the umpire be in line with the flight of the ball.

Diagram 2 shows the field umpire in a position to make a decision on a play at first base. Some umpires move into the diamond back of first base to make their decisions,

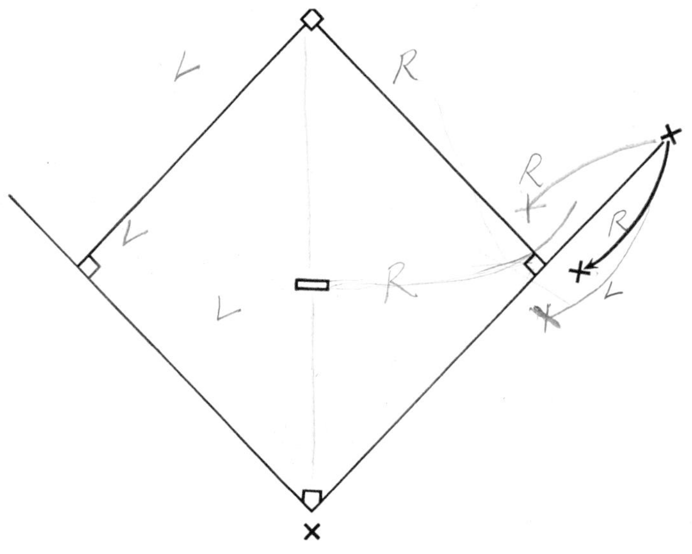

Diagram 2. Field umpire in position to make a decision on play at first base.

rather than assume the position shown in the diagram. The latter position is approved provided the umpire does not interfere with the throw from a fielder and provided he can see clearly the feet of the basemen in their relation to the bases.

If, in the opinion of the umpire, the runner is out, he should indicate this fact by throwing his hand with the thumb pointed up above his head. At the same time he

Turn away and rue the play

should declare the runner out. If the runner is safe, the umpire indicates his decision from a crouched position with arms outstretched in front of him. The palms of the hands are facing downward. In making a base decision, the umpire should not turn away from the play until the action is completely finished. The baseman may drop or juggle the ball. The runner may at first be safe and then an instant later be tagged out. If the umpire turned away too quickly, he could miss this kind of action. Figure 4(b) shows the umpire demonstrating the signal to declare a runner out, while figure 4(c) shows the motion to indicate that the runner is safe.

With a runner on first base, the field umpire should take a position behind and to the side of the pitcher and about midway between the pitcher's mound and second base. He should be sure that he does not obstruct the view of any fielder. From this middle position, he is able to cover plays

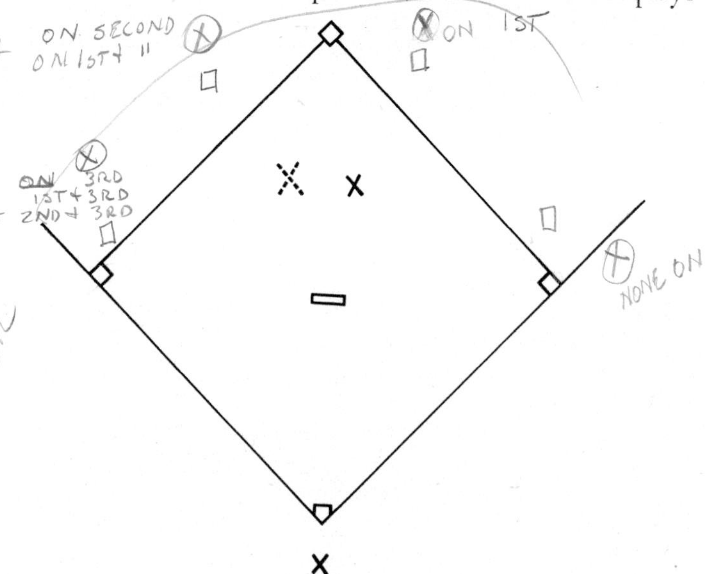

Diagram 3. Field umpire behind pitcher with runner on first base. Dotted-line x shows position when runner is on second base.

Was the fielder catching or throwing when the fumble occurred?

equally accurately at any base. He is also in an advantageous position to judge balk movements.

Diagram 3 shows the position of the field umpire with a runner on first base. If second base, first and second bases, or third base is occupied, the umpire usually stands on the opposite side of the line connecting the pitcher's mound and second base.

The umpire must be alert for throws to catch a runner off base. When the ball is hit to the infield, he must follow the movements of the fielder who catches the ball in order to be ready to make the decision at whichever base the ball may be thrown. The umpire should not decide on his own judgment that the play will be at a certain base and then turn his attention to that base. The fielder might decide to throw to another base, with resulting embarrassment to the umpire.

When there is a play at first or second base and at the same time or subsequently a play at third base on another

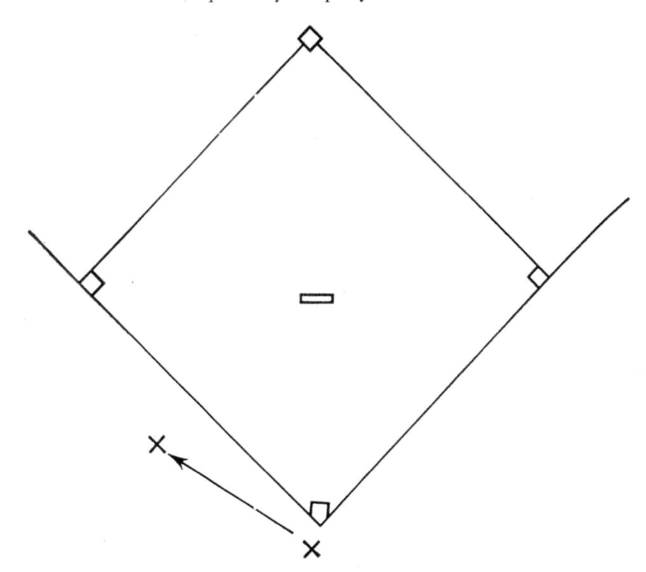

Diagram 4. Position of umpire-in-chief on a fly to right field with a runner on third base.

Get close to the play

runner, the field umpire should cover the play at first or second base. The umpire-in-chief must assist the field umpire by covering the play at third base. To be ready for such an eventuality, the umpire-in-chief should move along the foul line toward third base. (See diagram 4.) The umpire-in-chief will also make all decisions on runners at home base. He should remove his mask in readiness for these decisions.

6

Guides to Special Play Situations—Baseball

SEVERAL SITUATIONS ARISE DURING PRACTICALLY every baseball game which create difficult decisions for umpires. These are discussed here for emphasis, with the hope that fewer mistakes will be made in the future in these particular situations. Most of them seem to center around the plate.

BATTED BALLS HITTING PLATE

Pitched balls that are hit on top so that they are driven almost directly to the ground create difficult problems for the umpire. The ball may hit the plate, or the ground behind the plate or in the batter's box, and then roll and settle on fair territory.

If the ball has not hit the person of the batter while he is in the batter's box and has not been touched by the catcher while it is on or over foul territory, it is a fair ball. If the ball has hit the batter while he is in the box (this is the most common occurrence), or, the catcher while it is on or over foul territory, it is a foul ball. The umpire cannot always be certain whether or not the ball has hit the batter. As a consequence, many umpires have adopted the habit of calling every play situation of this kind a foul ball. This is not at all fair to the defensive team.

Balls hit directly down may be fair

The umpire should be on the alert for these plays. When it is clear that the ball has rolled fair without touching the batter and without being touched, it should be declared a fair ball. Of course, if there is doubt, it seems fairer to declare a foul ball.

HIT BATSMAN

Balls which without any apparent deflection barely graze the uniform of a batter may escape the attention of the umpire. He cannot rule that a batsman is hit unless he witnesses the fact. On the other hand, he must be very alert so that he does not penalize a batter when the ball actually hits him, however slightly.

The umpire must remember, however, that a batter may on a close pitch feign being hit. Dramatics should play no part in the decision. As a matter of fact, the decision should be made so quickly that there is no time for an act by the batter. Likewise, the umpire must remember that the batter is required to attempt to avoid being hit. He should not be awarded a base for deliberately getting hit or refusing to dodge a pitched ball.

STEPPING OUT OF THE BATTER'S BOX

Batters attempt to crowd the front of the batter's box for the purpose of hitting curve balls before they break or for meeting slow balls. They take a stand to the rear of the box to gain a little more time for swinging at fast balls. They leave the box to bunt a pitchout on a squeeze play. In following this strategy, it is not at all uncommon for them to have one foot out of the box.

By rule, the batter is out for leaving his box when batting a pitched ball. Umpires have a tendency to be lax in administering this rule. The usual reason for this is that the markings for the box become obliterated after a few innings. They should not, however, permit a batter to gain an unfair advantage by violating a rule.

Batters must avoid a pitched ball

INTERFERENCE BY THE BATTER OR THE CATCHER

If the catcher interferes with the bat or the batter and thus prevents him from swinging at a pitched ball, the batter is awarded first base. This violation occurs when the catcher takes a position in his box too close to the batter. In such a position, the catcher's glove touches the bat as he goes after the ball. There is also interference when the catcher leaves his box to catch a pitched ball in an effort to tag a runner on a steal of home or a squeeze play.

The umpire must be quick to catch these happenings. In the case of steals or squeeze plays, he can anticipate the possibility of interference and thus be ready for it. In the case of the catcher touching the bat or the batter, there is usually no warning unless it is noticed that the catcher habitually crowds the plate. The umpire must discriminate between a deliberate attempt by the batter to reach back with his bat and thus interfere with the catcher and bona fide interference by the catcher himself.

While the batter is entitled to stand in his box on plays at the plate, he may not move to block the attempt of the catcher to make a play on a runner. Certainly he cannot leave his box to block the catcher. Neither may the batter move his bat or body and by so doing interfere with the catcher who is throwing to a base. The batter may, of course, take a legitimate swing at a pitched ball.

STRIKING AT THE BALL

What constitutes an actual swing at the ball? According to the rule, the swing is not complete unless it is carried through to the point of the snap of the wrists, which constitutes the last of the sequence of movements in swinging at the ball. This means that a swing may be started and may go through to the final action, but if the batter can check his movement at that point, he has not struck at the ball.

The catcher or the batter may interfere

The umpire should rule on the pitch in accordance with whether or not the ball went over the plate at the right height. If the pitch was not a strike, then he should declare a ball. The umpire must continually anticipate this situation so that he does not penalize a quick reacting player who is able to make split-second judgments and regulate his swing accordingly.

TAGGING SITUATIONS

Four suggestions can be made which will aid umpires materially in rendering decisions on close plays at the bases when runners slide in an attempt to avoid being put out.

1. The umpire should observe what part of the runner is touched with the ball. The proper technique by the baseman for tagging is to hold the ball at the level of the base, between the base and runner. If this is done and the runner comes in contact with the ball with that part of his body (foot, leg, or hand) which is farthest advanced toward the base, the decision of the umpire is simple. The runner is out. If, on the other hand, as the runner comes into the base, the fielder reaches toward him and touches him farther back on his leg or body than the advanced portion which has made contact with the base, the probabilities are that the runner is safe. If there is any question in the umpire's mind, he should call the runner safe, because of the faulty technique in attempting to make the put-out.

2. The umpire should be within a few feet of the play. It is not possible to make accurate judgments on close plays from a distance. Tricky movements of runners may prevent the fielder from touching them with the ball. This cannot be detected unless the umpire is right on top of the play. The impact of the runner may cause the fielder to juggle or fumble the ball. Unless the umpire is right at the base with an unobstructed view of the ball throughout the play, the fielder may cleverly recover the ball and cover up his error.

Where did the baseman hold the ball to tag the slide?

3. The umpire should fix his gaze upon the play until the action is completed. The action is completed when the ball has been thrown or the fielder has come away from the play with the ball securely in his possession. This procedure will avoid missing fumbles or cases of oversliding or missing the base. Some umpires have developed the bad habit of immediately turning their backs on, and hastily walking away from, a play once they have rendered a decision. Such action invites trouble if one or the other of the above situations occurs subsequently. Figure 4(c) shows the umpire in the proper position to render a decision at a base.

4. At the instant action occurs at a base, umpires should indicate out or safe by their signals. If subsequent actions such as fumbles or missing or oversliding require a new or changed decision, one may follow. It is justified in view of new developments. It in no way reflects upon the first decision of the umpire. He should not hesitate to change his decision under these circumstances.

FUMBLING BALL BEFORE OR AFTER A CATCH

Questions frequently arise concerning the time when a fumble occurs. The umpire must have a clear view of the action in order to determine whether a fumble occurs as a part of catching the ball or whether the fumble was incidental to taking the ball from the glove preparatory to throwing it.

If the player is seen to hold the ball securely, that play whatever it may have been was completed. Any subsequent happenings are related to the next play. They will in no way require a change of decision on the previous play.

Several examples may be cited to illustrate this situation. A fielder catches a fly ball. As he attempts to retrieve the ball from his glove or starts to throw it, he juggles the ball or drops it. The fly was actually caught and that play

If ball is caught, the play is completed

completed. The fumble occurred as a part of the act of throwing the ball and not of catching it.

The first baseman catches the ball to retire a runner. He starts to step from the base to throw to third to catch a runner advancing from second base. In his effort to get the ball into his throwing hand, he drops it.

The second baseman receives a throw from the shortstop to force a runner coming to second base. In his haste to complete a double play he drops the ball as he starts his throw to first base.

The catcher catches a foul tip and strives to throw out a runner stealing second. He drops the ball in his attempt to transfer it to his throwing hand. Catchers have been known deliberately to drop the ball when they see that it is impossible to catch the runner at second base.

In all these situations, the fumble was part of the next play and in no way affected the completed one. The team affected adversely will often argue that the ball was never caught. The umpire must therefore be sure that he sees these actions in their proper sequence. If he has any doubt concerning the accuracy of his judgment, he may ask for an opinion from his colleagues. These are vitally important decisions to make. But, if the umpire has followed the movements of the fielder throughout, he should have no difficulty differentiating between the completion of one play and the start of the next.

LEAVING THE BASE AFTER A CAUGHT FLY BALL

This situation introduces the need for the exercise of split vision. The umpire must see the ball as it touches the glove of the fielder. At the same time, he must see the start of the base runner from the base. Here is a case where distance from both the fielder and the runner is an advantage. When possible, the umpire should be slightly off the imaginary line which connects the ball with the base. Of course, this is not always possible. But the umpire usu-

Sense the rhythm of the play when runner advances on a caught fly

ally has time to move so that he can approach this position.

For an extreme example, a runner is on third base. A fly ball is hit to right field. The umpire at the plate should move toward third base but as far away from the line as possible. If he can get halfway to third, he will be better able to encompass the ball and the base in his visual field. After the catch he will have plenty of time to return to home plate to cover the play there. Diagram 4 shows this situation.

The umpire must develop a visual sense of timing. He first sees the ball hitting the fielder's glove and then the dash of the runner from the base. So long as this rhythm is not reversed, he may be sure that the play is legal.

TOUCHING ALL BASES

On every hit ball when there is the possibility of base runners advancing more than one base, the umpires must observe whether or not the runners touch all bases. An umpire must condition his routine actions so that he is conscious of this responsibility.

When more than one runner is on base, this job is not a simple one if a long hit is registered. The duties of the umpires are divided, however, so that total coverage may be handled with facility. The umpire at the plate will watch the runners at third base and home while the field umpire observes first and second bases.

This is an action (leaving the base after a caught fly is another) which the umpires must notice, but on which they do not rule unless a ruling is requested by the team in the field.

SIGNALS

The baseball signals which the umpire employs to convey his decision to spectators and players are the fewest in number but the most revealing in all our sports. The seven signals shown on page 47 constitute his complete stock in trade. They are illustrated by actual photographs better to portray their use.

Each umpire may develop some mannerisms which would constitute a slight variation from the signals represented here. The illustrations, however, illustrate the fundamental pantomimes. Every umpire should learn these and employ them without fail whenever he is required to render a decision. His tool kit for use in carrying out his job is not complete without signals.

7

Softball

MOST OF THE TECHNIQUES WHICH WERE DESCRIBED for the baseball official apply with equal force to the softball official. The softball rule which does not permit a runner to leave his base until the ball leaves the pitcher's hand precludes the possibility of one umpire's successfully handling a softball game.

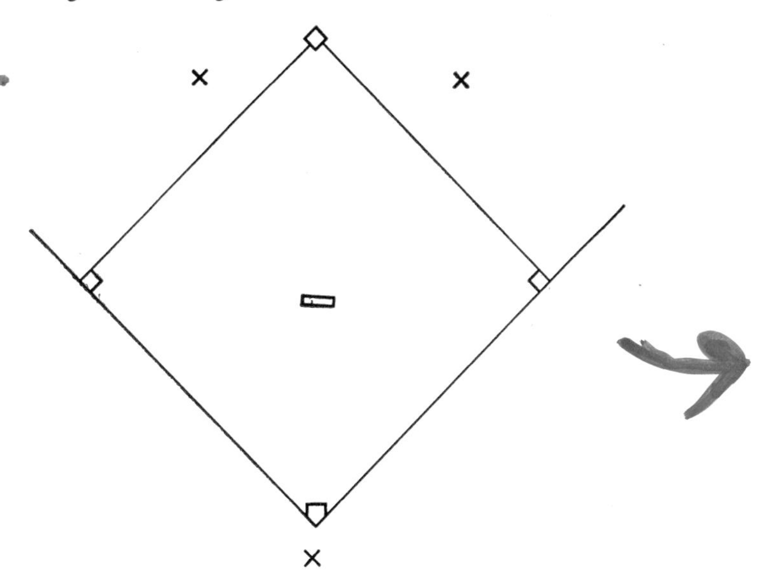

DIAGRAM 5. POSITION OF BASE UMPIRE WITH A RUNNER ON BASE IN A SOFTBALL GAME. THE BASE UMPIRE MUST BE ABLE TO SEE BOTH THE RUNNER AND THE PITCHER.

Two umpires are necessary

Also, because of this rule, the field umpire must always face so that he can see both the pitcher and the base runner. When more than one runner is on base and there is only one field umpire, he must, of necessity, take a position back of the infield rather than between the infield and the pitcher. (See diagram 5.)

No other alterations of the techniques of the baseball umpires will be necessary. The reader, therefore, is referred to the section on baseball officiating.

Then conclusion

8

Track

TRACK OFFICIATING, UNLIKE ALL OTHER SPORTS OFficiating, is diversified and non-professional. For the most part laymen are called upon to assume the responsibilities of officials. Except for the starter and referee (the two jobs are often combined), the track officials do not receive compensation for their services. This situation seems quite incongruous when one realizes that winners are determined and records set by the difference of a tenth of a second or an eighth of an inch.

Inasmuch as twenty-five to fifty officials are required to conduct a track meet in an efficient manner, one can understand why the officials for a track meet cannot be organized on the same highly professional and technical basis that has been attained in the officials' organizations for football, basketball, baseball, hockey, soccer, and wrestling. Track officials, with the exception of the starter, are volunteers.

Fortunately, through the years a certain prestige has become attached to track officiating. As a result, many prominent and capable persons have maintained an active interest in track. They volunteer their services readily for officiating purposes.

Unfortunately, a few of these continue to express their desire beyond the stage of their dependability as officials. Problems are created thereby. Out of gratitude for past

Track officials have been volunteers throughout the years

services it would be discourteous to eliminate these people. On the other hand, their unreliability due to the inevitable slowing up processes which are induced by age makes them useless as officials.

The best that can be done is to add extra officials whose judgments will be accepted and use the others in honorary capacities in recognition of valued services rendered in the past.

Because of the nature of the personnel for track officiating, those responsible for organizing and conducting the meets must allow for the shortcomings and the lack of training and preparation of lay officials. Written instruction should be given to each. These instructions should cover the technique and procedure to be followed in carrying out his duties. The instructions must of necessity be short. They must, nevertheless, be adequate. It has been found that sufficient information for each official can be typewritten on a 3x5 card. W. H. McCurdy [1] has worked out instructions along this line for some field events.

The discussions, explanations, and directions which follow have been worked out to include the implementation of this procedure. Since the rules of the National Collegiate Athletic Association [2] are most universally adopted, these are used as the basis for this presentation. It is recognized that some other associations and conferences have their own rules. However, the departure from the NCAA, which is the parent body to most of the others, is not sufficiently significant to justify the space to discuss the differences.

THE OFFICIALS

The officials for a track meet include:

referee

[1] W. H. McCurdy, *Unpublished Thesis* (Springfield, Mass.: Springfield College, 1949).

[2] *Official Track and Field Guide* (New York: A. S. Barnes and Company, 1949).

Provide short, concise written instructions

starter (assistant starter)
clerk of course (assistant clerk of course)
scorer
announcer (assistant announcers)
5 timers
judges of finish (twice as many judges as places to score)
head field judge
field judges (3 for each event—there can be some doubling up)
4 track inspectors
1 inspector of implements
surveyor (usually the track is measured and certified before the meet)

The foregoing includes a comprehensive list needed to conduct a large meet. Dual meets can be handled with fewer officials. For example, the starter usually acts as referee and head field judge. No assistants are needed for the starter, announcer, or clerk of course. The field judges can double up in some of the field events. Two sets of judges can handle the weight events and two sets can handle the jumping events.

In many meets, officials are requested to conform to a uniform dress. There is no official uniform for track, but white trousers and blue coat are customarily worn. In some indoor meets, the officials appear in full formal dress. On some occasions, dark blue trousers and white shirts are worn. Uniform dress is desirable to provide an attractive appearance on the field and for the purpose of easily identifying the officials.

Duties and Instructions to Officials

More space is devoted by track rules to the specific duties of officials than by the rules of other sports. Itemizing the pertinent job for each official is thus a comparatively simple task.

25 to 50 officials are needed for a meet

The Referee

The referee has general over-all supervision of the meet. He is the final authority when any disputes arise. If the rules do not specifically cover the point at issue, it is his responsibility to decide the matter. He reviews the general organization of the meet to make sure that all competitors receive equal opportunities. He checks the plans for each event to see that they are run in accordance with the rules of the meet.

While the rules designate that the referee shall name the head judges, this has usually been done in advance by the management in charge of the meet as a part of the preliminary preparation.

The referee should be provided with a copy of the rules under which the meet is run. He is expected to be familiar with the rules which govern each event. The referee may not have a single decision to make. He should, however, keep in close touch with the progress of each event and be available for consultation at all times. As previously stated, in many meets the starter, who is the only paid official, is often named as referee.

The duties which are commonly his, and which arise most often during the course of a meet, are the following:

1. To decide on disqualification for reported violations of track rules such as leaving one's lane, cutting in too soon so as to cause interference, crowding, exchanging baton outside of restraining lines, bad sportsmanship, illegal hurdling.
2. To act on the validity of a record after checking watches, wind velocity, heights, distances, verification of legality of implements, surveyors' affidavit, etc.
3. To determine questions of procedure when protests or disputes arise.

The referee is the final authority

The Starter

The starter is considered by far the most important track official. His success in getting races started fairly, in not exciting the runners, and in gaining their confidence is a mark of his ability as a starter. He must be consistent. To hold runners unduly long one time, to start fast the next, and so on, upsets the emotional control of the runners and ruins the races. Research [1] has shown that the best results are obtained when runners are held approximately two seconds after the command "Get set!" Of course, all runners must be stationary before the race is permitted to start. If this steadiness is not obtained without undue delay after the order to "Get set," the starter should call all runners off their marks and make a new start. If a competitor makes a false start, he should be warned. If he makes a second false start, he should be disqualified. (These are the NCAA rules.) A quiet, unhurried but firm voice will do much to calm the jumpy athlete and get all runners away to an even start.

The starter should wear some kind of an identification so that he may be located easily by the timers. A bright colored hat or coat is a typical identification. Recently, a green arm band has been recommended so that the starter's gun may be seen readily when the gun is up. Figure 5 shows the starter in position to start a race. The gun is up. Attention is called to the arm band on his upraised arm. He should stand in front, and to the side, of the runners so that they may see him. In a race where all start from scratch, he should stand at the outside edge of the track. In staggered races, he will find that he can best see all runners if he stands in advance of all runners but on the inside lane. He is sufficiently far away from the runner

---

[1] Breshnahan and Tuttle, *Track and Field Athletics* (St. Louis: C. V. Mosby Co., 1937).

The starter—the headlineman of the meet

on the pole so that he will have plenty of time to get off the track after firing his gun.

He should have two guns, one of which is a recall gun. His starting gun should be one that can be cocked for instant firing. A .32-caliber gun is best. At least, nothing less should be used because a .22-caliber gun does not give off sufficient smoke.

FIGURE 5. STARTER WITH GUN UP, READY TO START RACE. NOTE THE RECALL PISTOL IN HIS LEFT HAND AND THE ARM BAND WHICH IS A VISUAL HELP TO THE TIMERS.

A steady start is an acquired art

If an assistant starter is used, he would act as the recall starter and handle the second gun.

The starter takes charge of a race as soon as the clerk of course has placed the runners for the race and has given them their necessary instructions. Before calling the runners to their marks, he shall determine by means of a whistle, or other signal, the readiness of the timers and judges. The head timer should return the signal when judges and timers are ready. Immediately after all are ready, the starter should get the race under way. He is responsible for starting events promptly.

No written instructions are necessary for the starter since he is probably the one professional official in the meet. He should be well acquainted with the rules.

The Clerk of Course

The most arduous assignment at a track meet, particularly a large one, is that of clerk of course. He will find it necessary to spend many hours in his preliminary preparation for a large meet or relay carnival. When the necessary data on entries are not available until the day before the meet, he may find himself working far into the night arranging heats and preparing his records of entries in each race. This information must be available for the coaches and competitors in advance of the meeting. While the rules hold the competitors responsible for prompt reporting for a race, the clerk must check the entries in each race, assign each competitor to his proper lane, give the necessary instructions covering the race (that is, whether the race is run in lanes or not; starting positions for staggered starts; touch-off points in relay races; position for second, third, and fourth runners; the number of laps; the finish point; number of places in case of heats); make decisions concerning rearrangement of heats and lanes when all competitors do not report or all lanes are not filled; and

The clerk—the workhorse at a meet

finally report to starter that all is in readiness and turn race over to him.

The clerk must, if humanly possible, maintain the time schedule which has been set up. He may not start events in advance of the time schedule.

The drawings for heats are usually made in advance of the meet by the clerk. He is usually aided in this tedious task by information from the coaches concerning the ability of the competitors.

If semi-finals are necessary, the qualifiers of the preliminary heats are assigned to the semi-final heats in advance. For example, if there are to be six preliminary heats and two semi-final races, it may be determined in advance that the qualifiers in the first three preliminary heats shall make up the first semi-final race, and the last three heat qualifiers the second semi-finals.

Usually the clerk has the competitors draw for lanes in the semi-finals and finals when they report for the start of the race. A simple device for making such drawings is to use blank cartridges which have the lanes numbered on the end. The clerk should keep a record of the drawings for purposes of reference in case of dispute, errors in judging, or violation of rules.

In meets which have a large field of competitors or in relay meets, the clerk will need assistants. One assistant may be organizing the event which follows the one about to start. In relay races, his assistants conduct the second, third, and fourth runners to their starting places and point out to them the restraining lines. They signal to the starter when all runners are ready.

The following list of duties and instructions may be handed to the clerk of course several days before a meet:

1. Secure list of competitors in each race.
2. Arrange competitors in heats according to record of previous performances. (Fastest men as heat leaders—runners from same school in differents heats.)

If the meet is on time, the clerk is fine

3. Make record of drawings. (A program and clip board are useful for this purpose.)

4. Check contestants five minutes before each race. Make any rearrangements necessitated by withdrawals and make a record of any changes.

5. Number a blank cartridge for each lane to use for drawing for places in semi-finals and finals.

6. Keep a record of placements for finals and semi-finals.

7. Instruct runners.

8. Maintain time schedule.

9. Send record of all starters to scorers.

The Scorer

The scorer should be stationed in a place on the field where he is easily accessible throughout the meet. He needs a table on which he may place his score sheet and file the results of the various events as they are brought to him.

He should prepare a master score sheet upon which to record the point winners of each event, their schools and their records. Each entry on the score sheet should be carefully checked and the original record kept for auditing purposes if necessary.

He should make no entry except from the official results which are delivered to him.

If a score board is kept, he should furnish the information for this board and through assistants see that it is kept up-to-date. His record should be the source of information for the announcer.

The record of the official scorer is the basis for awarding all medals and trophies. He should prepare the award cards for each place after each event. These should be signed by each competitor as he receives his award. The signed card represents a record of the fact that the award has been received.

At the end of the meet, all records should be turned over to the manager of the meet or the Games Committee.

The scorers accept officially signed results only

The duties of the scorer may be condensed as follows on a 3x5 card for his guidance.

1. Establish headquarters in central place.
2. Prepare master score sheet.
3. Record only from official results signed by the Head Judge of the event.
4. Record name, school, points of each winner in proper space.
5. Furnish official results to announcer and custodian of public score board.
6. Prepare award cards for each place in each event.
7. File original results for auditing purposes.
8. Deliver all records to manager of meet at conclusion.

Announcer

The announcer at a track meet (at any athletic contest for that matter) has a single task and duty. His one and only job is to be informative so that those attending the meet may follow its progress in an intelligent fashion and so that their interest may be maintained at a high pitch throughout.

To fulfill his role effectively, he must maintain an impersonal attitude toward any team. His main requisites are a clear, resonant voice and a sense of good taste. It is wise for him to say too little rather than too much. He must not act as a cheer leader for any person or group. He should remember that he is not an entertainer, a comedian, or a clown. The spectators came to see a track meet and not to listen to a vaudeville act nor a dramatic production. Neither is it his duty to excite or to incite. His facilities are not to be used for advertising purposes, as a social calender, or for general announcements of any kind.

Specifically he should:

1. Give a background of records and performances in previous runnings of the same event.

The announcer is not a cheer leader

2. Give the calls for all events.

3. Announce the official results of all events as soon after their completion as possible. (Give names, school, times, heights, distances.)

4. Give the lane positions of runners in each event.

5. In field events, announce the qualifiers, those still remaining in events, and from time to time the height of the bar and who has cleared, and the best distances and who made them.

6. Give a periodic résumé of the scoring of the teams and their standing on the basis of the number of events completed.

7. Assist the marshal when necessary by requesting spectators to help maintain conditions which will help everyone enjoy the meet to the fullest.

8. Give information concerning rest rooms, exits, etc., which are for the convenience of the spectators.

9. Present the winners as they receive their awards.

10. At the close of the meet, give the final scores and standings of the teams.

11. Thank the spectators and bid them good afternoon.

Timers

Accurate timing requires good eyesight, quick eye–finger reaction and co-ordination, and correct technique. It is assumed that reliable stop watches properly synchronized are available. Watches should measure to one-tenth of a second.

In the 100- and 220-yard dashes, the high and low hurdles (and on some tracks, the 440-yard dash and ½-mile run) which start at the end of the straightaway, it is necessary to be able to see the flash of the starting gun clearly. When the signal is given that all is in readiness, the timers should be alert. It is customary for the head timer to call "Gun up!" as a command to bring everyone to attention. All must concentrate on the starter. Each must have an unobstructed view of the starter's gun. Figure 6 shows a timer in readiness to start his watch.

The announcer is an informer and guides the eyes of the spectators

Simultaneously with the flash of the gun (light travels faster than sound), the timers must start their watches. Two techniques have been developed which produce more accurate timing. First, it has been discovered that the

FIGURE 6. WITH WATCH POISED AND READY TO START, THE TIMER WATCHES INTENTLY FOR THE FLASH FROM THE STARTER'S GUN. NOTE THAT THE FOREFINGER IS ON THE STEM OF THE WATCH.

forefinger reacts more quickly than the thumb.[1] As a consequence, the forefinger should be used to push the stem of the watch to start and stop it. Second, the stem of the watch should be pressed to the point where all the slack in its movement has been removed. The stems of most watches will move a short distance before activating the hand. If this slack is taken up, there will be less lag between the firing of the gun and the actual start of the

[1] Breshnahan and Tuttle, *Track and Field Athletics* (St. Louis: C. V. Mosby Co., 1937).

The finger reacts more quickly than the thumb

watch. These same procedures should be followed when the watch is stopped at the finish of the race.

When the watches are checked out to the timers, they should practice starting, stopping, and reading them. In this way they will familiarize themselves with the characteristics of their watches. Such practice will give the timers greater confidence in carrying out their responsibilities and will tend to produce more accurate timing. No two watches operate exactly alike.

The ability to read the watch correctly is also necessary. Practically all watches now used for timing track events are calibrated to one-tenth of a second. One should, however, check the markings on the dial. He should take several practice readings. It is a good practice for the timers to read each other's watches in order to check each other. A small magnifying glass, commonly used for reading, is a desirable and useful aid in making accurate readings.

The synchronization of watches may be checked by starting watches simultaneously by pressing the stems of two watches together. To the extent that the tension in the two stems is the same, the watches will start together. They should be stopped in the same manner. They should be tested over a short period (ten seconds) and over a long period (one or two minutes). If the watches read the same, one can be fairly sure that discrepancies in timing the meet will be due to differences in the individual timers.

After the race has started, the timers should obtain positions on either side of the track opposite the finish line. They must be able to sight directly across the track along the finish line. The timers may watch the runners until they approach within ten yards of the finish. Then, they should sight along the finish with their watches poised in readiness to stop them. The watch should be stopped the instant any part of a competitor's torso reaches the finish line.

Learn about your watch before the race

After stopping the watch, each timer should read his own watch and record this reading on the cards provided for the purpose. The card should be handed to the head timer. The hand of the watch should not be snapped back to its starting position until clearance is given by the head timer. The head timer may desire to check all readings in case wide discrepancies arise.

The timers should not announce their readings nor compare the time which their watches recorded. This is the responsibility of the head timer. Strict adherence to this policy will avoid controversies in races which are run against time or where records may be at stake.

Occasionally it is necessary to recall competitors because of an unfair start. When this happens, the timers must be doubly sure that they snap their watches back in readiness for the next start.

The head timer should remind the timers repeatedly to check their watches before the start of a race. He should also review with them all the procedures mentioned above before the meet begins. These precautions will tend to prevent timing problems during the progress of the meet.

Three timers are necessary to establish an official time for each race. For this reason three timers are designated as official and one as a substitute. In case one of the three fails to record the time of the race, the watch of the substitute timer is used as extra insurance. The head timer should also operate a watch. His watch may be used when necessary to supply the third timer. He may also desire to check the time of his watch against that of the other timers.

When the official time for a race is determined, the head timer should record the time on the proper card, sign the card, and send it to the scorer.

One set of instructions should be prepared for each of the timers and one set for the head timer:

Record the time—don't discuss it

Instructions to Timers

1. Check out watch from head timer.
2. Operate several times for practice.
3. Use forefinger to start and stop.
4. Take up slack in stem in readiness to start at "Gun-up" signal. Stop with the same technique.
5. Start watch at flash of gun (sight of smoke).
6. Stop watch when torso of first runner reaches finish line.
7. Sight along finish line when runner is within ten yards of finish.
8. Record watch reading on blanks provided for purpose, sign, and hand to head timer.
9. Preserve reading on watch until cleared by head timer.
10. Do not discuss or compare time with anyone.

Instructions to Head Timer

1. Check out watches from manager.
2. Distribute watches to timers, review timing procedures, suggest practice (see timers' instructions).
3. Appoint official timers and substitute.
4. Assign positions on either side of track.
5. Signal to starter when ready.
6. Collect recorded times, compare, determine official time. (Middle time, if watches are all different—if two watches agree, that is the official time.)
7. Check readings of all watches, if necessary.
8. Record official time and send to scorer.
9. Organize and prepare timers for next race.
10. In case of records, have referee check watches.

JUDGES

The judges of the finish have the most delicate job of all the track officials. Tremendous responsibility rests upon their shoulders. It is their job to determine the order of the winners. In races where several competitors are bunched at the finish, mistakes in judgment are likely

Preserve the reading until released

to be made in spite of the most concentrated and conscientious effort. Instances are not uncommon where winners have been overlooked entirely because the same contestant has been chosen for two places. It is also comparatively easy to overlook runners who are in the lanes closest to the judges. Here is one phase of officiating where closeness to the play is not an asset. As a rule, first place is not difficult to pick; but second, third, and fourth places can create a nightmare for the judges. Above all else, the judges must not be excitable individuals. They must be keen, discriminating, and dependable. If possible, men with track experience are preferable.

FIGURE 7. JUDGE WATCHING THE APPROACH OF A RUNNER.

Through experience, some techniques have been developed which have proven to be helpful. For purposes of double checking, two judges are recommended for each place. One judge is stationed on one side of the track and one on the other.

A judge can be more discriminating in his judgments and see the relative positions of runners more clearly if he is some distance away from the track and elevated above it.

Judging is delicate work—experience is essential

As a consequence, platforms built at graduated heights like stairsteps and placed as much as twenty feet from the edge of the track are now available at most tracks.

Judges should watch the runners as they approach the finish line. (See figure 7.) But when the runners are about ten yards away, the judges should sight across the

FIGURE 8. JUDGE'S ATTENTION HAS MOVED, WITH THE RUNNER. HE IS NOW SIGHTING ALONG THE FINISH LINE TO PICK THE WINNER OF THE RACE.

track along the finish line. Figure 8 shows judge intently sighting along the finish line in readiness to pick winners. The first contestant whose torso reaches the finish line is the winner. The judges who are to pick second, third, and fourth places must carefully and quickly count the runners who cross this line in order to select the place for which they are responsible. As the runner who fits the place the judge is picking reaches the line, he should follow this runner down the track in order to identify him. He is identified by a number on his back, or, in dual or triangular meets, by the color of his jersey, which represents his school.

Follow the runners as they approach the finish

Each judge should write down on a card the number or school of the winner of the place he is picking and hand this card to the head judge. He should do this without consulting the other officials or anyone else. The head judge will then record the results and send them to the scorer.

When conflicts in judging arise, the head judge should draw the judges apart from contestants, coaches, other officials, and spectators for consultation. By this means, it is usually possible to straighten out any irregularities without confusion. If errors in judgment cannot be solved, the matter must be referred to the referee. If, perchance, official pictures were taken of the finish, these may be used to settle the matter.

The head judge should always appoint judges to pick one more place than the number to score.

Instructions for Head Judge

1. Assign place each judge is to pick, including one more than the number to score. Two judges for each place.
2. Review procedures to be followed (see instruction to judges).
3. Tabulate results turned in by judges and send to scorer.
4. In case of discrepancies, assemble judges apart from others to straighten out.

Instructions for Judges

1. Judges picking same place get on the opposite sides of track.
2. Watch race until runners approach within ten yards of finish line, then sight across track along line.
3. When any part of torso reaches line, runner has finished.
4. A fallen runner must be completely across line.
5. Write on finish card the number or name of school of winner of place you are to pick.
6. Sign and hand card to head judge.
7. Do not consult or discuss decision with anyone.

Privacy is golden when conflicts arise

TRACK INSPECTORS

There should be at least four track inspectors. They should be stationed along the start and finish of each curve. In hurdle races, they should be spread equally along the hurdle route. Their job is to report any violation of the rules to the referee. The inspectors have no authority. They are observers, but they must know the rules which control the contestants on the track. There are five rules which the inspectors must know:

1. In races run in lanes, each competitor must finish in the same lane in which he started.
2. In hurdle races, hurdlers may not run around a hurdle or advance or trail a leg around the side of a hurdle.
3. A runner must be two strides ahead of a competitor before cutting across his path or it must be clear that he does not interfere with his competitor.
4. A competitor may not jostle or impede another.
5. In relay races, runners must exchange batons within the restraining lines.

As a rule, there are not many violations of the track rules. When violations occur, they usually involve jostling or passing illegally. The fact that few violations occur does not minimize the importance of the duties of the inspectors. The potential of their presence may act as a deterrent in a heated race. They may find it expedient to remind runners as they pass that they must not cut across too soon or jostle.

Instructions to Inspectors

1. Report to referee for direction and placement.
2. Review rules on passing a runner, staying in lanes, jostling, and hurdling.
3. Report violations immediately to referee by giving a full description of what happened. Inspectors have no authority to make decisions.
4. Caution runners to prevent fouls.

9

Field Events

IN LARGE MEETS, THE FIELD EVENTS ARE SUPERVISED by a head field judge. He assists the referee. He has a threefold job.

1. Through the inspector of implements, he checks all implements to be used in the meet to see that they conform to the standards specified in the rules.
2. He sees that the proper relationship is maintained between the field events and the track events. Time schedules must be maintained. Those who compete in both track and field events must be handled so that no unnecessary delays in running off events are permitted.
3. He supervises the administration of all field events to the extent that they are conducted according to rule. He is available to rule on disputes or other problems which may be referred to him. He must know the rules under which the meet is being conducted.

In small meets, there is not usually a separate official for this job. The referee assumes these duties.

The field events may consist of as many as eight events. These divide themselves into the continuous type of field events—the high jump and pole vault—and the limited trial field events such as the shot, discus, broad jump. In general, the duties of the officials in each may be classed

Implements must be checked

under four headings. These should be included when a list of instructions is prepared for the judges.

1. *Determining the order of competition.* In the continuous type of events, the order is usually determined by lot. In dual meets, the contestants are often alternated. The visitors are permitted to choose whether they shall be first or second in the order. Occasionally in large meets the contestants may be divided into flights of as many as ten in a flight. One flight jumps in order, until all have successfully cleared the bar or been eliminated. Then the next flight starts.

In the limited trial events, the common practice is to perform in pairs. Each pair takes two trials in order. Then the next pair follows. This procedure is continued until all have competed, then the second round of trials is started.

If the field of competitors is large (40 or more), the pairs may be grouped into flights. Each flight completes all of its trials before the next flight starts.

The general practice in pairing and in arranging the sequence is to pair contestants of comparable ability and to place the pairs in the reverse order of their ability. The pairs with best performances compete last.

In the finals or semi-finals of all limited trial field events, the competition is in reverse order of the best performances in the preliminary rounds.

2. *Measuring the results of performance.* In the continuous field events—high jump and pole vault—the height of the bar is measured at the conclusion of the event or at the height at which a record is broken. If a record is broken, the height of the bar must be measured before the bar is moved. All measurements are made from the ground vertically to the upper side of the bar at its lowest point.

In the limited trial events, two practices are followed by necessity. In the shot, 35-pound weight, and the broad jump, measurements must be made and recorded

The order of competition may be determined by agreement

after each trial. If performances were marked to be measured at the conclusion of the trials, some of the marks would be lost or distorted by subsequent performances which lighted in the same area. In the other events, markers may be used to indicate the best distance of each contestant until all trials are completed. Then, measurements are taken and recorded to determine the qualifiers or the winners.

The distances in the broad jump and javelin are measured at right angles to the scratch line to the nearest break in the ground. The distances in the events in a circle are measured along an extended diameter of the circle. (See page 89 for detailed instructions.)

3. *Judging the legality of performance.* Each event has a list of those acts which constitute a foul. They are listed below under the specific instructions on the duties of the officials in each event. In general, they constitute touching the ground or advancing beyond the scratch line, or restraining line, for that event.

4. *Recording and reporting the results of the event.* At the completion of an event, the results must be recorded. Then the records must be studied to determine the winners of the various places. When the winners have been indicated, the head judge of the event signs the reports and delivers them to the scorer. The assistant judges return all implements and tapes to the proper custodian.

There are, in addition, some duties which are peculiar to a particular event. These are listed below under the special instructions to the officials for the event.

Instructions for High Jump

1. Report to head judge.
2. Secure entries and record cards from scorer.
3. Call roll and arrange for draw by lot if order is not already established. Call jumps in order of drawings.
4. Start bar at height to fit class of competition,

If the mark can be lost, measure it

but at as great a height as is reasonably possible. (The better jumpers may pass the lower heights.)

5. Raise the bar by one- to two-inch increments. It is customary to determine the height at which to start the bar and the increment at each change after consultation with the contestants before the event begins. The weak performers will practically always ask for the lower limits while the better performers will insist on greater heights. The judges must make the final decisions. Remember that the best performances are not attained by prolonging the event.

6. Give each jumper three trials at each height. Trials must be taken in order. A record must be kept of each jumper's performances at each height. (See form I for sample record sheet.)

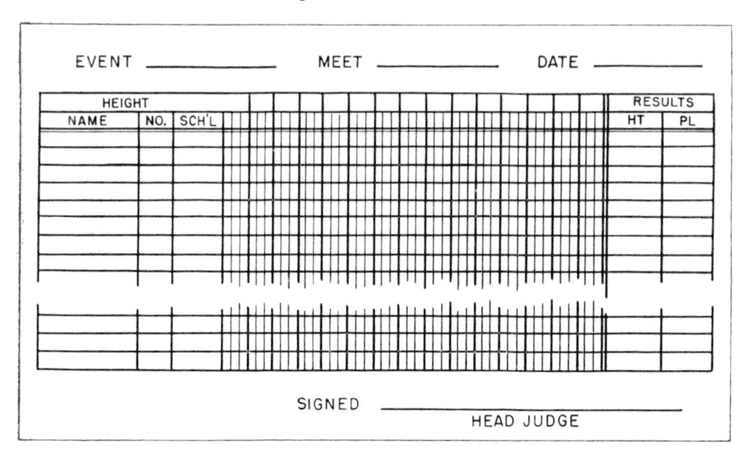

EVENT ______ MEET ______ DATE ______

HEIGHT				RESULTS	
NAME	NO.	SCH'L		HT	PL

SIGNED ______
HEAD JUDGE

FORM I. A SIMPLE CHART FOR RECORDING THE RESULTS OF A CONTINUOUS TYPE OF FIELD EVENT, SUCH AS THE HIGH JUMP OR POLE VAULT.

7. A trial consists of clearing the bar with all parts of the body, knocking the bar off the standards, passing under the bar or the line of the bar extended, or leaving the ground in an attempt.

8. Jumpers must take off from one foot to make a fair jump.

9. Continue event until all have failed to clear the bar or all but one are eliminated.

Raise the height of the bar by increments far

10. Measure the greatest height cleared. (See diagram 6.)

11. Check records to designate place winners. In case of ties, the points are divided equally between the contestants concerned, unless other provisions or rules are announced in advance.

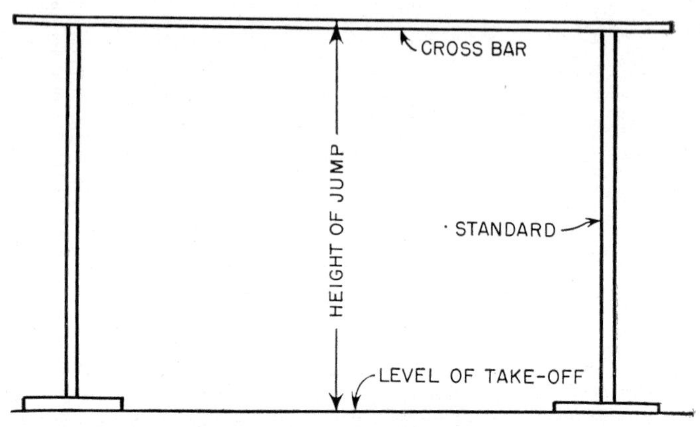

DIAGRAM 6. THE CORRECT MEASUREMENT FOR THE HIGH JUMP. THE POLE VAULT IS MEASURED IN THE SAME MANNER.

12. Sign report and return records and tape to scorer's table.

13. Special arrangements may be made for those competing in other events at the same time.

Instructions for the Pole Vault

With the following exceptions, the officials should follow the same procedure for conducting the pole vault as listed for the high jump:

1. The bar may be raised as much as six inches for the first or second raises. Thereafter, three- to four-inch increments should be used.

2. A trial consists of displacing the bar, passing under it, crossing the line of the bar extended, carrying any part of the competitor's pole beyond the line of the bar extended, or leaving the ground in an attempted vault.

Measure a record when it is made

3. The top hand may not be moved up nor the lower hand moved above the top hand.

Instructions for the Broad Jump

Instructions 1, 2, and 3 for the high jump apply. In large meets, the drawings by pairs and by flights will undoubtedly be made in advance. Form II shows a sample chart for recording the results of limited trial field events.

EVENT ________ MEET ________ DATE ________

NAME	NO.	SCHOOL	TRIALS									FINALS						RESULTS		
			1		2		3		4		Q	1		2		3		DIST.		PLACE
			FT.	IN.	FT.	IN.	FT.	IN.	FT.	IN.		FT.	IN.	FT.	IN.	FT.	IN.	FT.	IN.	

SIGNED ________
HEAD JUDGE

FORM II. A SAMPLE CHART FOR RECORDING THE RESULTS OF LIMITED TRIAL FIELD EVENTS, SUCH AS THE BROAD JUMP, SHOT PUT, DISCUS OR JAVELIN.

4. Give each jumper four jumps or trials in the preliminaries and three in the finals. If the meet is a two-day event and semi-finals are held, two trials are permitted in the semi-finals. The number of jumps may vary according to the rules under which the meet is conducted.

If the candidates are competing in pairs, then each pair shall take two jumps or trials before the next pair competes.

5. A trial occurs when a contestant's shoe extends over the scratch line when taking off for a jump or if

Use a chart to record the mark

he runs across the scratch line or scratch line extended.

6. Measure each jump at right angles to take-off board and from front edge of board or board extended to nearest point on ground which is touched by the jumper. (See diagram 7.)

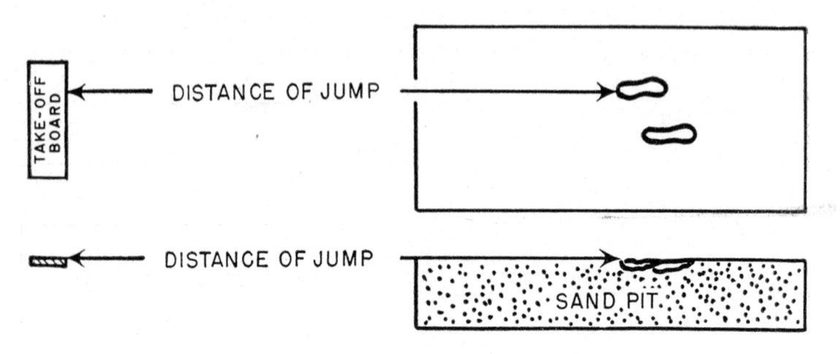

DIAGRAM 7. METHOD OF MEASURING DISTANCE IN THE BROAD JUMP.

7. Use knife-edge or flat blade to mark nearest point of jump.

8. Have zero end of tape at jumping pit.

9. Head judge calls order, records distances, and calls fouls. Other two judges mark point of jump and measure distance.

10. Judge at pit keeps sand at same level as take-off before each jump.

11. Judge at take-off keeps ground in front of scratch line smooth and at same level as take-off.

12. Determine qualifiers and place winners, sign results, and deliver to scorer. Twice as many as places awarded (but not exceeding ten) qualify for the semi-finals, and one more than places awarded qualify for the finals.

Instructions for Shot Put

Procedures 1, 2, 3, 4, 7, 8, 9, and 12 of the broad jump apply to the shot put. Numbers 5 and 6 are as follows:

5. A foul occurs when the foot touches the top of the toe board or the circle or when the contestant

Measure the shortest distance

steps outside the circle before the put is marked. A foul counts as a trial but is not measured. Figure 9 shows the head judge of discus, watching feet of contestant in order to determine legality of throw.

6. Measure each put from the nearest edge of mark made by put to the nearest point on the inside edge of the circle. This point may be found by moving the tape through an arc along the inside edge of the circle until the shortest distance is found. (See diagram 8.) The zero end of the tape should be held

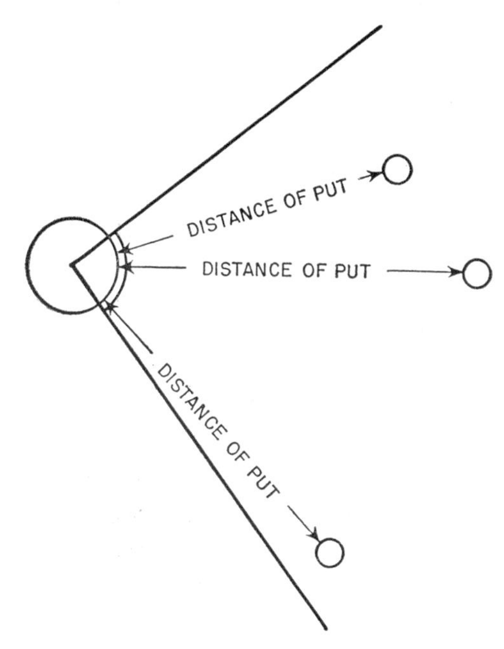

Diagram 8. Method of measuring distance in the shot put. The discus would be measured in the same manner.

at the mark of the put. The other end extends through the circle and should coincide with the diameter of the circle. The exact point on the edge of the circle may be determined by moving the tape slowly back and forth through an arc. The zero end is used as the center of rotation. The shortest dis-

The radius extended is the distance intended

tance from the mark of the put to the inside edge of the circumference of the circle is the correct distance to record.

Instructions for Discus Throw

The shot put and discus are conducted in exactly the same manner with two minor exceptions:

1. Throws to be legal must fall within a 90-degree sector which is marked on the ground.

FIGURE 9. TO DETECT ANY OF THE DISCUS THROWER'S FOOT FAULTS THE HEAD JUDGE MUST HAVE HIS EYES FOCUSED ON THE FEET OF THE CONTESTANT AND UPON THE RING.

2. The best throw of each competitor is marked by means of metal or wooden pins and measured at the end of preliminary and final throws.

Instructions for the Javelin Throw

The distance for the javelin throw is measured the same as for the broad jump.

The discus must park in a 90° degree arc

The point of the javelin must strike the ground first to constitute a legal throw. The javelin must be held at the grip.

The thrower must not touch the scratch line, scratch line extended, or the ground beyond the line until the throw is marked. Figure 10 shows the judge watching thrower until he regains his balance after a throw.

FIGURE 10. THE JUDGE OF THE JAVELIN THROW CHECKS THE THROWER'S POSITION RELATIVE TO THE SCRATCH LINE UNTIL HE REGAINS HIS BALANCE AFTER THE THROW.

If perchance the implement should break while in flight, the trial does not count and a substitute trial should be awarded.

Aside from the above, the javelin event is conducted the same as the other implement events.

Instructions for the Hammer Throw

The hammer and discus events are conducted in the same manner. It is not illegal for the head of the hammer to

The point of the javelin must stick to make the trial tick

hit the ground during the swing. The contestant may not, however, stop his throw and start anew.

Inspector of Implements

The inspector of implements works under the supervision of the head field judge. It is his job to check all implements against the specifications in the rules. He needs a standard steel tape and scale.

The following standards must be maintained in the various implements:

Shot—College, 16 pounds minimum; High School, 12 pounds minimum.

Hammer—Weight, 16 pounds minimum; over-all length, 4-foot maximum.

Discus—Weight, 4 pounds, 6.4 ounces minimum. (Some high schools use the modified discus, weight 3 pounds, 9 ounces.)

Javelin—Length 8.53-feet minimum; weight, 1.765 pounds minimum; grip, 43.31 inches to 35.43 inches from point.

35-Pound Weight—Over-all length, 16 inches maximum; weight, 35 pounds minimum.

When implements are approved, they should be stamped with an appropriate mark. Judges will then permit the use of approved implements only. In many meets, the implements are furnished by the games committee and no others are permitted.

Surveyor

Before the beginning of each season, the track should be measured by an engineer to make sure that all distances from start to finish are correct. An affidavit attesting the results of his work should be filed for use in case of records.

Likewise, all take-offs, circles, scratch lines, and the level of the track and broad jumping pit should be carefully checked.

Professional attest assures that the track is the best

An anemometer should be available on the day of the meet to determine wind velocity and the direction of the wind.

The surveyor can be used to inspect the implements in the absence of an inspector for this purpose.

10

Swimming and Diving

THE CONCEPT THAT A SWIMMING AND DIVING OFFICIAL can be any person who is interested but untrained as an official is no longer tenable. A growing need exists for district organizations of swimming and diving officials. Such organizations could establish certification standards and officiating technique standards, serve as the accrediting body, and conduct training clinics. Interest in competitive swimming and diving on the part of the spectator, contestant, and administrator is growing constantly. To maintain this growth in interest, adequately trained and accredited officials must be readily available, or the dignity and prestige of competitive swimming and diving will not attain the high position it rightfully deserves in the physical education program.

NUMBER OF OFFICIALS

One of the first questions confronting either the swimming coach as he prepares for a dual meet in his pool or the planning committee for a championship meet is: "How many officials are needed to conduct the meet efficiently?"

Ten officials are needed to conduct properly an interscholastic or intercollegiate meet. Of course, when competent officials are available in excess of the following assignments, they should be utilized to the fullest extent.

To judge diving is technical—the judge should be professional

1. One official serves as the meet referee, starter, diving referee, and inspector of lanes and turns at the end of the pool opposite to the starting end.

2. Three officials serve as judges of finish and judges of diving. Two of these judges serve as touch-off judges and one as inspector of lanes and turns at the starting end of the pool. One of these officials is also appointed head judge of finish.

3. One official serves as announcer and clerk of course. This official is usually the manager of the home team.

4. Two officials serve as computers of the diving scores. These officials are usually assistant managers and their work should be checked by the referee.

5. Three officials serve as timers. The possibility of record breaking performances should be anticipated and a fourth timer secured to serve as an alternate in case one of the three regular watches fails to function properly. One of the three regular timers should be appointed head timer.

The number of officials needed to conduct a championship meet depends upon such factors as: (1) number of lanes, (2) use of time or place as the method of qualifying the finalist, and (3) changes of assignments for timers from trials to finals.

A championship meet conducted in a six-lane pool requires the following officials:

1. One official serves as meet referee.
2. One official serves as starter.
3. One official serves as head judge of finish.
4. Twelve to eighteen officials serve as judges of finish.
5. One official serves as referee of diving.
6. Five officials serve as judges of diving.
7. One official serves as secretary of diving.
8. Two officials serve as computers of diving.
9. One official serves as head timer.
10. Eighteen to twenty-four officials serve as timers. One of each group of three or four uses a split-

At least 10 officials are needed

timer to record the split times for that lane. One of each group of timers is appointed head timer for that group.

11. One official serves as the announcer. This official is usually the manager of the host swimming team.

12. One official serves as clerk of course. He should have several assistants.

13. Six to twelve officials serve as inspectors of lanes and turns.

14. Six officials serve as touch-off judges.

When the finalists are determined on the basis of time, then each performer must be timed by at least three timers during the trials. Therefore, eighteen to twenty-four timers are needed depending on the use of alternate timers. This same procedure may be followed for the finals, or the number of timers may be reduced by using four timers to time only the first place winner and one split-timer to take splits in each lane.

DUTIES OF REFEREE

The referee should meet with the other officials at least twenty minutes before the start of a dual meet to make the following assignments:

1. At least three finish judges; one judge to serve as head judge.
2. Three diving judges.
3. Two touch-off judges. If the meet is held in a sixty-foot pool, four touch-off judges will be needed.
4. Two inspectors of lanes and turns.
5. At least three timers; one to serve as head timer.
6. Clerk of course and announcer. (The home team manager usually serves in this capacity.)

At this time the referee should review briefly the duties of each official.

Before the first event the referee should approach each captain or coach to receive the entries written on an entry

Organize and instruct before the start

slip provided by the home team in plenty of time to assure the start of the meet on time. Before each of the remaining events the referee should repeat this procedure in time to avoid any unnecessary delay. All entries are turned over to the clerk of course to be recorded and announced.

The referee has complete authority over the actual conduct of the meet. He should confer on all infractions of the rules with the acting official and report his decision to the clerk of course for announcement.

Some time before the start of a championship meet, the referee should confer with representatives of the host's school and key officials to complete the assignment of the remaining officials.

DUTIES OF STARTER

The starter should thoroughly familiarize himself with the action of the starting gun and carry with him an ample supply of blank cartridges.

He may elect to start the events from a position on the pool deck about twenty feet from the starting mark or from a point about three feet in front of the starting mark.

The starter has complete control of the competitors after they are assigned to their lanes by the clerk of course. Inexperienced competitors should be instructed where to stand while awaiting the initial command "Swimmers Ready!"; to step up together to the mark in the erect position; to assume the bent trunk starting position following the command "Take your Marks!"; to be absolutely motionless while waiting for the pistol shot; and to avoid anticipating the sound of the gun.

When the starter is serving as both referee and starter, he attracts the attention of the judges and timers by saying "Judges and Timers, Ready" and receives a signal of readiness from the head judge and head timer before proceeding with the start. In a championship meet, the starter re-

Be sure the swimmers are motionless before the start

ceives a signal from the referee indicating that the judges and timers are ready.

When the crawl or breast stroke competitors are standing on the starting blocks or starting elevation about four inches behind the mark, the starter gives the initial command "Swimmers Ready!" in a clear, unhurried voice. After the competitors step to the mark, the starter gives the second command "Take your Marks!" and as soon as the competitors hold the conventional starting position for a brief, motionless period, the starter fires the pistol. After the back stroke competitors are in the water holding onto the starting grips, the starter repeats the foregoing procedure. The starter should hold the starting gun above his head in such a manner as to protect spectators and competitors from flying wads.

In the case of a false start by competitor or starter, the starter recalls the competitors by several rapid pistol shots. A recall rope lowered into the water at the thirty foot mark by two assistants will recall the competitors if the pistol shots are not heard.

DUTIES OF FINISH JUDGES

The chief judge should assign the judges to their places at the finish, provide them with finish cards, indicate to them where they are to turn in the finish cards, and review briefly wall and line finishes.

The finish judges observe the finish from opposite sides of the pool and should have an unobstructed view of the finish until the last competitor has finished. To improve the efficiency of the judges, a portable stairway type of elevated platform should be provided.

Although the fastest swimmers are usually placed in the center lanes, the judges should avoid the mistake of overlooking the finish of swimmers in the outside lanes during a close finish.

Judges should not confer with each other until they have

Starter, be calm

submitted their judgment in writing to the chief judge. When more than one judge for each place is used, they should judge from opposite sides of the pool to assure maximum accuracy. Judges should be on the alert at all times for an underwater finish touch by a swimmer. This touch is not so easily seen as an above the surface touch but the possibility should be recognized and given credit.

When the chief judge is serving in that capacity alone, he should observe the finish of each event in order that he can submit his judgment in case of disagreement and thereby arrive at a final decision.

DUTIES OF TIMERS

The host institution is responsible for securing sufficient watches for dual or championship meets and having them examined for accuracy by an expert. The chief timer should check on this point before the start of the meet.

When a watch is assigned to a timer, he should acquaint himself thoroughly with it by starting, stopping, and snapping it back several times. Errors of judgment will be avoided if the timer knows the watch that he is using.

After the assignment of the watches, the chief timer calls the timers together:

1. For assignment to lanes (championship) or position at the finish.
2. To assign a head timer in each group (championship).
3. To assign the three official timers and alternate or alternates by number.
4. To provide them with timers' cards.
5. To instruct them not to snap back their watches until they have been read and recorded by the head timer or chief timer.
6. To instruct them that if two or more of the watches agree, that is the official time; if all three watches disagree then the middle time is the official

If two watches agree, that time is official

time. If one or more watches do not function properly, then the assigned alternate or alternates become the official timers.

7. To instruct them not to obstruct the finish judge's view of the finish.

8. To instruct them to start their watches on the flash of the starter's pistol and to stop their watches when the first place winner touches the finish wall or finish pennant, or when his hand passes under the finish line.

DUTIES OF DIVING REFEREE

The diving referee carefully checks the list of dives submitted by each diver, to avoid mistakes in degrees of difficulty, terminology, repetition of dives, use of nonlisted dives, and signature of the diver.

Just prior to the start of the diving competition the diving referee calls the diving judges together to explain any rule changes, to provide them with score cards, and to assign them to their positions for judging. When the diving board is in the center of the pool and sunlight is not reflected from the surface of the water, the judges should be placed on opposite sides of the pool. However, when the diving board is not in the center of the pool, the diving judges may be placed along one side of the pool, opposite the end of the diving board, with the sun at their backs. All diving judges should have a clear view of the diving.

During dual meets, the diving referee usually serves as a diving judge and may appoint the clerk of course or announcer to blow the whistle following each dive and read off the scores flashed by the diving judges. During championship meets, he should not serve as a diving judge, but he should blow the whistle following each dive and read off the diving scores so they can be recorded by the diving secretary. During the diving competition, he should be constantly alert to any infractions of the rules and be ready

Judges must have a clear view of the dive

to instruct the diving judges and diving secretary regarding the nature of the ruling.

DUTIES OF DIVING JUDGES

The technique of judging diving cannot be mastered over a brief period. To become a competent diving judge, one must know the mechanics of diving, see the best divers perform, frequently observe diving, have access to slow-motion pictures, and be intensely interested in this aspect of swimming competition.

There are several methods that are used by expert diving judges to evaluate diving. When these methods and others are based on the principles of diving, the slight difference in the awards will be insignificant. However, when diving judging is based on an inaccurate interpretation of body movement and the physical principles involved, then a wide divergence of opinion is the rule rather than the exception.

The following standards will serve as a basis for judging diving:

1. *Approach:* The approach shall be smooth, erect, forceful, and confident. No penalty should be incurred because of individual mannerism.

The running approach includes the starting position, the steps preceding the hurdle, the hurdle, and the landing on the board in preparation for the take-off.

The term "run" is used in connection with any dive preceded by three steps and a hurdle, and should not be construed to mean a "run" in the true sense of the word.

2. *Take-off:* The take-off shall be forceful.

The take-off includes the angle of lean, the co-ordinated action of arms and legs from the time that the board is fully depressed until the diver's feet leave the board.

There are six parts of a dive to judge

3. *Elevation:* The elevation or height shall be sufficient to permit proper execution of the dive.

Elevation is the result of a properly executed take-off and signifies the distance or height of the diver above the board or the water.

4. *Execution:* The execution shall be graceful and controlled.

The execution is the performance of the dive from the time the diver leaves the board until his body disappears beneath the surface.

5. *Drop:* For all dives, excluding the plain dives, there should be a marked "breakout" followed by a definite drop with the body aligned for entry.

The drop is the distance from where the diver completes his dive to the surface of the water.

6. *Entry:* The entry should be clean-cut and as nearly perpendicular as possible.

The entry is the vertical or nearly vertical flight of the body into and beneath the surface of the water.

Judging a dive may be thought of as a comparison of the actual dive performed with a mental impression of what constitutes a ten-point dive. The preceding six basic parts of a dive should help the diving judge achieve a well-rounded concept of each dive. As a dive is performed, the diving judge should compare it with his impression of what the dive would look like if it were a ten-point dive. As the dive fails to achieve this high standard, it should be penalized according to the amount of difference that exists.

The following table should be used as an over-all guide: [1]

---

[1] Charles McCaffree, editor, *Official Swimming Guide* (New York: A. S. Barnes and Co., Inc., 1948), p. 167.

Compare the dive with your image of the perfect dive

Completely failed				0	points
Unsatisfactory	1	–		2	
Deficient	3	–		4	
Satisfactory	5	–		6	6.5
Good	7	7.5	–	8	8.5
Very good	9	9.5	–	10	

Four penalty standards have been established: (1) the score awarded a dive other than the dive announced must be 0, (2) the score awarded a dive following a balk is reduced by one third, (3) the score awarded following two successive balks is 0, and (4) the score awarded a running dive preceded by two steps rather than by three or more steps is 0. It would be exceedingly difficult to establish exact penalty standards for all aspects of diving.

DUTIES OF DIVING SECRETARY

The diving secretary records the individual awards on the score sheet as they are called out by the diving referee. When five judges are used, he cancels the highest and lowest awards or any two when the five awards are identical and adds the three remaining awards. When three judges are used as in dual-meet competition, no cancellation of awards is made. He announces the sum and degree of difficulty to the two computers who quickly complete the multiplication and check with each other for error in their calculations. He then records this number on the score sheet and announces it to the spectators, who may wish to keep a progressive score. Following this procedure, he adds the score to the previous sum total and passes the score sheet to the computers for checking. When the competition is finished he divides the sum total by three to obtain the final score. Then, in collaboration with the diving referee, he lists the order of the competitors, adds his signature with that of the diving referee, and passes the final results to the announcer for announcement.

Carefully check the divers' scores

DUTIES OF ANNOUNCER

The announcer should be supplied with complete information immediately following each event, such as: order in which contestants finished, name of each contestant, school or club he represents, first-place time for final events or the time for each contestant for trial events, and all records and previous holders and dates in case a new record is established. His announcement of results should be carefully and clearly presented.

DUTIES OF CLERK OF COURSE

The clerk of course must know the scope of his job and carry out his responsibilities effectively or the progress of the meet will be seriously hampered. He must provide himself with adequate assistance, particularly for a championship meet, because he and his assistants are responsible for many details. The clerk of course and his staff are responsible in whole or in part for:

1. Entry forms and mailing of same.
2. Preparation of entry scratch lists for coaches.
3. Preparation of blank trial forms.
4. Paper and numbers for organizing trials and drawing lanes.
5. Preparation of sufficient copies of the trials, heats, and finals for the coaches, officials, and contestants.
6. Seating arrangements for contestants.
7. Dressing room facilities and towels.
8. Securing sufficient stop watches and recording cards for timers and judges.
9. Securing diving score cards and score sheets.
10. Securing necessary officials, starting gun, and whistles.
11. Securing finish pennant.
12. Securing services of a scorer.
13. Protecting valuables.
14. Record forms and signatures of the officials.

Announcing can be educational

15. Supplying the announcer with correct and ample information.

16. Organization of the results for the records and publicity.

17. Notifying contestants of their events at least five minutes before they are due to compete.

18. Placing the contestants at the starting mark for each event at the proper time.

DUTIES OF INSPECTORS OF TURNS AND LANES

The inspectors of turns and lanes must determine the legality of the:

1. Breast stroke, particularly the kick.
2. Breast stroke turn and push-off.
3. Breast stroke finish.
4. Backstroke turn and push-off.
5. Backstroke finish.
6. Crawl turn.
7. Position in lanes—swimmers must stay in assigned lanes.

Infractions of the rules must be reported to the referee immediately after the finish of the event with full particulars. These officials should station themselves directly above the end of the pool when inspecting turns and push-offs and should observe the breast stroke from the rear, front, side, and above, before making the final decision. Whenever possible, there should be one inspector for every two lanes at each end of the pool. Disqualifications should be based on what is actually seen, not what is imagined. Refraction errors are possible when observing a contestant from the side only.

DUTIES OF TOUCH-OFF JUDGES

The touch-off judge should kneel at the side of the relay swimmer who is on the mark about to leave, with the little finger of the near hand in contact with the top of the swimmer's little toe. He leans forward over the edge of

Report what you see—not what you imagine

the pool in order to see the incoming swimmer's finish touch. In this way he sees the incoming swimmer touch and feels the starting swimmer leave. When the contact of the finger and toe is broken simultaneously with the finish touch, the relay take-off is legal. Of course, the starting swimmer may leave after the finish touch is made, but if the starting swimmer breaks the finger contact (leaves the mark) before the finish touch is made, the relay take-off is illegal and the touch-off judge must report the infraction to the referee for disqualification of the relay team.

The touch-off judge does not signal the starting swimmer in any manner whatsoever. He simply uses the hand–eye method of determining the legality of the take-off. He should resist the tendency to duck back to avoid being splashed by the incoming swimmer.

II

Tennis

TENNIS MAY BE CHARACTERIZED AS THE SPORT WITH the fewest players and the most officials. One singles match which involves two players requires thirteen officials if a full coterie is used. In a dual meet where six singles matches are underway at the same time, seventy-three officials would be necessary if all places were filled. Only twelve players would be participating.

It is clearly evident that the problem of furnishing a sufficient number of competent officials for a dual match between two schools or for a tournament becomes practically insurmountable. Except in very few instances it is impossible to obtain the number of officials required by rule to conduct a match. Even if they were available, they would have to volunteer their services. If they demanded remuneration, the cost would be prohibitive, except probably in the large national and international tournaments.

It is much more desirable to do without officials than to secure untrained and incompetent ones. Wrong decisions of any type in tennis do more to annoy the players and, many times, to decide the outcome of a match than erroneous decisions in any other sport. It must be remembered that the decision of an official which is based on judgment is final. He may not be overruled on a question of judgment.

No officials are better than poor officials

The problem of officials may be the reason for the high ethical standards and good sportsmanship that has developed in tennis competition. The contestants are forced to officiate their own games. Each player makes the decision on the balls on his side of the net. As a consequence, a spirit of fairness pervades practically all play. In case of doubt, a player almost invariably rules against himself.

On the surface, this practice may seem to be the ideal solution to a difficult problem. Experience has shown, however, that the practice of self-officiating is not satisfactory at all and in many instances decidedly unfair. For instance, in the case of foot faults, it is impossible for a player to be sure that he has or has not violated the rules. In a crucial stage of a match, the pressure of circumstances requires that he rule against himself on a decision which is questionable to him but which may have been actually in his favor.

For these reasons efforts should be made to train, develop, and provide officials for all tournaments and league and conference matches. While it is recognized that a full quota of officials may be impossible to attain, a fairly satisfactory partial solution may be worked out. There is tremendous social interest in tennis and students and followers of the game are eager to assist in its administration. If the leadership and the stimulus for training officials are furnished, surprisingly favorable results may be attained. The discussion of the officials and their duties which follow are directed toward supplying this need. The United States Lawn Tennis Association[1] has done much to encourage an interest in tennis officiating.

THE OFFICIALS

The officials for tennis consist of a referee, two umpires, and ten linesmen.

---

[1] *Rules of Lawn Tennis* (New York: United States Lawn Tennis Association, 1948).

It is difficult to self-officiate foot faults

It may be of interest to point out that the rules of tennis do not list the officials required for a match, nor do they, except in one instance (Rule 28), refer to the officials and their duties in any way. Only in the umpire's manual are these instructions found.

The Referee

The referee is the final authority on appeals which involve questions of law. He has the general over-all supervision of a match or tournament. He must be available at all times when play is in progress.

In general, it may be said that his authority covers those factors incident to the play, such as assigning officials; changing or removing officials; assigning courts; starting, stopping, postponing, defaulting, and delaying matches; and excusing players from competition for a definite period, as his judgment based on the conditions which prevail may indicate.

Only in cases of appeal or referral on points of rules does he enter into the decisions which govern the actual play.

The Umpire

The umpire is the principal official of a match. An umpire should be provided for each contest, even though it is not possible to enlist the services of any other official. To a limited extent, he can cover the assignments usually assigned to the ten linesmen. With an umpire in charge, considerable responsibility is removed from the shoulders of the contestants and greater fairness can be administered to both on most of the play situations which require decisions.

The umpire should have a seat on a platform which is at least five feet high. The platform should be centered on the line of the net extended and several feet away from the net post. Figure 11 shows such a platform, with an umpire seated and ready for duty.

Wrong decisions annoy contestants

The duties of the umpire in chronological order follow.

Preliminary Duties

Like the officials in other sports the umpire in tennis has the usual routine pregame duties. He must:

1. Measure height of net at posts and at center and observe the net's condition and placement.

FIGURE 11. UMPIRE IN POSITION IN UMPIRE'S CHAIR AND READY FOR DUTY.

The umpire is the principal official

2. Check facilities for other officials.
3. Check necessary supplies at the umpire's platform (that is, balls, etc.).
4. Secure score card and pencil.
5. Learn correct pronunciation of names of contestants.
6. Supervise the toss for the choice of court and service.
7. Prepare score card for first set.
8. Check and instruct other officials.
9. Start match promptly at scheduled time. Three minute warm-up is sufficient.
10. Determine readiness of other officials and announce match.

Duties during Match

1. Announce each player as he serves for the first time.
2. Record each point and then announce the score.
3. Announce all decisions which effect the play (for example, "out," "let," "fault," "not up").
4. Repeat any decisions made by other officials.
5. Change balls when necessary. The decision to replace the balls is the sole responsibility of the umpire.
6. Announce game, set, and match scores.
7. If no other officials are available, assume their duties.
8. Control disturbances by gallery.
9. Suspend play as circumstances require and make such other decisions as the proper conduct of the match may indicate.

Concluding Duties

1. Announce the final score and winner.
2. Record final score and winner.
3. Sign score card and file with proper officials.

Net Umpire

The net umpire is in a sense an assistant to the umpire. In this capacity, he should keep a duplicate score. In addi-

The umpire announces the match, controls the crowd

tion, he is responsible for calling "let," "fault," or "through." When the ball goes under or through the net and when requested by the umpire, he calls, "not up." His position is on the court level and near a net post.

There is usually insufficient personnel, so that net umpires are not available. As a result, the umpire assumes the duties of the net umpire.

The Linesman

If a full component of officials is at hand, there would be ten linesmen for each court. They are stationed in accordance with the positions shown in diagram 9. The positions of the linesmen are designated by the number next to the square. Assignments are usually made by number. By superimposing the diagram on the court, one may locate without difficulty the position to which he has been assigned.

The linesmen should sit in chairs which are placed as far from the boundaries of the courts as possible, in order to avoid interference with the players. The chairs should be of a dark color, preferably green, and the uniforms of the linesmen should be of dark color.

If all positions are not attended, the linesmen should be assigned to cover those stations which are most difficult for the umpire to see. These would be the base lines and the side and service lines farthest from the umpire.

The primary job of the linesman is to call "outs" on the lines which are assigned to him. He does not make decisions on any other lines. Neither does he make any comment if a ball is in play. The base linesmen who are stationed at positions 3 and 4 (diagram 9) have the additional responsibility of calling foot faults. Figure 12 [1] is reproduced to show the five types of foot faults which may be committed. Figure 12 also shows the legal position for

---

[1] *Umpire's Manual and Rules of Lawn Tennis* (New York: United States Lawn Tennis Association, 1948).

Linesmen dress dark—sit quietly

serving. See the two pictures in the lower left-hand corner.

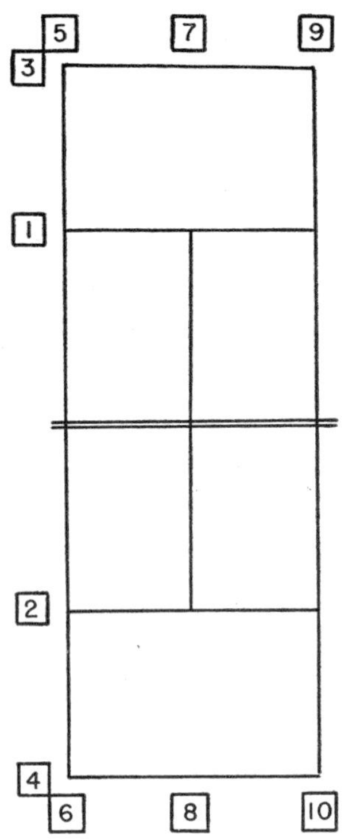

DIAGRAM 9. POSITION OF LINESMEN FOR TENNIS MATCH. LINESMEN 5, 6, 9, AND 10 ALSO JUDGE SIDELINE AND DOUBLES MATCH.

The following guides, if followed by linesmen, will aid in raising the efficiency of their work:

1. Be constantly on the alert and concentrate on the job at hand. Most decisions are not difficult. However, if one permits oneself to be distracted or if one relaxes one's vigilance for a moment, that is likely to be the moment when a close call escapes one.

2. Anticipate decisions but do not make an announcement until the ball hits the surface.

Focus on court ahead of the ball

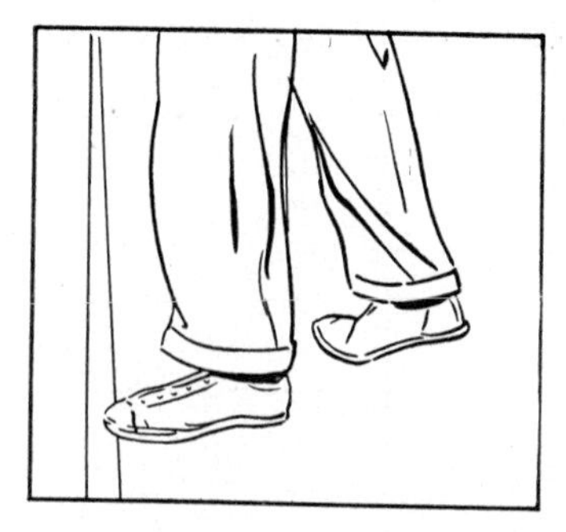

If you step on the line, or if your foot just touches the line, it is a foot fault.

Swinging your foot over the line or into the court before you hit the ball is a foot fault.

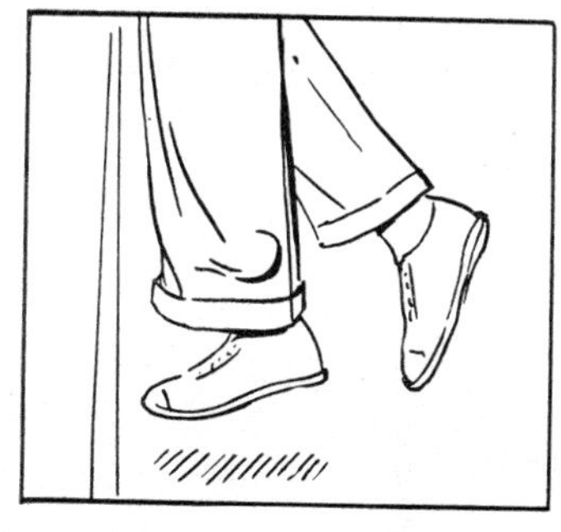

Maintain contact with the ground. A jump is a foot fault.

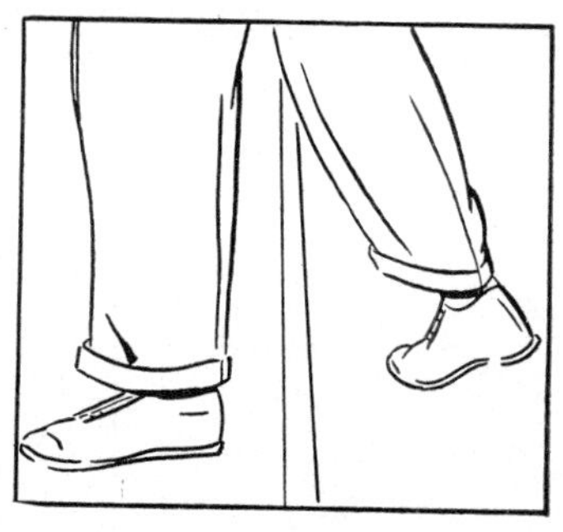

Stepping into the court is a foot fault.

Keep both feet back of the line until the racket hits the ball—this is a fair service.

Keep a little back of the line, as shown above, and avoid trouble.

FIGURE 12. THE FIRST FOUR DRAWINGS SHOW TYPES OF FOOT FAULTS THAT MAY BE COMMITTED DURING A SERVICE. THE LAST TWO SHOW LEGAL POSITIONS FOR SERVING.

3. Watch the ball. If the direction of the ball is such that it may in the judgment of a linesman fall in the area for which he is responsible, the linesman should quickly focus his gaze on about the spot where he thinks the ball may hit. When the eyes are moving rapidly from one spot to another, one's vision is not accurate. For this reason, it is important that the focus be on the surface in advance of the ball in order that reliable judgments may be made.

4. The linesman should announce his decisions in a loud, clear voice. He announces a decision only when the ball is "out" or there is a "fault." No decision is ever announced when the ball is in play.

5. The linesman must not move about and must be quiet while play is in progress. Movements such as retrieving balls, smoking, and disturbances by talking are very disrupting to the players.

6. If, after making a decision, a linesman discovers that he is wrong, he should not hesitate to correct his mistake.

7. The dress of the linesman should be of a dark color. White shirt or trousers create a bad background for the ball when it is in the line of sight between the linesman and the player who is facing him.

ANNOUNCING TECHNIQUES

A specific form and etiquette has been developed for announcing. It is important that the umpire learn the announcing procedures and that he follow them strictly. By conforming to the established practices the spectators will be served best. The proper dignity and refinement peculiar to tennis will be maintained.

In the first place, all announcements should be timed so as to secure the greatest audience. The umpire should pause until any applause or confusion has subsided and then make his announcement in a clear, strong, unhurried voice. The manner in which announcements are made can add much to the enjoyment of the match.

No decision is announced on ball in play

At the beginning of play, the umpire makes the following statement:

"This match is between Mr. Doe and Mr. Roe. Mr. Doe is serving." If the contest is between schools or if it is a tournament between schools, the name of the school which the player represents should also be given.

It is important to get the correct pronunciation of each name. Most people are annoyed when their names are mispronounced.

It is also customary to ask, "Linesmen, ready?" and then, when all is in readiness, to declare, "Play!"

The score of the game is announced after each point. The score of the server is always announced first. Thus, if the server wins the first point, the announcement is, "15-love." If he wins the second point and then loses the third, the announcements are, in order: "30-love"; "30-15"; and so on until the game is finished.

If there is a deuce game, the point after deuce is always announced in the following manner: "Advantage Mr. Roe." No other terminology is acceptable.

At the end of the game, announce the winner thus: "Game, Mr. Doe" or just "Game Doe" omitting the formal titles.

At the completion of each game, the games score should always be given, for example: "Game Mr. Roe. Games are 3 to 2, first set; Mr. Roe leads."

If a game also determines the winner of a set, the announcement should be: "Game and first set, Mr. Doe, 6 to 4."

After the first set, the set score is announced after every 3 or 4 games. As an example: "Games are 3 to 1; Mr. Roe leads, third set. Sets are 2 to 0; Mr. Doe leads."

At the conclusion of a match, the umpire says: "Game, set, and match, Mr. Roe; score, 6–4, 8–6, 3–6, 0–6, 14–12." The games won by the winner of the match are always announced first.

There is etiquette and art to announcing

If, during the progress of a match, the umpire should make an error in announcing a score or a decision, he should correct the error immediately after it is discovered.

If it becomes necessary to ask the spectators to avoid the possibility of disconcerting the players, the umpire's statement should be a dignified, courteous appeal. Such an approach will not fail to gain the co-operation of the people in the stands. Applause during a rally and before a point is won, excessive mass movement, etc., can cause considerable annoyance to the players. When it persists, the umpire should speak up.

PLAYERS CHANGE SIDES AFTER 1ST GAME, 3RD GAME, ETC.

C B		SERVERS INITIALS	POINTS—SET NO. 1	JB (GAMES)	MS (GAMES)
	1	JB		1	0
	2	MS		1	1
	3	JB			
	4	MS			
	5	JB			

Form III. A sample score card for tennis, showing the order in which the points were scored in the first two games of set number 1.

SCORING

Regulation score cards are available for all matches. If special ones are not provided, printed forms will be found at the bottom of the boxes which contain a dozen balls.

A sample of such a score card is reproduced in form III to illustrate the form and the method of keeping a score.

Prepare the score card in advance

In the upper left-hand corner of the card is space for the initials of the players. These initials head the columns in which a progressive game score is kept. To illustrate: J. B. won the first game, which is shown in column bearing his initials. The score of the opponent at this stage was "love" and is shown by the zero. M. S. won the second game. The next score in the column is thus shown as "1–1," and so on. It is wise for the umpire also to write out the names, so that he will have a ready reference.

In the left-hand column, the numbers refer to the game. The initials in the next column designate the player who serves each game. The service is alternated so, after the toss when the player who is to serve first is determined, the umpire should insert the initials of that player for the first game. He should then alternate the initials of the servers for each game for the first set. This should be done before play starts to prevent error in the record. For each succeeding set, the server's initials for each game should be inserted after the proper game before the set begins.

The tally marks in the squares on the body of the card indicate the winner of each point. The tallies in the top row of squares represent the scores for the server, while the tallies in the lower row of squares record the points scored for his opponent. It will be noted that the order in which the points were scored is shown by the progressive position of the tally along the row. For example, in the first game, the order of scoring was as follows: J. B. was the server, he scored first, 15–love; 15–all; 30–15; 40–15; 40–30; deuce; advantage J. B.; game J. B.

This is a simple method for keeping a complete record and will avoid the possibility of mistakes. Umpires should record a score before announcing it, to reduce errors.

The score card should be signed on the line at the bottom, when the match is completed. If, later, question about a score should arise, it may be referred to the signing umpire.

12

Volleyball

OFFICIATING OF VOLLEYBALL DEMANDS THE SAME qualifications that hold in any other sport: intense love of the game, many and varied experiences in officiating from ordinary class games to national tournaments, thorough training, being a student of and intimately acquainted with the annual Rules and Guide,[1] having a philosophy of officiating which helps players and spectators enjoy the game to the fullest, and being truly amateur in spirit.

This last point needs explanation. Volleyball is one of the few remaining world sports that is absolutely amateur in letter and spirit. No player or official gets paid. The sport is never a job. Players and officials pay in time, money, and effort for the privilege of competing.

STEPS TOWARD CERTIFICATION

The basic development of an official should begin in the class games of school, college, YMCA, or club. He should act as linesman, umpire, scorer, and then referee, and at the same time become a student of the Rule Book. Under supervision of experienced officials he graduates to interagency matches. Next, he seeks a rating from the regional chairman of the USVBA (names may be found in the Annual Guide) by officiating in regional tournaments. He

[1] M. L. Walters, *Official Volleyball Guide*, (Berne, Indiana: U. S. Volleyball Association, 1950).

Volleyball—a truly amateur sport in letter and spirit

is then ready for national certification by the USVBA's Officials Committee. This group administers a true–false rules knowledge examination, and certification judges judge the applicant on his competence in action. He must officiate in a national or regional tournament at least every three years to hold his national or regional rating.

OFFICIALS

The officials necessary for tournament volleyball are: referee, umpire, scorer, timer, linesmen.

Good players are not developed by playing without training, coaching, and study. The same is true of officials. Not only must a person have the desire to help the game by his officiating, but he must develop himself to the highest level possible in order to enjoy the experience to the ultimate.

Clinics are an excellent method of training officials. These can be of a single day's or evening's duration, or they may be a series of such affairs. These clinics should make use of a lecture session by some well-qualified official discussing what makes good officiating, with chalk talk and rules interpretation. Movies, slides, or charts will aid in these presentations.

Two good teams may then play a match so that good officiating can be demonstrated and the officials get an opportunity to work the games and obtain suggestions, criticisms, and ratings of their ability.

These clinics can be set up in colleges, schools, YMCA's, or clubs and should be planned, promoted, and conducted by those who know the game. Help can be procured toward this end by contacting regional chairmen or asking local YMCA officials to help set up such clinics.

Another excellent training device is to have the trainee work with an experienced official and then later to referee as he umpires.

Competent officials are developed by officiating

The Linesman

The position of a linesman seems insignificant, and yet upon his alertness has hung the balance of many points determining a championship. It is so easy to become absorbed in the game and fail to watch closely the line and its relation to the ball when it hits the floor.

A line ball is good. The linesman should indicate *immediately*, as soon as the ball hits the floor, whether or not the ball is good (in the court or touched the line). His signal is exactly the same as the umpire's in baseball: palms of the hands toward the floor, fingers extended. (See figure 13.) A ball is out if: (1) it hits outside the line, (2) it touches a player any part of whose body is outside the line, or (3) it hits any apparatus outside the court.

Figure 13. Linesman's signal indicating ball is in play.

Figure 14. Linesman's signal indicating ball has hit floor outside of court boundary line.

The baseball call of "out" is used, the thumb being thrown over the shoulder in a "hitchhiker's" motion (see figure 14).

Two or four linesmen may be used. With two, places are taken at opposite corners of the court. Each man watches one sideline and a backline. With four men, each man watches one line.

Linesmen may stand or be seated. In any case they must be six feet off the court, constantly alert, and ready to retreat out of the way of players who have to come out of the court for a ball.

The advantage of four men is obvious. Each man has only one line to watch. He can be placed exactly in line with the part of the court he is to call and he can be moved back from the court and out of play further than if only two men are used.

No whistle is used in calling balls (only the hand signals) because players and referee immediately look to the linesman for his call.

Service foot fault is also called by the back-line linesman. *Stepping on* or over the service line *before* the ball is *hit* by the server should be instantly indicated to the referee by a whistle or horn.

The Timer

Games may be played on a time basis. (See official Rules.) In a time game the timer must be extra-alert to catch the referee's motions as to when the ball is in play and when it is dead. The best device is an electric timer, visible to players and officials, with an electric light in the circuit which goes on when the clock is running. It is important that, lacking an electric clock, a mechanical device be used so that the timer may show time remaining to be played.

The timer should use a gong to indicate the end of the game.

The Umpire

The umpire is seated on the floor under the net, opposite the referee. His main purpose is to assist the referee in case of questionable decisions. He also signals a foul for

Touching the service line is a service foot fault

stepping *over* the center line and for net contact. He should have a horn which is different in tone from the device used by the referee.

Other than the above two fouls, the umpire does not call plays, unless asked for his help by the referee when the referee was not in a clear position to see the play.

The umpire also keeps time out and aids in the checking in of line-ups and substitutions.

The Scorer

The score on the record of the scorer is the *official* score. The score displayed on the scoreboard, or someone's memory of the score, is not official. Therefore, the scorer must be a meticulous and rapid worker. This is one case in which "practice does make perfect." Because there are many methods of scorekeeping, being ultrafamiliar with the system is imperative.

The scorer is seated at a desk opposite the referee. He should obtain the line-ups at least fifteen minutes before match time. Before the line-ups are entered on his score-sheet he should see that the umpire or referee has had the captains flip for service, inasmuch as the line-ups should be written down in serving order, including name and shirt number.

The gamut of scoring methods runs from the simple one of keeping a team tally to the F. C. Martini system of keeping a play by play record, which results in a box score similar to basketball or baseball. See forms IV and V.

Whatever system the scorer uses, the score card should at all times indicate the team score at the moment. An assistant scorer should be seated at the table to see that the official scoreboard matches the official score card. And in most cases this assistant has on the desk a signcloth scoring device, which he turns over as scores are made, and which

The umpire calls center line and net contact fouls

is visible to the referee, both teams, and the scoreboard operator.

Second, the scorer should at all times know from his record which team is serving so that points and side-outs are never confused.

Third, the scorer should know which players have and have not served. He must keep the serving order straight. If the serving order is questioned, the scorer's record is used as the basis for settling the dispute.

VOLLEYBALL SCORE SHEET

PLACE ________ COURT ________ EVENT ________

DATE ________ TIME ________ MATCH NO. ________

REFEREE ________ UMPIRE ________ LINESMAN ________

WINNER ________ SCORE ________

FIRST GAME

TEAMS	1	2	3	4	5	6	7	8	9	10	11	12	13	14	15	16	17	18	FINAL
L.A.	X	X	X	X	X	X	X	X	X	X									10
CHIC.	X	X	X	X	X	X	X	X	X	X	X	X	X	X	X				15

Form IV. A simple score sheet which merely shows the running score of a game.

Fourth, the scorer must keep record of substitutions and the position of original starters and substitutions. (See rules on substitutions.)

Fifth, the scorer's sheet should show number of time outs.

Sixth, he may show how points or side-outs were made and by what players: ace serve, bad serves, block, spike, net ball, foul, etc.

Seventh, his score should show date, time, line-ups, officials, place, tournament, match number, court.

The scorer keeps the order of the serve

The Referee

The referee is the official in charge and must look and act the part. He should be dressed in long blues, white

VOLLEYBALL SCORE SHEET

EVENT ______________ DATE ______________

WINNER ______________ SCORES ______________

MATCH NO. ______________ COURT NO. ______________

REFEREE ______________ UMPIRE ______________

SCORER ______________ LINESMAN ______________

L. A.	NO.									FINAL
GREEN	11	X	⊗	X78	X	X14				15
BROWN	2	X	X45	X9	X	X15				
WHITE	10	X12	X6	⊗	X					
GRAY	8	X	⊗	X1011	X13					
KING	6	X3	X	X12	⊗					
PARSONS	4	X	X	X	X					

DAVIS	1	X	X	⊗	X	X				5
THOMAS	5	X	X	X3	X4	X5				
WELLS	24	⊗	X2	X	X	X				
MOORE	15	X1	X	X						
FLEET	7				X					
JONES	2	X	X	⊗	X					
SMITH	12	X	X	X	X					

Form V. A sample of the F. C. Martini system of keeping a play-by-play as well as a box score of a volleyball game.

Martini is a system for scoring in volleyball

ducks, or some neat looking trousers and wear a white, open-collared shirt or sweater. Certified officials should wear their insignia. His carriage, friendliness, businesslike attitude, clean appearance, and absolutely fair and consistent calls should add dignity to the game. Upon every one of those characteristics the future of the game depends.

His signaling device may be a whistle, horn, or buzzer which can be heard easily by players and spectators. It should have a tone different from those used by other officials.

PREMATCH DETAILS

The referee should introduce himself, or be introduced by the tournament committee, to the team captains, coaches, and players. He should see that the flip of the coin for choice of serve or court is done early so that the line-ups can be procured before match time.

The referee should ascertain that the linesmen know where they are to place themselves, which lines they are to watch, and which signals they are to use. He should check the scorer to see that he has line-ups and that he understands substitutions, correction of scoring on the boards, and checking of serving order. He needs to check the timer to see that he understands what his duties are and when the clock is and is not to be running. The referee also makes sure the umpire knows which plays he is to call and when the referee will call for help on plays.

The ball should be checked by the referee to see that it is round (by rolling it slowly across the floor to see that it goes in a straight line), properly inflated, and official in all respects. He should also use a measuring stick to see that the net is at the right height and that all overhanging hazards are out of the way. He also must see that the net

The referee should look and act his part

tapes are on the net parallel to the side lines, for the guiding of the linesmen in calling balls being played back into the court from out-of-bounds. (See Rules.)

In many cases it is also well to see that players are introduced and that spectators and players know the match, number of games, and other information which makes for more enjoyment by all.

GAME DETAILS

Position

The referee must be even with the net and with his head above the net. (See Guide and Rule book.) It is impossible to see over-the-net infractions from the floor accurately. Provision of a referee's platform is a must in conducting top-grade volleyball.

Starting Play

At the beginning of a match and after any time out, the referee should ask each captain if he is ready to play. He should have instructed them beforehand to raise their hands when asked if "ready." The referee should then point to the server and with a sweep of the arm toward the opposite court and a short blast on the whistle call "Play!" This makes clear when play is to begin and no ball may be legally served until this takes place.

Several devices may be used by the referee to aid him in remembering which team has served. One is to hold the whistle in the hand on the side of the serving team. Some men keep the whistle in the mouth during play so that instantaneous calls may be made, and have the whistle

Referee—your head must be above the net

on the side of the mouth from whence the serve was made. Other referees turn slightly toward the serving team and hold that position until a side-out. Some place a towel on the guy wires leading from the net on the serving side and shift it on side-outs. Some such routine is important.

Just before the serve is made, the referee must also give a quick glance to see that all players are within their zones. (See Rules.) As the serve is made, he should also watch for foot faults in case the linesman should not see it. No warning is given on foot faults.

After "play" has been declared, if it is necessary to stop the game before the ball is served, the referee should give two sharp whistle blasts and hold up both hands with palms open. (See figure 15.) The necessity for stopping the game would arise if a ball from another court were in the way of the players, if some of the officials were not ready, if a line-up was not complete, etc.

Ball in Play

Once the ball is in play the referee should keep his eyes on the ball, with his peripheral vision ahead of the play. Both this direct concentration and the "field of play" vision are equally important and are attributes too few officials develop.

This attention on play can be keen and the referee can still be physically relaxed. To be taut is fatiguing and will destroy one's acuity in a long match. (For best results, no official should work two matches in succession.)

Net Play

When the ball is played near the net and the resulting play calls for hairline decision, the referee must crouch down with one eye glued on the top of the net. Calling of over-the-net violations are made easy to the official if he

Have a plan to check the serve

will use this technique. A swimming-finish judge or a track-finish judge does not stand to the side of the finish line. He stands absolutely in line with it and on close finishes closes one eye and aims the other down the tape just as one aims a gun. This same method is essential in refereeing net play. The instant either player or both get a finger or hand over the net, the whistle or buzzer should sound. Immediately the referee should point to the man over and call out "Number 6, over the net." At the same time, he should signal the violation. If the violation was by

FIGURE 15. REFEREE'S SIGNAL TO STOP PLAY. HANDS ARE RAISED, WITH PALMS FACING EACH COURT.

FIGURE 16. REFEREE INDICATING THAT A NET VIOLATION HAS BEEN COMMITTED BY THE PLAYER TO HIS RIGHT.

a player in the right court, the referee should place his right hand over the net with the fingers pointing into the left court. (See figure 16.)

In case both teams are over, indicate such by crossing the extended hands at the wrists and calling out "Number 6

Be technical on over-the-net violations

and Number 11 over; double foul." (See figure 17.)

It is important not to anticipate over-the-net. If it happens, admit it and have a replay. Do not call it, *until* it occurs. When it does occur, do not wait; call it immediately, for waiting until another play has been made is too late. Volleyball is played in hundredths-of-a-second timing, while most other games involve tenths of seconds in reaction.

Be friendly but firm in the call. The referee is present to aid the game, and his attitude should be in that vein. Neither players nor spectators are in a position to see over-the-net plays.

To be strict in calling net violations at the beginning and lax or lenient thereafter is certain to invite trouble. Consistency is the essence of refereeing.

Touching the Net

Very few sports have as high a code of ethics of play as volleyball. From interclass play to the finals of national tournaments, players have called their own fouls. No greater thrill exists for those who have seen players call "touching the net" on game point when the foul was not seen by the referee. Referees accept these self-called fouls. To be consistent, if a referee calls a net foul on a player who consistently calls himself but who has not, in this instance, called a violation on himself, then the referee must accept this man's word of honor and have the ball replayed rather than penalize the man and stick to his own decision.

Touching the net any time the ball is in play is a foul, and the referee must watch closely. In debatable cases he may ask the umpire for his help.

An excellent method of determining if the ball "ticks" the net on the serve is to place the hand lightly on the net cable as the serve is made. Any touch of the ball on the top of the net can be felt better than it can be seen or heard.

A man's word is honored in volleyball

Contacts

Each team is allowed three contacts of the ball before returning it over the net. It is well to have the referee get the habit of counting to himself "one, two, three," in order to keep alert on number of contacts and settle any dispute when the referee is not certain. If some such system is not used, even the best officials once or twice in a tournament will miss the count on this simple rule. One needs also to remember that the player may use anything above his knees in playing the ball. And that on playing a spiked ball the defensive man is charged with only one contact even though it may strike his thigh, hand, and thigh in succession.

Playing the Ball

Only one point in the game of volleyball has created any wide divergence in the method of refereeing it—the point of holding or pushing. The rules state that the ball must be clearly hit or batted, and not pushed. Some officials hold that a player using an overhand or underhand play who does not clearly shove or scoop the ball is within the rules. Others believe an ultrastrict call should be used, and that any follow-through on an overhand pass, practically any underhand played ball, and any flexing of the wrist so that the hand follows the ball momentarily in the spike—that all these are pushing.

Physics teaches us that when any object changes direction, there is a momentary halt. Therefore, from the standpoint of physics, every ball hit comes to rest for a measurable amount of time. Cameras and instruments can record the thousandths of a second of this hold. The human eye is limited and so is the ability of the cerebrum to gauge this time.

Only by studying the work of other officials and by minute attention and practice can a referee pace himself in these calls. He needs primarily to keep in mind that the ball must be *batted*. In passing, spiking, or recovery, any deviation from hitting the ball should be called *instantly, without fail!*

Some technique must be worked out to suit the personality of the referee himself to keep attention focused on these touches. He may say to himself: "Hit, hit, hit, hit, push (whistle)." Or he may say: "OK, OK, OK, OK, Carry. . . ." Eventually, after such training, the official is able to relax more and recognize an illegally played ball. It is however practically impossible to attain perfect uniformity in judgment for all situations. The difference in human interpretation is too wide for that. The referee's criteria must be consistency, how near he calls in line with other nationally approved referees, and how the better players accept his calls.

Point or Side-Out

When a point is scored, the referee should call out "Point!" and raise his arm with forefinger pointed upward on the side of the team that scored the point. This will make it clear to the scorer, the teams, and spectators that a point has been made. (See figure 18.)

If the play results in a side-out, the referee should point the arm on the side of the team which is to receive the ball, and with the arm lowered describe a circle with his hand which will indicate "rotation" by the team getting the ball for service. (See figures 19 and 20.)

Use of Whistle

Whether whistle, horn, or buzzer is used, it should be used with discretion. Some officials overuse the instrument and annoy players and spectators alike. Never use the whistle when not necessary, and when using it, have some system—a sharp, short blast on routine play, two short

Was the ball batted or pushed—a ticklish call

FIGURE 17. REFEREE'S SIGNAL TO INDICATE A NET VIOLATION BY EACH TEAM.

FIGURE 18. REFEREE'S SIGNAL TO INDICATE THAT TEAM IN COURT ON HIS RIGHT HAS SCORED A POINT.

FIGURE 19. REFEREE INDICATING SIDE OUT AND POINTING TO TEAM THAT IS TO SERVE NEXT.

FIGURE 20. REFEREE INDICATING ROTATION OF PLAYERS AFTER SIDE OUT SIGNAL SHOWN IN FIGURE 19.

blasts to resume play, three short blasts or a long one for a close play involving a foul, to add emphasis.

The underuse of the whistle is equally disturbing. Those present are entitled to know when play starts and ends, and when a foul has been made. And they need to know it at the instant it occurs, and not some time later.

Attitude

Rarely, very rarely, in top-notch volleyball is there ever a question about the official's decision. When that occurs, only the captains should ask the referee for an interpretation.

The referee should see that this is carried out in a firm, fair, and extremely courteous manner. The best officiated match is that in which the spectators are hardly aware that an official is present, and one in which the players are impressed with the conduct of the match and thank the referee for a well-worked contest.

13

Badminton

THE JOB OF OFFICIATING A BADMINTON MATCH IS IN many respects similar to that of handling a tennis match. While the action is fast, the shuttle, because of its construction, moves more slowly and tends to float or sail. It does not bounce like the tennis ball. Consequently, it is much easier to make decisions on the shuttle than it is on the tennis ball.

Fewer officials, particularly linesmen, are needed for a badminton game. An umpire and eight linesmen conduct the match. This is two linesmen less than for tennis. Actually four can handle the match effectively. The umpire can make the short service line decisions easily because this line is only six and one-half feet from the net. This eliminates two linesmen. The four linesmen who cover the side boundary lines can also rule on play at the back boundary line and the long service line in doubles matches. This eliminates two more linesmen. There may be a referee. This official is customarily present in a tournament but may not be appointed for other matches.

UMPIRE

The umpire should be on an elevated platform as in tennis. He is the head official of a match. In the absence of a referee, he is the court of final appeal on any point in dispute.

Officiating—similar to tennis—but simpler

It is his duty to appoint linesmen at his discretion. While the umpire's decision is final, he should uphold the decision of a linesman. The umpire shall call "fault" or "let" when either occurs, without an appeal from the players.

For the positions of the officials on the court, the reader is referred to diagram 10. The officials who are indicated by an "X" with a circle about it are the linesmen who may be eliminated.

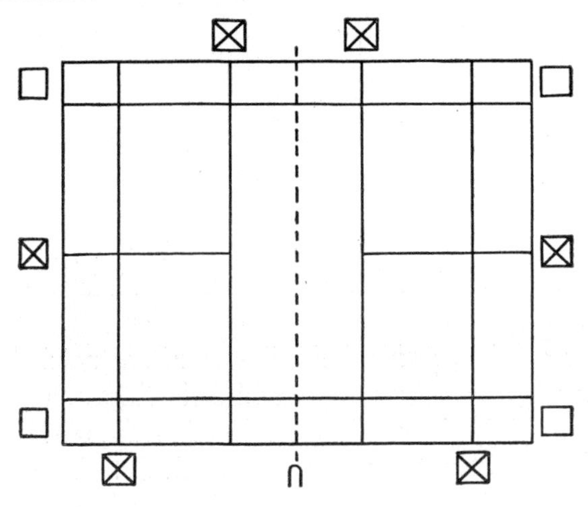

DIAGRAM 10. THE POSITIONS OF THE LINESMEN AND UMPIRE ARE SHOWN. THE LINESMEN INDICATED BY THE BOXES MARKED X MAY BE ELIMINATED, BECAUSE OF THE SIZE OF THE BADMINTON COURT, WITHOUT JEOPARDIZING THE EFFECTIVENESS OF THE OFFICIATING.

HELPFUL GUIDES TO EFFICIENT OFFICIATING

Pregame

1. Check the height of the net.
2. Place and instruct linesmen.
3. If the rules of the match permit, have three or four correctly-weighted shuttles ready for play.
4. Do not change shuttles without good reason.

Umpire—uphold the decision of a linesman

During Service

1. Watch to see that the shuttle when struck is below the server's waist. Linesmen, who are on the floor, are in a better position to judge this point. This duty should be delegated to a linesman.

2. Watch for a "let."

3. Watch that the player on the "out" side does not leave his court before the service is delivered.

4. Watch for scoop or throw shots. They are illegal.

During Play

1. Always watch the shuttle.

2. The player who strikes a shuttle before it passes the net loses the point.

3. Touching the net or supports with the racket, person, or clothes before the shuttle is dead, costs the point.

4. Keep track of the number of hands in. It is easy to make mistakes on this point unless great care is exercised. It may be advisable to keep a written record of this point. See form VI for a suggested method. As a player fin-

BADMINTON SCORE CARD

~~SINGLES~~ / DOUBLES — MATCH *BILL J.* / *FRED M.* VS *JOHN D.* / *TED S.* DATE *10/10*

HAND IN	*B.J.*		*J.D.*		*T.S.*		*B.J.*		*F.M.*		*F.M.*									
PLAYERS																				
B.J.–F.M.	X	~~2~~	3	4	5	6	7	8	9	10	11	12	13	14	15	16	17	18	19	20
J.D.–T.S.	1	2	3	4	5	6	7	8	9	10	11	12	13	14	15	16	17	18	19	20
	21	22	23	24	25															
	21	22	23	24	25															

FORM VI. UMPIRE'S SCORE CARD FOR KEEPING A RECORD OF HAND IN AND OF CONTINUOUS SCORE IN A BADMINTON GAME.

Number of hands in—be alert on this point

ishes his serve, an "X" is drawn through his initials. This indicates that the next player in order is the next to serve. It will be noted that the initials of the players are in rotation.

5. When a score at which setting is permissible is reached, the player who first attained this score should be asked if he wishes to set.

6. See that the players change sides at the proper score in the third game.

GENERAL

1. Officials should not be influenced by the player or spectators in making their decisions. Promptness in making decisions will avoid this.

2. An official should not make a decision if he is unable to do so. The opinion of the players may be accepted if they agree. Otherwise, the official must call a "let."

3. Decision should be given promptly, but they should not be anticipated.

4. The score should be announced at the end of each rally. This should be done in a clear, loud voice which can be heard by both the players and spectators.

5. A linesman's decision on all points relative to the line over which he has jurisdiction is absolutely final.

6. The umpire should keep a written record of the score. A sample score card is shown in form VI.

7. At the conclusion of a match, the score should be filed with the proper authority.

8. The reader is referred to the chapter on tennis for further suggestions in the techniques of officiating a badminton match. Much of the procedure recommended for tennis is applicable to badminton. The reader must, of course, make the necessary adaptations in accordance with the rules and nomenclature for badminton.

14

Handball

TWO SETS OF HANDBALL RULES EXIST: THE YMCA RULES and the AAU rules. Only two officials are needed: a referee and a scorer. It is a distinct advantage if both men have had long experience as players and as students of the game. It is not impossible, however, to train good officials without this background. This training will need to include more than a study of the rules. It must also include the study of match play and the observation of other good officials handling a match.

Both officials should be seated in the gallery, above the court, so that they can easily see every play. They should be seated together.

THE SCORER

The scorer must have an official score sheet on which is shown the date, place, tournament, officials, and time, a place for players, a place to check service, and the running score. This must be so organized that at any moment he knows the exact score and which player served last. (See form VII.)

After each series of plays, when the referee calls point, or handout, the scorer should announce the score loud enough so that players and spectators can hear. He should always give the server's score first. For example, if a player is serving and is in the lead and makes a point, the

Two sets of rules exist—decide which to use

scorer would announce "18—11." Some officials use the expression "18 playing 11." When the man or team behind is serving, the same principle holds—give the server's score first. If, in the above case, there was a handout, then the scorer would say "11—18."

HANDBALL SCORE CARD

PLACE ________ COURT NO. ______ DATE ______ TIME ______

EVENT ____________ MATCH NO. ____________

WINNER ____________ SCORES ____________

PLAYERS	1	2	3	4	5	6	7	8	9	10	11	12	13	14	15	16	17	18	19	20	21	22	23	24	25	26	FINAL
JONES	X	X	X	X	X	X	X	X	X	X	X	X	X	X	X	X	X	X	X	X	X						·21
DAVIS	X	X	X	X	X	X	X	X	X																		9

JONES	X	X1X2X	X	X3X	X4X	X5X6X 7X	X8X9X	X10X11X
DAVIS	X1X	X2X	X	X3X	X	X4X	X5X	X

X12X13X 14X	X15X16X	X17X	X18X19X	X20X21				21
X6X	X	X7X8X	X9X					9

Form VII. A sample score card showing two methods of keeping score. The record at the top merely shows the score at a particular stage of the game. That at the bottom gives a complete record of the order in which scores were made together with a serving record of each player. The latter is preferred.

THE REFEREE

The referee may or may not use a whistle. Many do not.

The referee should introduce the players to each other and flip a coin for service before match time. A few minutes before time of play, he should announce, "Match will begin in three minutes," so that players may complete their warm-up and have no excuse for delaying. The referee should test the balls for official rebound and choose the ball

The server's score is announced first

that is to be used. He must also be certain before the match begins that all towels, shirts, or extra balls are removed from the court.

Just before the match begins, the referee introduces players to the spectators. (The committee in charge should have introduced the officials.) He then asks each player if he is ready and calls, "Play!" He should have some system of remembering who is serving, so he can immediately after each play call "point" or "handout." He may do this by having a card with the player's name on it in front of him and turning up the name of the server each time. In singles, have one player's name on one side of the card and the opponent's on the other. Or he may have blank sheets in his hand with the players' names on them, and keep the server's sheet in his right hand.

The referee's difficult task centers around the calling of "hinders" and "intentional interference." Only thorough experience, study, and observation will enable the referee to judge these plays. These are not easy plays to call, however, because no rule of thumb can be applied. A man may move and commit an intentional interference, or he may stay put and do the same. In other words, an opponent is entitled to a clear view and an unobstructed chance to play the ball. *Any unintentional hinders* should be called immediately. Never wait for players to ask for a hinder. The referee has lost control of the game when that occurs.

At the same time, any intimation of intentional obstruction should be cause for awarding the ball to the opponent for a handout or a point. A firm, fair, courteous stand will result in fast, clean play.

Another call the referee should make clear is that of foot faults. Many players get the habit of stepping over the service line, and they are not called. All referees should call this, as well as every other, fault shown in the rule book.

A third point of dispute arises in the matter of stalling

In case of doubt, call for a replay

for time. The first item to watch is that of not bouncing the ball more than three times in making a serve. The next is either serving before the opponent is set to receive, or of taking more than ten seconds in serving. Either of these is a handout. The referee must also enforce the time limit of three minutes after the first game and ten minutes after the second.

The referee should have extra balls available so that when the playing ball becomes wet he can throw in a dry ball.

A fourth point important in refereeing is that of calling a "short." If the referee calls a "short" on the first ball served and the opponent does not play the ball, it remains a "short." If he does play it, the play continues as if the ball had been good. However, on the second consecutive "short" there is no choice. It is a handout and the referee must call it as such. The receiving player has no option. The referee must make it stand as a handout. On foot faults the referee should allow no such option; the call must stand and the ball may not be played.

In case of a doubtful decision the referee may call for a replay.

Because of the proximity of the players, the speed of the ball, and the keen intensity of the competition, refereeing top-notch handball competition is not easy. To be qualified to accept such a position means a thorough knowledge of the rules, a fast reaction time, keen eyesight, experience, and the ability to make clear-cut, strong decisions, and smile while making them.

Study the game, the rules, the infractions!

Part III

The officiating techniques which are discussed in this section of the book include those for football, basketball, soccer, wrestling, hockey, lacrosse, skiing. These are the sports which, for the most part, require in their administration the discriminating judgment of the official. They are the sports in which the decisions depend upon the effect created.

The rules in these sports permit the official to exercise discretion. Because of this fact, considerable space is devoted to the development of guides to specific play situations for the official. This is by way of implementing the philosophy expressed in Part I and of providing bases for uniformity in officiating.

15

Football

ANY DIRECTIONS WHICH ARE GIVEN IN THE FOOTBALL rule book for the guidance of the officials in carrying out their duties will be found in the back of the rule book [1] under the heading, "The Officials—Jurisdiction and Duties." With these as a pattern, and from years of experience in the administration of contests, a rather definite plan of operation has been developed. This plan will be presented in the order in which the officials perform their duties. Since games are conducted by both three and four officials, their duties and methods of working are presented under both conditions. The commissioners of college conferences have worked out a manual of football officiating [2] which is now rather universally adopted. The treatment here follows the outline of this manual in some respects, but goes beyond this manual by attempting to give a background upon which to develop the art of football officiating. In addition, specific play situations are discussed. The procedure here is intended to assist the novice as well as the seasoned official. As a general guide, the following seven hints are given at the outset. Detailed development follows.

---

[1] *Official Football Rules* (New York: A. S. Barnes & Company, Inc., 1949).

[2] Manual of Football Officiating, National Association of Football Commissioners, Eastern College Athletic Conference, Biltmore Hotel, New York.

OFFICIALS

1. All officials have concurrent jurisdiction.
2. Head linesman's chief responsibility is to call offside.
3. Only the referee's whistle kills the ball. He covers the ball on most plays.
4. Umpire's chief duties are to cover legal use of hands and blocking in line of scrimmage.
5. Field judge is the timekeeper. He covers return of punts.
6. Signals for fouls do not stop the play.
7. If three officials, umpire assumes duties of field judge.

These points are listed here to emphasize the primary jobs of each official and thus to give a bird's-eye view of the total co-ordinated job of officiating a game. In doing this, there is no intention of minimizing the importance of other duties which are discussed subsequently.

Pregame Duties

The officials have four specific duties to perform before the game actually begins.

1. The first of these duties might be classed as partly social. It consists of getting acquainted, of reviewing duties, of discussing methods of co-operation on the field, of checking personal equipment (such as horns, guns, watches, pencils, record cards, and signal devices).

The referee should take the leadership in this meeting. If he desires any special arrangements, here is the place to instruct his fellow officials. In this way clashes of personalities on the field can be avoided and full harmonious co-operation secured.

2. The officials have duties with respect to equipment and facilities. The referee must inspect the ball and then turn it over to the field judge. He must also inspect the field to see that it is properly laid out and marked. Many

Don't neglect pregame duties

times, through oversight or error, mistakes which may create embarrassing problems have been discovered. For example, on one occasion an end zone was found to be fifteen yards long on one side. On another occasion, when a severe storm had hit in the morning before a game, the lines were entirely obliterated. Special corner markings had to be set up by the officials, and chains were strung on both sides of the field so that the officials might sight across to get bearings. Fields that are not marked off in five-yard distances make certain phases of officiating difficult.

As a result of spilled lime or poor marking, the goal line sometimes is irregular—too broad in some places and indistinct in others. Close goal-line decisions—and there are many of them—can be made very difficult unless situations of this kind are observed and corrected before game time.

The surroundings should also be checked for obstructions and hazards. The yard line markers may be constructed of hard, sharp materials and may be placed too close to the side lines.

Any serious conditions should be corrected before the game begins. For this reason, the referee should make his inspection fifteen to thirty minutes before game time.

The umpire is required by rule to inspect the equipment of players to see that it is legal according to the rules. He must also inspect the taping and bandaging of players to make sure that nothing is worn which might be dangerous to an opponent.

The head linesman should secure the chain which is to be used and check its length and condition.

The field judge should check the timing devices if an electric field timer, which is operated from the side lines, is to be used. If there are only three officials, then the umpire assumes these responsibilities.

3. The head linesman will need three assistants. He should select an assistant linesman who will hold the down marker at the side lines and two chainmen who will hold

Check the field, check the chain, check the timepiece

each end of the chain. Sometimes, it is possible to have a neutral assistant linesman, but usually both the assistant linesmen and one of the chainmen are associated with the home team. The other chainman will be assigned from the visiting team.

The instructions to these assistants are most important. It must be emphasized to them that they must not make any moves whatever unless directed to do so by the head linesman. To act otherwise could cause great confusion.

For example, if the chainmen were to move the chains and the assistant the stake, after a punt, before being directed to do so, and a penalty should occur which would require that the ball be brought back and played over, it becomes evident what problems would arise.

Specific instructions for the assistant linesmen are:

a. The assistant should place his stake on the side line at the forward point of the ball as directed by the head linesman.

b. He should turn his stake to indicate the proper down.

c. He should never move the stake nor change the down until directed to do so by the head linesman.

The chainmen should:

a. Be placed so that the chainman associated with the home team is holding the end of the chain which is toward the goal defended by his team. The other chainman will, of course, hold the opposite end. In this way the head linesman will have no worries about the chain being held taut at all times. The head linesman will always direct the placing of that end of the chain on the side line which is nearer the forward point of the ball at the beginning of each new series of downs.

b. Be cautioned never to move the chains until directed to do so.

c. When play comes close to the side line, in order to prevent injury, the chainman nearer the point where the

An officiating sin—to move the chain without orders

play may go out-of-bounds should move his stake away from the side line. If the other end is held in place, the position of the chain will not be lost.

The field judge, when time is to be kept with an electric timer, must check with those who are to operate the clock:

a. To make sure they know when to start the clock. (The clock starts only when the ball is put in play after time is out, except by order of referee.)

b. To demonstrate the signals for time out. The clock is stopped only upon signal from the referee. (The signal is always repeated by other officials.)

c. To advise concerning notification when five minutes remain in each half.

d. In cases where the field judge keeps time on the field, he should co-operate with the scoreboard operators. They will need regular information on time remaining to play in each period. He should also keep the referee informed concerning the time remaining to play, as the end of the second and fourth periods approaches.

Diagram 11 illustrates the arrangements of the chainmen and assistant linesmen.

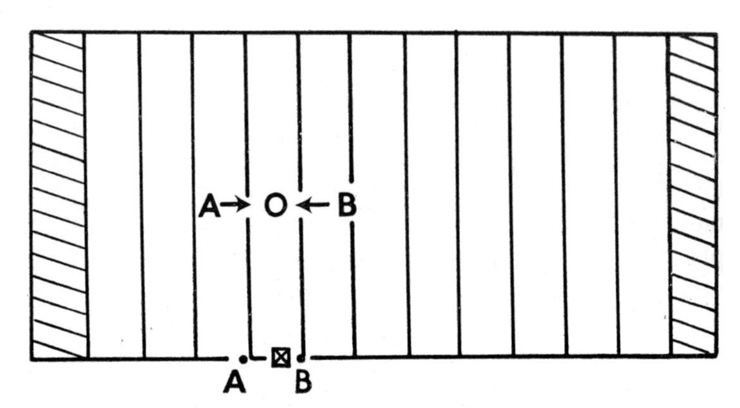

DIAGRAM 11. ARRANGEMENT OF CHAINMEN AND LINESMEN. ☒ INDICATES DOWN MARKER.

The time-out signal is most important

4. The last pregame duty of the officials is to meet with the captains in the center of the field for making the toss. It is customary for the umpire and field judge to go to the visiting bench before the game. They will escort the visiting team captain to the center of the field for the toss.

The referee and head linesman will escort the home team captain.

These duties are performed:

a. Everyone should be introduced. The officials should determine the playing positions of each captain.

b. Any special instructions should be given, special arrangements explained, any questions answered, and requested interpretations given.

c. The referee makes the toss after designating the visiting team captain to call it. The winner is indicated by placing a hand on his shoulder. The proper signal should be given to indicate the choice: a kicking movement to the leg for choice to kick, a catching movement to signal the choice to receive, a point to goal to indicate the choice of goal.

The choices left to the loser should be explained, and the selection made should be properly signaled. The referee should make a record of the winner of the toss.

The game is then ready to be started.

THE KICKOFF

The positions of the officials at the kickoff are shown in diagram 12. The positions indicated permit the officials to surround the play and at the same time to co-operate in covering all possible play situations which may occur at the kickoff. The positions of the officials on the field are determined by the position taken by the head linesman. He has previously placed his assistants and so must take a position on the same side of the field with them.

The head linesman will take a position between the ten-yard line and the goal line of the receiving team and from

At kick-off, the position of the head linesman sets the others

ten to fifteen yards in from the side line. He must be sure that he does not obstruct the view or interfere with any member of the receiving team.

The referee will take a similar position on the opposite side of the field from the head linesman.

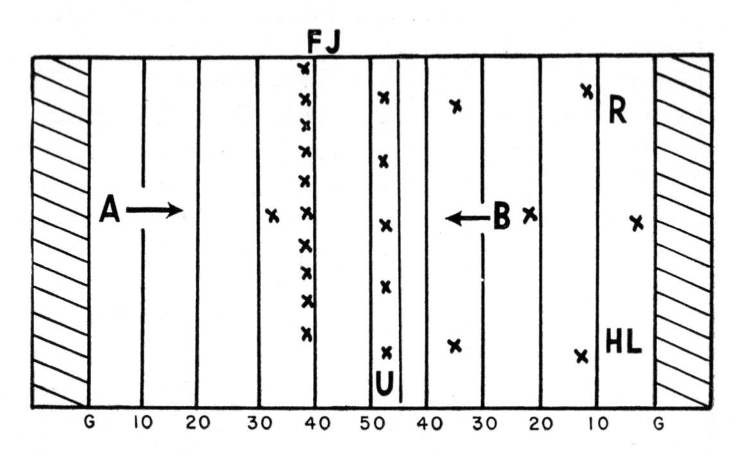

DIAGRAM 12. POSITIONS OF OFFICIALS AT THE KICK-OFF IN A FOUR-OFFICIAL GAME.

These two officials will cover the runback of the kickoff and all play immediately converging on the ball carrier. They will make decisions on out-of-bounds plays on their side of the field.

The umpire takes a position on the side line on the opposite side of the field from the head linesman and between the restraining lines of the receiving team. The chief responsibility of the umpire on the kickoff is to see that the receiving team does not violate the rules pertaining to the restraining line for the receiving team. After the kick, unless it is a short one, he observes the blocking of players as they move toward the ball carrier.

The field judge is responsible for the ball and for the enforcement of the rules pertaining to the restraining line for the kicking team. The field judge stands by the ball until everything is in readiness for the kick. He then goes to the end of the restraining line for the kicking team and on the same side of the field as the head linesman.

After the kick, his duties become the same as those of the umpire. In case of a short kick, he or the umpire would observe the play immediately surrounding the ball.

The field judge should help the referee to get the ready signal from the captain of the kicking team. The attention of the other captain should be secured by the official who is nearest to him. The head linesman, umpire, and field judge should indicate their readiness to the referee by an upraised hand.

When the captains, the officials, and the time keepers (when the time is kept on the side lines) have indicated their readiness, the referee who has had his arm raised above his head as a signal for readiness to play, sounds his whistle for play to begin.

When the ball becomes dead following the kickoff or at any other time during the game, the referee shall blow his whistle to indicate this fact. If an official other than the referee is administering the play of the ball carrier, he shall indicate a dead ball by raising his hand above his head. This is a signal for the referee to sound his whistle to officially stop the play. The referee will, of course, look to the official who has signaled the ball dead for guidance in any decisions incident thereto. This same procedure shall apply on all kickoff plays at any time during the game and on all kicks following a safety.

If three officials are used instead of four, they take positions as shown in diagram 13. The referee moves over to a position midway between the side lines. The head linesman assumes the duties of the umpire in the four-official pattern. The umpire takes over the job of the field judge.

As play starts, the officials should be on the alert for any rule violation. However, the usual situations on which decisions may be required on the kickoff are the following:

Only the referee's whistle stops the play

1. Restraining-line violation.
2. Kicks out-of-bounds.
3. Kicks into end zone.
4. Fouls with ball in possession of neither team.
5. Clipping and illegal use of hands.
6. Fumbles and legal possession.
7. Out-of-bounds play.
8. Dead ball.

SCRIMMAGE PLAY

On all scrimmage plays, the referee takes a position behind the offensive team. He should take a position behind the deepest backfield man and toward the nearer side line.

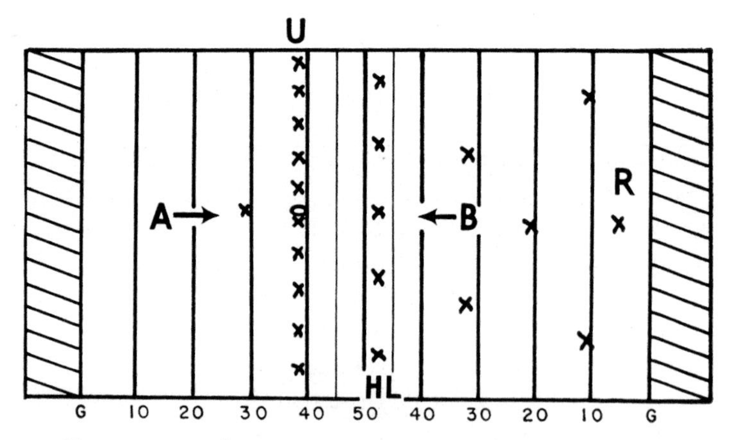

DIAGRAM 13. POSITIONS OF OFFICIALS AT THE KICK-OFF IN A THREE-OFFICIAL GAME.

If the ball is in the center of the field and he has discovered that a team is running most of its plays to the right, then the preferable position would be on the left side of the deep back. The referee must always be able to see the ball and, if possible, all backfield men, in order to be able to rule on the legality of the start of a play. He must always be able to see the ball throughout the scrimmage. The referee must be able to see the movement of the backs in rela-

The referee must always see the ball

tion to the snap of the ball. This is his primary job on all scrimmage plays.

The head linesman stays on the same side of the field as his assistants. He should take a position from ten to fifteen yards from the nearer end of the line of scrimmage, so that he can see clearly all players on the lines of scrimmage. His primary job is to administer the rules which govern the encroachment upon the neutral zone, before the ball has been put in play.

The umpire assumes a position behind the defensive team. He probably will not be closer than five yards to the line of scrimmage nor more than ten yards away. It is his primary duty to observe the blocking and the use of the hands of both the offense and defense on the line of scrimmage in particular, and on the line backers. The impossibility of sharply focusing attention on approximately fifteen players at one time requires the umpire to change his focus of attention on practically every play. Consequently, he will be ranging somewhere between the defensive ends. He must be careful that he does not obstruct the view of defensive line backers nor interfere with movement during forward pass plays. An effective umpire will not be concerned with the ball. Rather, he will be concentrating on all other players but the ball carrier. The players should find him looking at their blocking maneuvers. The potential of presence created by such a situation will do much to discourage illegal blocking. An umpire who is able to keep a game free from illegal play by such tactics deserves a very high rating. It is much more to the credit of an umpire to be knocked down during a scrimmage play because he is not watching the ball than it is to be constantly showing the referee where to place the ball at the end of a scrimmage. This latter is the duty of the referee.

The field judge stations himself on the side of the field opposite from the head linesman and from fifteen to twenty yards behind the defensive line. Under no circumstances

Umpire—observe the block—leave the ball to the referee

should the field judge be closer than ten yards to the defensive line. The field judge is a general assistant during scrimmage plays. He is far enough away from the play to be able to get an over-all view. He can spot any unusual situation which may develop, such as a quick kick or forward pass which starts as a running play. In particular, he can be of invaluable assistance to the umpire in watching the blocking on the line of scrimmage and on the secondary defense.

In a three-official game, the referee and head linesman have exactly the same duties. The head linesman must be ready to assist down the field on kicks and passes and be more alert to aid the umpire. The umpire assumes the duties of the field judge, in addition to his own. He will find it necessary to spend more time on the side opposite the head linesman.

The importance of the work of the referee and head linesman in the effect which their decisions and their manner may have upon the play of the two teams cannot be overemphasized. For the referee to be inconsistent, overtechnical, or lax in his decisions on the start of the backfield with respect to the snap of the ball, can be very demoralizing to either or both of the teams. He must keep play on an even level. Otherwise, he will throw off the timing of the teams completely.

Likewise, the decisions of the head linesman must be reasonable and realistic. To be hypertechnical is the greatest weakness of head linesmen. In carrying out their duties they should exercise the discretion allowed them by the rules. In this respect the same caution should be given to the umpire. It has been said that few plays in football have been completely free from illegal blocking. Nor is this fact particularly important. It is important, however, to see that a player is not unfairly affected by an illegal act. In such instances, the experience and good judgment of the official must be relied upon.

With three officials, umpire assumes the duties of the field judge

From scrimmage, the common situations which necessitate official attention and, frequently, action are the following:

1. *Shift or motion plays.* These are the primary responsibility of the referee, as already noted. However, the head linesman can assist in determining forward motion on spread plays or flankers where it is difficult for the referee to keep all backs and the ball in his field of vision.

It is important that the official discriminate clearly between illegal shifts and illegal motion. This requires a careful analysis of the rules, which is not a part of this text. Suffice it to say that officials are prone to recognize illegal shifts which carry the more serious penalty. As a consequence, most movements become illegal movements and not illegal shifts.

In any case, the referee must be sure that the offensive team does not get an advantage by a premature start.

2. *Offside play or encroachment on the neutral zone.* The head linesman is actually the only official who is in a position to make a decision on this play. He must use discretion in administering the rules on this phase of the game.

Inexperienced players quite often fail to get up to the line of scrimmage. In most cases, this violation is of greater detriment to the team committing it than to the opponent. The head linesman should bear this in mind and thus be realistic in his judgments.

Likewise, a finger or a swinging hand slightly ahead of the near point of the ball probably makes little difference in the play. A word of caution from the official is usually sufficient to correct an error of which the player is not conscious.

The situations from which a real advantage is gained are those which involve actual movement or change just before the ball is put in play. These are the violations which require action on the part of the head linesman in order that opponents will not be placed at a disadvantage.

Are you prone to call an illegal shift?

3. *Blocking maneuvers of all kinds.* These involve the blocking that occurs in the line to displace linesmen or to prevent them from getting to the ball carrier. They include the attempts of the offense to screen out the secondary defense in order to provide a breakaway for a ball carrier in case he gets beyond the line of scrimmage, and are particularly concerned with the hand, arm, and body tactics of the personal interferers for the ball carrier.

Here again the insignificant and inconsequential violations which invariably and unavoidably occur during a play do not constitute cause for action on the part of the official. As in other instances already mentioned, he must use discretion. His judgments must be conditioned by the possible effect such violations may have upon the play.

The acts of holding, locking a leg with the upper arm, extending the arms full length from the body in order to reach an opponent, use of the hands and forearms as a flail in driving an opponent back or striking him in the face or under the chin, slipping and grabbing the foot of the opponent in close line play so that he cannot lift it from the ground in stepping or retreating, are the types of fouls for which officials must be alert to take immediate action.

All four officials will be in position to make decisions on plays which involve the illegal use of the arms, hand, and body. The umpire, as previously stated, is in the best position to watch the close line play and the secondary defense. In addition, the head linesman will assist in watching the players on the end of the line nearer to him. The referee is in the best position to observe the action of the ball carrier, players immediately ahead of the ball carrier and particularly the personal interferers for the ball carrier. The field judge can best cover the down-field blocking and any other action that may come to his attention from his position where he can get an over-all view of the play.

4. *Delay of the game.* After the ball is ready for play, the offensive team has twenty-five seconds in which to get

Did the illegal block affect the play?

the ball in play. It is the referee's duty to enforce this requirement. He must be particularly conscious of this situation toward the end of a game. The team in possession of the ball is attempting to protect a lead by consuming as much time as possible on each play. It is expected, however, that the game will be kept moving with as little delay as possible throughout all periods.

Diagram 14 shows the position of the officials on a scrimmage play.

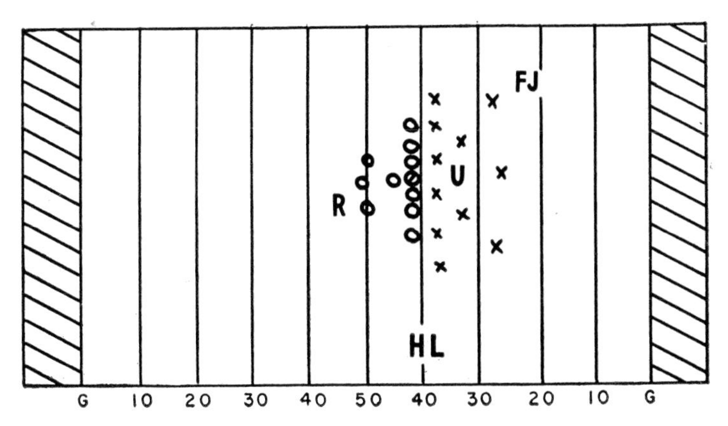

DIAGRAM 14. POSITIONS OF OFFICIALS IN A SCRIMMAGE PLAY.

RUNS FROM SCRIMMAGE

The positions shown in diagram 14 are the starting positions for running and pass plays from scrimmage. When the ball is snapped, the referee is the only official who moves with the play. He should watch the play carefully and follow closely enough to see the ball at all times and be able to catch the forward progress of the ball when the play is finished. He must not, however, be so close that he would interfere with a backward pass or a fumble. It is better for the referee to keep somewhat to the rear and to the side of the ball carrier, when he declares the ball dead. It is not a bad habit to inform the players that he sees the ball and has marked the forward point of progress. This practice tends to eliminate continued charging on the part of both teams. It also gives the players confidence in the referee. They feel that he is right on top of every play and will permit no unfair advantage.

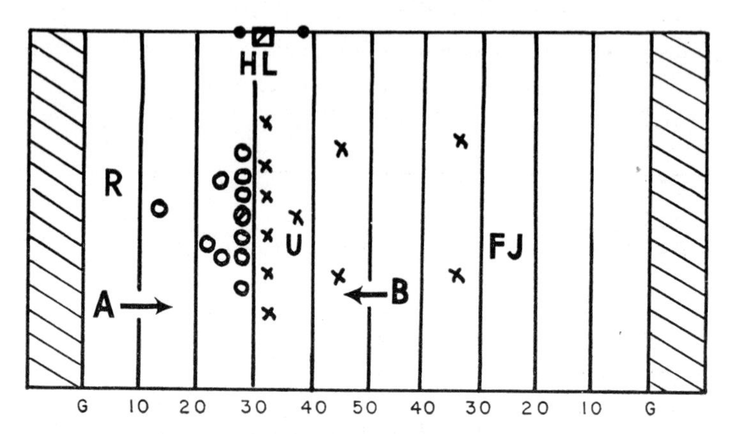

DIAGRAM 15. POSITIONS OF OFFICIALS ON A KICK FROM SCRIMMAGE.

The referee, of all the officials, must be in tiptop physical condition. He does more running than any player, because he is following the ball on every running play by either team.

When the ball is dead, the referee follows a set routine:

1. He looks toward the linesmen's chains to determine the distance to be gained for a first down. This is done before he rotates the ball into position for the next play.

2. He checks with the head linesman to determine the down.

3. He then places the ball in position for the next play. If it was in the outer third of the field, he moves it to the inbound line.

4. He declares the down and distance and calls play.

The head linesman must focus on the two lines until the ball is put into play. When this duty is finished, he follows

If you are out of condition—don't referee

the play. When the ball is dead, he places himself in line with the forward point of the ball so that the referee may determine the yardage to be gained for a first down. He next signals the down to the referee.

When the head linesman has checked to see that no penalty has been called, he motions the assistant linesman to place the center stake in line with the forward progress of the ball. After a first down has been declared by the referee, he motions the chainmen to move up with the chains and checks to see that they place the stakes correctly.

The umpire does not move during the scrimmage, except as necessary to keep out of the way of the ball carrier, blockers, and tacklers. If the ball is declared dead in the side zone and near to the side line or even out-of-bounds, he goes to the in-bound line to assist the referee. The referee will toss the ball to the umpire who will place it on the in-bound line as directed by the referee. This type of co-operation tends to eliminate unnecessary delay in getting the ball ready for play.

The field judge will probably move little during a run from scrimmage, unless there is a breakaway. Then he moves to avoid interfering with the play and in order to follow the progress of the run.

FORWARD PASS PLAY

The foregoing discussion applies to all running plays and, in general, to all other scrimmage situations. The officials must, however, be prepared to handle forward pass plays as well.

At times it is possible for the officials to anticipate passes by reason of the conditions incident to the score, the time remaining to play, the down, and the yards to go. Occasionally, the officials are aware of the strategy of the teams with respect to the use of the pass. In any event, they must never be caught unaware.

Headlinesman—check the down with the referee

In anticipation of a pass, the referee should note the numbers of the backfield men. He should check to see whether or not all are eligible to receive passes. (A player in a position to take a hand-to-hand snap is not eligible to receive a forward pass.)

If a pass develops, the referee should stay with the passer. It is his duty to watch the blocking for the passer and to observe the tactics of the defensive players after the pass has been made.

If the passer runs forward before passing, he must know whether or not the pass was made from behind the line of scrimmage. He should have a general view of the total play. If the pass is completed and the subsequent play is covered by a fellow official, he blows his whistle upon a signal of the upraised hand from the official who indicates that the play is finished.

He will receive a report from the other officials, which will indicate whether or not the play was legal from their standpoint. If there is a backward pass before the forward pass, the referee must be sure that the first pass is not forward.

If the pass was incomplete, the referee goes to the spot from which the ball was put in play; the other officials will retrieve the ball and relay it as quickly as possible to the referee.

The head linesman should note who is on the end of the line near him. If there is a flanking back the head linesman should look to see if the back is at least one yard back of the line. The head linesman, as the pass develops, covers the play down the field on his side of the field.

The umpire covers the play in the center area, while the field judge covers the play deep down the field and, in particular, the play on his side of the field. He notes the number of the player on the end of the line on his side.

If the pass is incomplete, the official nearest to the ball retrieves it quickly. If it was a long pass, the other officials get in a line between the ball and the referee in order to relay the ball to the referee without delay.

The particular situations which attend a forward pass, and the officials' responsibility are:

1. Pass from behind the line of scrimmage.
2. Blocking for the passer.
3. Continuing to block or tackle the passer after the pass has been thrown.

(These are all the duties of the referee.)

4. Interference of all kinds beyond the line of scrimmage.
5. Check of eligibility of receiver at time ball is touched.

(These are the responsibility of all the officials.)

6. Ineligible players crossing the line of scrimmage.

(This is the particular job of the umpire.)

7. Holding of eligible pass receivers to prevent them from getting down the field.

(When there are only three officials, the umpire covers the side opposite from the head linesman. Both the umpire and head linesman cover the center. It is necessary for them to spread their attention over a wider area.)

KICKS FROM SCRIMMAGE

When the ball is kicked from scrimmage special situations occur, in addition to the general scrimmage points already mentioned, to which officials must give attention:

1. *Illegal play against kicker.* The referee should stand back and to the side of the kicker. If a team is known to quick-kick, the referee should be alert to this possibility. He stays with the kicker after the kick to see that there is no foul play committed against him.

2. *Out-of-bounds kick.* The referee watches the flight of the ball in cases where it seems evident that it will go out-of-bounds before hitting the ground in the field of play. If it does go out, the field judge marks the spot

where it crosses the side line, as directed by the referee, and then retrieves the ball.

If the ball first hits the ground in the field of play and then goes out-of-bounds, the field judge assumes the responsibility for marking the spot where the ball crossed the side line.

3. *Conditions surrounding the ball when violations occur.* In the case of kicks from scrimmage, the official must note whether or not the ball has been touched when a foul occurs. This fact determines the point from which the penalty will be assessed.

4. *The freedom of movement of the receiver.* The receiver has the right of way while the ball is in the air. This is the particular responsibility of the field judge.

When a kick is expected, the field judge drops back to a point behind and to the side of the safety man. The field judge covers the runback of the punt for the referee. He signals to him by an upraised hand when the ball is dead and marks the spot. In cases where possession of the ball is at issue, the field judge furnishes this information to the referee.

The other officials hold their regular positions, as in other scrimmage plays before the kick. (See diagram 15.) After the kick, the head linesman moves down the field to observe blocking and to assist in case of out-of-bounds.

The umpire holds his position but turns to watch the blocking and particularly the clipping by the receiving team. The referee assists in such observations. As soon as the ball is dead, all officials hurry to assume their regular positions for a new scrimmage by the opposite team.

The chainmen and the assistant linesmen should be cautioned not to move their stakes to the new location of the ball until ordered to do so by the head linesman. When the stakes are moved after a kick, the head linesman should mark the spot on the side line where the rear stake

Anticipate the possibilities on a foul after a kick

should be placed. In this way, there will be very little delay in setting the stakes for the next series of downs.

When there are only three officials, the umpire must drop back to take the position of the field judge. The head linesman will then assist the umpire in covering his original assignments.

POSITION AND DUTIES IF OUT-OF-BOUNDS

If the ball goes out-of-bounds in a running play from scrimmage, the referee should mark the spot. He is the one official who is following the ball carrier. If, however, the play gets away from him, then the head linesman should be ready to assist on his side of the field, and the field judge on his side of the field.

If the ball is carried out-of-bounds after a completed forward pass, whichever official is covering the play (umpire, field judge, or head linesman) will mark the spot and signal to the referee with the time-out signal.

On pages 163, 164, the methods of handling out-of-bounds situations on kicks from scrimmage are discussed.

When the ball carrier goes out-of-bounds during a run-back of a punt, the field judge is the responsible official.

In all cases of out-of-bounds, the official who has marked the spot, holds that point until the ball is accurately placed for the next scrimmage.

The umpire always goes to the in-bound line in order to place the ball.

Of the other two officials, whichever is nearer to the ball secures it and passes it to the umpire.

A question concerning the down is determined from the spot where the ball crossed the side line, before the official who has marked the spot leaves it.

GOAL LINE PLAY

When the ball is within the defensive team's five-yard line, one change is made in the positions of the officials on

Out-of-bounds—the umpire places the ball

scrimmage plays. The field judge comes up on the line of scrimmage at the end opposite from the head linesman. The total area to cover is, of course, reduced because of the proximity of the goal line. There is no need for the field judge to be back of the defensive team. By this change, the play is completely surrounded with the head linesman and field judge within five to ten yards of the ends of the line, the umpire in the center behind the defensive line and within five yards of the line, and the referee in his usual position. The referee is even more alert to see the ball at all times. Diagram 16 shows this arrangement.

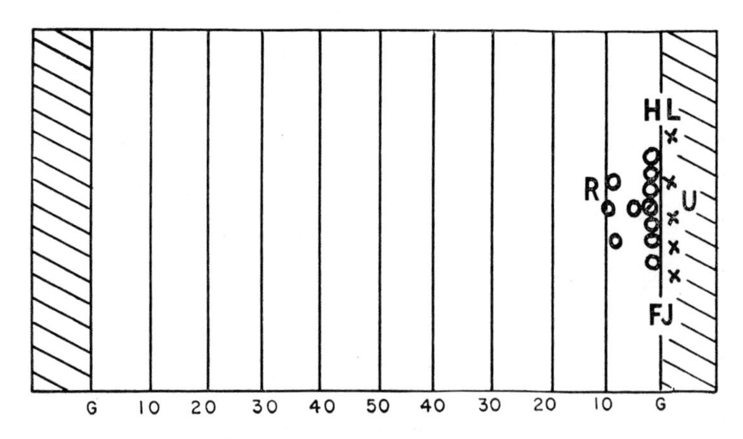

Diagram 16. Positions of officials on a goal-line play.

By such a formation of the officials, valuable assistance can be given to the referee on the vital goal line play. In situations where there may be a question in the referee's mind as to whether or not the ball was carried over the goal line before the carrier was thrown back, he may look to the official nearest the play for advice.

If the play went through the center, the umpire can by a prearranged unobtrusive signal convey his judgment to the referee. It should be remembered, however, that the principal duty of the umpire, as on all scrimmage plays, is

On the goal line, the field judge is stationed on the line of scrimmage

to watch the blocking in the line. This is equally true, if not more important, on the goal line. Likewise, the field judge, if the play hit toward his side, or the head linesman if the ball carrier plunged over his side, indicates his observations. The head linesman and field judge by reason of their positions are better able to judge the forward point of the ball. They can sight along the goal line.

The appropriate signal may be a nod of the head or a movement of the body, hand, or foot. Placing the foot to indicate the point of forward advance of the ball is a simple and effective signal.

Since the referee has sole authority for the score and since it is impossible for the other officials to know what the judgment of the referee may be on a goal line play, they should not use the official signal of arms raised above the head to indicate their opinion. This is the duty of the referee only.

It should be emphasized that there should be little or no lag in announcing the decision on a touchdown play. Consequently, the transfer of information to the referee must be instantaneous.

TRY FOR POINT

There should be no delay between the scoring of a touchdown and the try for point.

On a try for point, the officials assume the same positions as for the goal line play. The importance attached to the attempt for the extra point after a touchdown requires this close supervision of all movements. The referee should stand directly behind the kicker so that he can follow the flight of the ball and rule accurately on the success or failure of the try.

The position of the field judge varies in some sections of the country. An earlier practice of placing the field judge behind the goal posts, so that he can determine whether or not the ball goes over or under the crossbar, is still carried out to a limited extent. However, it is now felt that the referee is sufficiently close to be able to make this decision without the assistance of the field judge.

Immediately after the kick, the field judge should secure the ball and place it on the forty-yard line of the kicking team for the next kickoff. The referee will immediately determine the choice of the captain of the team scored upon.

TRY FOR FIELD GOAL

A try for a field goal takes place from scrimmage or occasionally from a free kick after a fair catch. The position of some of the officials is different in each situation.

On both a scrimmage and a free kick, the field judge drops back to the goal posts so that he can see whether or not the ball goes over the crossbar. The distances of some kicks from the goal is over thirty yards, so that the assistance of the field judge is needed in making this decision.

The referee takes a position behind the kicker and directly in a line from the ball to the goal posts, so that he can follow the flight of the ball. Upon completion of the kick he should quickly check with his fellow officials and immediately render his decision on the kick. The arms extended above the head indicate a goal. Hands and arms crisscrossing in a horizontal plane in front of the body signal no goal.

The umpire and head linesman assume their regular positions as on all scrimmage plays when the kick is from a scrimmage. If the try is on a free kick, the umpire stations himself on the side line at the end of the restraining line for the defensive team and on the opposite side of the field from the head linesman. The head linesman takes his position on the side line at the end of the restraining line for the kicking team. (See diagrams 17 and 18 on next page.)

It is the duty of the umpire and head linesman to see

Field judge—did the ball clear the bar on the try for field goal?

that the teams do not cross their respective restraining lines before the ball is kicked.

If the kick does not score a goal, the duties of the officials become the same as on a kick from scrimmage. It must be remembered, however, that after a free kick, either team may legally recover the ball.

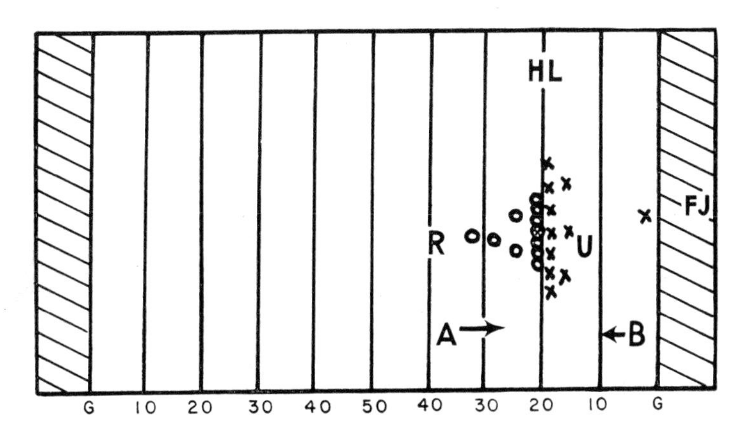

Diagram 17. Positions of officials on a try for field goal.

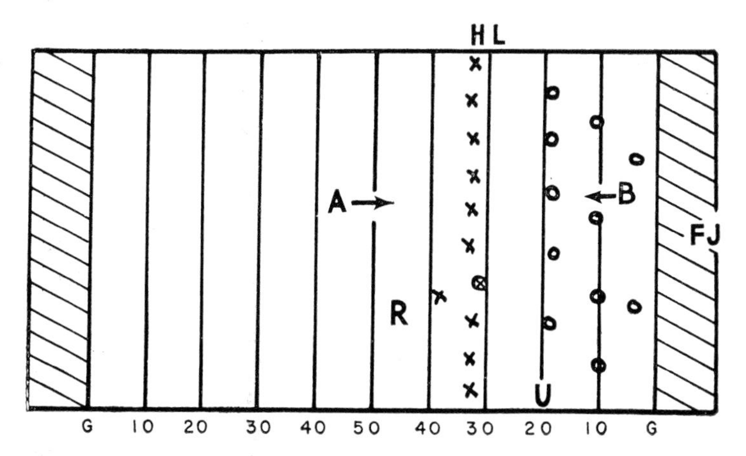

Diagram 18. Positions of officials on a try for field goal from a free kick. (Manual of Football Officiating reverses positions of head linesman and field judge.)

Handle a missed try-for-field goal from scrimmage the same as a punt

TIME OUT

Because of the rules pertaining to substitutions, it is important that all officials signal clearly so that both coaches may know when time is out. The time out signal is indicated by crisscrossing the hands while the arms are extended above the head. In all cases where time out is taken as a result of an incomplete pass, out-of-bounds play, a foul, a touchdown, touchback, safety, or field goal, the officials proceed with their duties and to their positions as required speedily to make ready for the start of the next play. These situations have been described previously.

If a time out is taken at the request of a captain, because of injury to a player, or for the referee:

1. The umpire immediately goes to the ball and marks its forward point. He covers the ball until play is ready to be resumed.

2. The referee makes a record of the time out if it is to be charged to either team. He signals by extending both arms horizontally and points in the direction of the team to indicate the team for which time was taken. If he takes time out on his own authority, he so indicates by pointing to himself. After the above procedure, the referee is then free to confer with captains, to discuss points of play with the other officials, or to give any assistance or comment that may be necessary. While a team is allowed two minutes for a charged time out, the referee should get the game underway as soon as possible if the teams are ready before the expiration of two minutes. Before play is resumed after a time out of any kind, it is necessary for the referee to ascertain from the captains if they are ready. Delay can be prevented in this function if the referee prearranges with the captains that unless they voice themselves to the contrary he will assume they are ready if he hears nothing from them after his question, "Are you ready?"

All officials signal time-out

3. In order that the signal for play may be given at the end of the two minutes, the field judge should give a fifteen-second warning with his horn. This will get trainers, attendants, and others off the field within the two-minute limit. In addition, the field judge should go to the defensive team to give any assistance necessary. He should watch the bench for this team so that any requests to come on the field may be recognized instantly.

4. The head linesman should station himself near the offensive team and watch the bench of this team for any requests which may come from the side lines.

Upon the expiration of the time out period, the officials should quickly assume their respective positions for play. When the referee whistles for play to begin he should begin his twenty-five-second count. If this procedure is not followed, there will be an inevitable dragging out of time-out periods. There is a tendency for football games to extend unnecessarily long. The officials should use every means possible to keep the game moving along. Two hours and thirty minutes is too much time for playing a game. Yet most of our games which are played in fifteen-minute quarters last this long or longer. Diagram 19 shows officials in a typical time out situation.

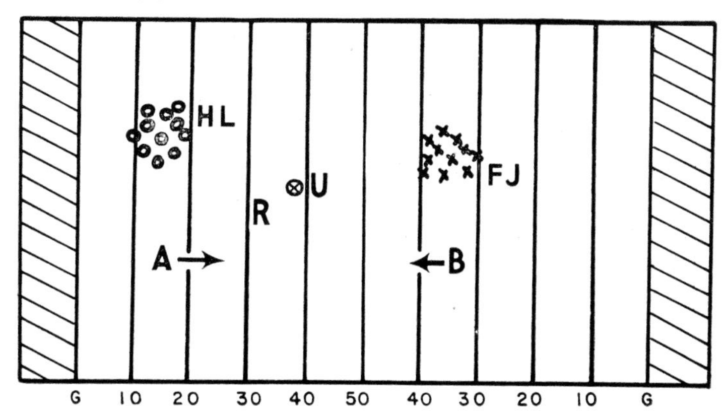

DIAGRAM 19. POSITIONS OF OFFICIALS DURING TIME OUT.

Get the ball in play promptly after time out

BETWEEN QUARTERS

At the end of the first and third quarters, one minute is allowed for the teams to change goals and for the officials to transfer the ball to the same relative spot at the opposite end of the field.

1. The referee immediately locates the position of the ball with respect to its distance from the in-bound line and a yard line. He should record this information together with the down and distance to be gained for a first down. He then transfers the ball to the same relative spot on the opposite side and end of the field. He checks the down and distance with the head linesman.

As soon as the ball is in place and the head linesman has changed the chain, play should be resumed. This is not a time out period for the teams.

2. The head linesman should check the down and distance with the referee immediately at the expiration of time. He should next go to the side line and mark a spot either with a metal snap or with his hand on the chain which corresponds to a yard line between the stakes. He should then pick up the chain and have his chainmen reverse the stakes and move to the opposite end of the field. He should place the mark on the chain on the corresponding yard line at that end of the field and then have the chainmen set their stakes after pulling the chain tight in each direction from the yard line on which the chain is held.

When the tasks of the referee and head linesman are finished and they have rechecked the location of the ball, the down, and the distance, the game is ready to continue.

3. The umpire accompanies the offensive team to the opposite end of the field, sees that it complies with all rules, and recognizes any requests from the bench of this team.

4. The field judge administers to the defensive team in like manner. He also keeps a record of the length of the

Between quarters—Referee—Headlinesman—double check the ball, down, distance

time out, so that play will not be delayed longer than one minute.

Diagram 20 illustrates the method of changing ball and chain between quarters.

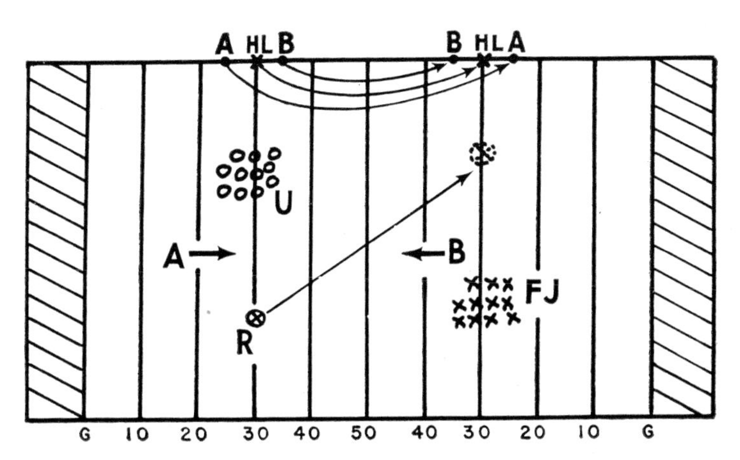

DIAGRAM 20. PROCEDURES AND POSITIONS OF OFFICIALS BETWEEN QUARTERS.

MEASURING POSITION OF BALL

At the end of every play the referee must be conscious of the approximate distance to be gained for a first down. He should glance toward the chain stakes to check when the decision is a close one. In case of doubt or upon request of a captain in a close situation, he should first call time out and then signal the head linesman to bring the chain in for a measurement.

The proper procedure for the officials in making a measurement follows:

1. The referee holds the ball in its original position on the ground when it was declared dead. If it was out-of-bounds, he holds the spot on the side line until a decision is reached. If the ball is in the side line zone when declared dead, it is left there until the measurement is made.

Don't rotate the ball until after the measure

The referee stays over the ball while the measurement is made and makes his decision with respect to the position of the forward point of ball and forward edge of the chain stake. If a first down has been gained, he immediately signals accordingly.

2. The head linesman on doubtful first-down situations should go to the side line and place his foot at the point which he judges to be in line with the forward point of the ball. If a measurement is decided upon, he should first tighten the chain from the rear stake, because this is the stake which he personally sets at the beginning of each series of downs. Next, he grasps the chain or fastens a snap at a point on the middle of the yard line which is farther from the ball. The farther line is used because in making the measurement with the longer part of the chain, greater accuracy can be attained. By using the longer portion of the chain to measure with, it is possible to establish a more nearly perpendicular direction from the yard line to the ball. Then, by using the point of the chain which is on the yard line as a center, the other end of the chain may be swung through an arc to determine the farthest distance toward the goal from the center of rotation.

After securing the point on the chain from which the measurement is to be made, he, with his two chainmen, moves quickly with the chain to the position of the ball.

The assistant linesman remains at the side line with his stake at the forward point of the ball.

3. When the chain has been brought to the ball, the umpire holds the stake which is next to the ball. The umpire and head linesman then make the measurement under the supervision of the referee.

After the measurement, the umpire returns the chain stake to the chainmen. If a first down has been declared, the head linesman releases the chain. The chainmen hurry back to the side line and set the chain stakes in position for the next series of downs, as directed by the head linesman.

Measure from the farther yard line

If the offensive team has failed to earn a first down, the head linesman holds his mark on the chain and returns with his chainmen to reset the chain stakes carefully into their former position. He checks the down with the referee and signals when all is in readiness to resume play.

4. The field judge is the emergency official. He stands in a position such that he may acknowledge any requests from either player's bench. He should permit no delay greater than necessary to make the measurement.

Diagram 21 shows the method of measurement.

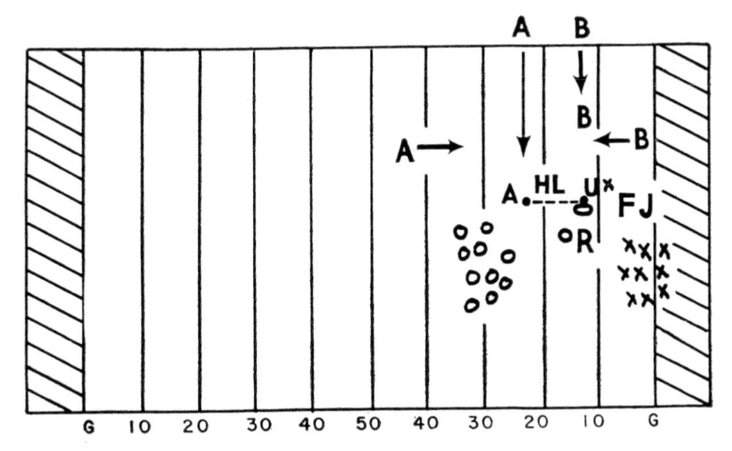

DIAGRAM 21. POSITIONS OF OFFICIALS WHEN A MEASUREMENT IS TAKEN.

BETWEEN HALVES

The following procedure should be followed during the fifteen-minute intermission between halves:

1. The field judge immediately starts his watch when the ball is dead after the expiration of playing time, in order to time the intermission.

2. The field judge secures the ball from the referee.

3. The head linesman directs his assistants to take the chain to the opposite side of the field in readiness for the second half.

Use the intermission for review

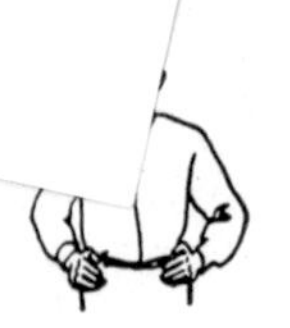

Offside

Illegal position or procedure

Illegal motion or shift

Delay of game

Unsportsmanlike conduct

Defensive holding

Illegal use of hands and arms

Intentional grounding

Incomplete forward pass

Penalty declined; no play or no score

Crawling; helping the runner or interlocked interference

Ball dead

DIAGRAM 22.

Learn the signals

Personal foul

Clipping

Roughing the kicker

Illegally passing or handling ball forward

Forward pass or kick catching interference

Ineligible receiver down field on pass

Ball illegally touched, kicked or batted

Touchdown or field goal

Safety

First down

Start the clock, or No more time-outs allowed

FOOTBALL SIGNALS.

4. It is customary for the officials to go to the visiting team's bench.

5. The officials should use the time during the intermission to review any phases of their work which may be helpful to a better administration of the game during the second half. Sometimes questions, problems, and controversies arise during the first half which should be discussed and clarified during the intermission.

All such discussions should be carried on in privacy.

6. As the teams return to the field, the referee seeks the captain who lost the toss, to receive his "choice" for the second half. He or the umpire then secures the choice of the other captain.

7. The field judge waits at the center of the fifty-yard line with the ball for instructions by means of signals to indicate the direction of the kickoff.

8. The head linesman reorganizes his assistants in readiness for the kickoff.

9. When all is ready, the officials assume their proper positions for the kickoff, as previously described.

AFTER THE GAME

1. The referee should obtain possession of the ball at the end of the game and deliver it to the home management or dispose of it in accordance with any instructions which may have been given to him.

2. The head linesman should thank his assistants and see that the chain and stakes are returned to the proper persons.

3. The officials should be wary of making any comments to the press or public concerning the game.

4. The officials should go immediately to their dressing room.

SIGNALS

The signals which are reproduced on the following pages represent the common code which is used by officials throughout the United States. It is the duty of every offi-

When the game ends—leave—don't talk

cial to know these signals perfectly. He should be able to give them instantly.

Signals are the only means by which the action of the officials on the field may be relayed to the public address system and the spectators.

It is not enough to know the signals. The official must have a sense of timing and a flair for the dramatic, so that everyone may clearly receive his message. When it is necessary to signal a foul, a first down, a score, etc., the official should pause momentarily before signaling. This pause draws the attention of everyone. Then, in clear, staccato fashion, the official should act out his decision. Both before and after a penalty has been assessed, the official should signal the foul for which the penalty was given. (See diagram 22 for a list of the approved signals.)

Careful attention to the art of giving signals will add much toward a satisfactory reception by the spectators of the work of an official.

16

Football—Guides to Play Situations

When a foul occurs, the officials have well-defined duties to perform. These are partly covered by the section on "The Officials" at the end of the rule book. There are, however, procedures which are not covered by rule. In addition, an analysis of Rule 10 suggests certain axioms which may be used by officials to guide them in the difficult job of applying the rules which relate to penalties. These procedures and guides are presented and discussed below.

1. The referee does not blow his whistle until the ball is dead.
2. The official, other than the referee, who detects a foul immediately blows his horn.
3. The official who detects a foul drops his marker at the spot of the foul.
4. All officials follow the play until the ball is dead. (The penalty may be declined.)
5. The official who has announced by blowing his horn or dropping his marker that a foul has occurred, must be sure to get the number of the offender, to mark the spot of the foul, and to notice whether or not the ball is in possession of either team. In the case of a kick from scrimmage, he must know whether or not the ball has been touched at the time the foul occurred.

There is orderly organization to handling a foul—learn it

6. The field judge stops the watch immediately upon signal from the referee.

7. All officials signal time out.

8. The head linesman makes sure that the chainmen or the assistant linesman does not move the stakes.

9. The official who calls the foul reports the foul and the player, and indicates to the referee the spot of the foul and the penalty.

10. The referee explains the foul to the captain of the offended team and states the alternatives.

11. After the captain makes his decision, the referee signals the foul, and if the penalty has been declined he so indicates by crisscrossing his hands and arms in a horizontal plane in front of his body.

12. If the penalty is accepted, he locates the spot from which the penalty will be assessed. He then notes a similar spot near the proper yard line where the ball should be placed after the penalty is assessed. He never steps off the distance penalty.

13. The referee checks the down and distance with the head linesman and resumes play immediately.

ENFORCEMENT OF PENALTIES

In the enforcement of all penalties, there are three factors involved:

1. *The spot from which the penalty shall be assessed.* The penalty for the violation of rules states the spot from which the penalty shall be assessed. An analysis of this part of the rules indicates that the spot from which most penalties are assessed may be indicated under two general headings:

a. All personal (contact) fouls are penalized from the spot of the foul, except fouls against the passer or kicker, pass interference by the passing team (these fouls are penalized from the spot of the preceding down), and pass interference by the defense behind its own goal line (ball placed on the one-yard line).

Explain the options

b. All technical fouls, noncontact fouls, are penalized from the spot where the ball is put in play (except hurdling, illegally touching a kicked ball, illegal forward pass). Whether or not the penalty is from the spot of the previous play or the succeeding play depends on the time at which the foul was committed. If the ball was in play, then the penalty is from where the ball was put in play; if the ball was dead, then the penalty is enforced from the spot from which the ball would next be put in play had no foul occurred.

2. *The penalty for fouls.* In general, the fouls with which officials are most often concerned carry a penalty of five or fifteen yards. There are a very few which involve the loss of the ball. Illegally touching the ball is the most frequent. Two handy axioms for determining the yardage involved in a penalty follow:

a. Most personal fouls carry a penalty of fifteen yards. Exceptions: interference with an opponent after the ball is ready for play, holding by the defense, flying block or tackle.

b. The technical fouls which are commonly committed carry a five-yard penalty. Exceptions: ineligible player touching pass beyond line of scrimmage, hurdling, unsportsmanlike conduct, misconduct by persons other than players, illegal shift, grounding pass, intermission rules, not ready to play. It will be noted that the exceptions listed above seldom if ever occur.

c. When the ball is not in possession of either team, the penalty is the loss of the ball. The one exception is the case of a foul after the ball has been kicked from scrimmage and before it has been touched by any player. This foul carries a fifteen-yard penalty from where the ball was put in play.

3. *The down following a penalty:*

a. After the assessment of a penalty for a foul, the down and the point to be gained before the foul occurred

Enforcement involves—the spot, the penalty, the down

remain the same unless the ball after the penalty is beyond the point to be gained for a first down. The exceptions to the above statement occur when the ball is awarded to the offended team as a result of the foul, and cases of pass interference by the offensive team. In the latter case, the play counts as a down.

GUIDES TO AN UNDERSTANDING OF SOME RULES

It is the duty of every official to know the rules thoroughly and to know the intent and purpose of each one. It is not, however, the purpose of this text to discuss the rules in detail.

There are a few guides and some analyses which have been developed after more than twenty years' experience in teaching classes in officiating which may prove helpful. Many feel that the football rules are the most difficult of all our rules to master. While they do appear somewhat complicated because of the many different situations and fouls which arise during the progress of a game, those rules with which the officials are actively engaged are not too numerous. There is a consistency in the present code which greatly simplifies the job of learning and interpretation.

A few suggestions have been given to aid the official in knowing what to do in the enforcement of penalties. The reader may find the following syntheses of additional value for building a comprehensive working pattern for some of the more vexing practical problems.

Fumbles

The decisions which must be made in connection with fumbles can be clarified by four simple statements which bring together all the situations which puzzle many officials.

1. Any fumbled ball which is recovered before touching the ground by the team which did not fumble the ball may be advanced. This applies to a

Who fumbled? Who recovered? Did the ball touch the ground?

fumble of a kicked ball as well as a ball fumbled on a running or forward or lateral pass play.

2. Any fumbled ball which touches the ground and then is recovered by the team which did not make the fumble is dead at the spot of recovery.

3. Any fumbled ball which is recovered by the team which fumbled the ball may be advanced until declared dead by the referee.

4. A ball which is fumbled and then goes out-of-bounds belongs to the team which fumbled the ball.

If one will take these simple statements and apply them to any situation involving possession by the kicking team, he can hand down accurate decisions. He should not let himself become confused by conditional clauses or by the introduction of numerous and complicated incidents.

For example, Team A kicks off. The ball is touched in the field of play, rolls across the goal line, is recovered by Team B, run out to the twenty-yard line, lateraled to a teammate who runs to the fifty-yard line where he is tackled and then laterals to another teammate. This pass is fumbled, hits the ground and is picked up by a player of Team A who runs for a touchdown.

Much of the foregoing is superfluous verbiage. The fact that the ball was fumbled, hit the ground, and then was recovered by the team which did not fumble the ball precludes the possibility of any subsequent play. The ball was dead at the spot of recovery. Had it been recovered before hitting the ground, then the run and touchdown would have been legal.

Touchback, Safety, Touchdown

Misunderstanding often exists concerning what constitutes a touchback, a safety, and a touchdown, and what play may be made on a ball which crosses the goal line. Mistakes are made because officials permit extraneous circumstances to divert their thinking. If three questions are asked and answered correctly every time the ball crosses the goal line, and no attention is paid to any other factor, no doubts would ever arise concerning a touchdown, safety, or touchback. These questions are:

1. Which team caused the ball to go across the goal line?
2. Is the attacking team eligible legally to recover the ball?
3. Who gained possession of the ball in the end zone?

If the attacking team caused the ball to cross the goal line and is eligible to recover the ball and does recover it, it is a touchdown. If the attacking team does not recover the ball behind the goal line, then, under no circumstances can it score a touchdown. If the attacking team is not eligible to recover the ball, it is not possible to score a touchdown even though the ball is recovered over the goal line by this team. If the ball is caused to go over the goal line by the defending team and is legally recovered by the attacking team, it is a touchdown.

A safety can be scored only if the defending team causes the ball to cross the goal line and it is declared dead in the end zone in possession of the defending team or rolls out-of-bounds behind the goal line. It should be remembered that a punt by the defending team which is blocked and rolls over the goal line and is declared dead in possession of the defending team is considered to be caused to cross the goal line by the defending team. A safety may be scored as a result of a foul—that is, illegally batting or kicking a free ball in a team's own end zone.

A ball which is caused to cross the goal line by the attacking team and which is declared dead in possession of the defending team, regardless of attempts to run it out, is a touchback. A touchback may be scored as a result of a penalty—that is, illegally batting or kicking a free ball in an opponent's end zone or illegally touching a kicked ball inside the opponent's ten-yard line.

Answer three questions to solve touchdown, safety, touchback problems

A punt or place kick by the attacking team which is not touched by the defending team and which crosses the goal line becomes a touchback unless the receiving team advances the ball into the field of play.

These statements should help officials to avoid mistakes on play situations involving touchdowns, touchbacks, or safeties.

As a further aid to officials, a specific rule should always be taken as qualifying and refining a general rule. The general rule states the principle involved. A specific rule places limitations on a particular play and goes beyond the general rule. This is analogous to the federal laws in contrast to the state laws. The state laws may not violate the federal law, but they may go beyond it, and in so doing take precedence.

The application of these principles may be illustrated in the case of interference by the defense on a forward pass. In general, the penalty is loss of the ball at the spot of the foul. But in the specific case of interference behind the goal line of the defending team, the penalty is a first down on the one-yard line.

Likewise, a kick which goes out-of-bounds before being recovered goes to the receiving team. But in the case of a first kickoff, the ball is brought back and kicked again.

The penalty for fouls committed when neither team has possession of the ball is loss of the ball at the spot of the foul. However, in the case of a foul after a kick from scrimmage and before the ball has been touched by any player, the penalty is fifteen yards from where the ball was put in play.

Specific rules qualify general rules

17

Basketball

THE POSITION AND MOVEMENT OF BASKETBALL OFFICIALS on the court in order best to observe and administer each type of play, and to co-operate with and supplement each other, is known as court mechanics. It is the modus operandi for the official. To a very limited extent, the rules direct the actions and procedures of the officials. However, for the most part, their pattern of action has been developed through a process of trial and error during actual officiating experience.

There are slight differences in the plans of operation adopted in the different sections of the country. In general, however, the plan is quite uniform, so that officials from east, west, north, south, and midwest may come together and officiate with little lack of harmony.

The National Association of Approved Basketball Officials[1] has done much constructive work to develop a uniform pattern. Mr. Porter and Mr. Tower, in their book on Basketball Play Situations,[2] have given space to methods of covering the court. Many of the organized conferences have developed manuals, which they distribute to

---

[1] Handbook of The National Association of Approved Basketball Officials. Biltmore Hotel, New York, 1949.

[2] H. V. Porter, and Oswald Tower, *Basketball Play Situations* (New York: A. S. Barnes Co., 1948).

Know your modus operandi

their officials. These manuals constitute the instructions under which the games in the respective conferences are to be conducted. There is now a single manual by the National Organization of Commissioners[3] so that, in fact, all sections of the country will follow the same pattern.

The following is a presentation of the more widely accepted court mechanics. The few variations which exist at present will be pointed out. An explanation of, and the reason for, the position and movement of each official for each court situation will be given. This should be of great help to the inexperienced official. It will direct his attention to the important points on which he should focus his attention in each situation. While he is going through the stages of gaining experience and developing his judgment, he can at least look like a good official by being in the right place at the right time. He can be looking in the right direction, even though in the early stages of his experience he may not be able to see clearly or judge correctly.

Only the plan for the double officiating system will be discussed. Practically no organized game today is conducted with one official. The elimination of the center jump and the advent of the fast break have created the necessity for two officials. It is not physically possible for one official to handle a game effectively under present conditions. For this reason, to present the technique of the single official would be of historical value only.

PREGAME DUTIES

The pregame activities of the official may be divided conveniently into four categories:

1. Pregame conference of officials.
2. Checking equipment and court.
3. Instructing timers and scorers.
4. Meeting with coaches and captains.

---

[3] *Manual of Basketball Officiating* (Kansas City, Mo.: National Association of Collegiate Commissioners, 1948).

Be in the right place even though you don't see

Pregame Conference

The conference of the officials in the dressing room before the game can be the means of smooth and co-operative action on the court during the game. This is especially true if the two officials who are assigned to work the game have seldom or never worked together. There are sufficient variations in court procedures to necessitate a discussion for the purpose of a common understanding before the officials go onto the court. It is also true that some officials are sensitive or jealous of their prerogatives and resent what they term interference or encroachment upon their duties by the other official. The enumeration of several of these points will tend to clarify the issue. A discussion of the different techniques will be presented later on in their proper sequence.

1. What method of switching will be used?
2. Who will toss held balls at the free-throw line?
3. How will out-of-bounds play be covered?
   a. Will both make out-of-bounds decisions anywhere?
   b. Will each have authority in certain areas, except when help is asked of another official?
   c. How can another official co-operate without delay or confusion when asked?
   d. What signal system will be used?
4. Is each official to call violations and fouls wherever or whenever he sees them?

These are pertinent and sometimes touchy questions which must be resolved before the officials leave the dressing room. Harmony in working the game is dependent upon a common understanding. To neglect to work out a uniform pattern of action may mean a poorly officiated game.

Other matters also lend themselves to a dressing room discussion. The referee may have some specific assignments for the umpire. These should be given at this time.

Did you confer with your colleague before the game?

For example, he may desire that the umpire work with the scorers and timers before the game, while he is checking other matters. He may also have a specific plan for the umpire to follow with the scorers and timers in checking decisions with them during the progress of the game.

Occasionally peculiar and puzzling play situations arise during the season. Interpretations have not always been clarified. The dressing room conference affords an opportunity to discuss these, so that the officials will not be opposing each other on the court if the same situation should occur. In addition, the dressing room provides a meeting place for a general rules discussion. The best way to develop a thorough knowledge of the rules and uniformity of interpretation is through continued discussion of the moot points.

Many teams because of the style of play which they employ present special problems. It is also true that rivalries between teams create conditions which make some games more difficult to officiate than others. Some coaches and some players are more serious problems than others. Audiences in certain localities are more unruly than in others.

If the game at hand presents any of these special situations and they are known to the officials, a plan of approach can be adopted in advance. Such advance preparation may be the means of handling cases satisfactorily and with ease, whereas failure to anticipate and be ready may produce embarrassing moments and may mar contests. A couple of situations which represent actual experiences may demonstrate the wisdom of forethought. The identities of those involved are not revealed for obvious reasons.

A certain team which did considerable barnstorming was known always to test the officials in the opening minutes of the game. In the first place, because they carried limited personnel, a request was made to set aside the disqualification rule for too many personal fouls. Next, the players would determine by their court tactics just how

Are you in tune with your colleague?

technical and how free the officials were, and how much courage they possessed. They would hold, they would block, they would charge, in a clever fashion. If caught, they would evince great surprise and attempt a bit of official baiting—typical professional tactics. If the officials could be intimidated, then this team would run the game as it pleased and proceed to make life miserable for both the officials and the opponents. If forced to do so, the players, who were finished performers, would play by the code.

This team had played in a certain locality the previous year and had gotten away with "murder." The following year, when they came for a return engagement, officials refused to work the game. Finally, two competent men were secured. They knew of the reputation of this particular team. Without prejudice they proceeded to keep the game in check from the very beginning. After several attempts by the players of the team to dominate the scene, a time out was called. In the huddle, the following remark was overheard: "Cut out the funny stuff. These officials are going to run this game. They can't be bluffed."

Thereafter, the game went along smoothly and without further incident. The barnstorming team won handily because it was far superior. But it was forced to play according to the rules, because the officials before the game had determined to keep the game under control. The fact that there had been pregame planning to meet this particular situation made it possible to handle a difficult situation with ease.

On another occasion, two officials dared to enforce the rules for unsportsmanlike conduct on a particularly unruly coach. This coach had been browbeating officials for years from the side lines during the progress of the game. His actions caused the crowd to follow a similar pattern. The worst sportsmanship imaginable was displayed by both the coach and the spectators.

Can you be intimidated?

Two officials in their pregame planning determined that for such tactics to persist was unfair to the opponent and a disgrace to the game. They also decided that they as officials were at fault for permitting such practices to continue in brazen violation of the rules. Together, they determined that if the usual display occurred during this particular game, they would first warn the coach, then penalize him if their friendly appeal was not heeded.

They had occasion to put their plans into practice. A foul was called on the coach several times. Their courage not only controlled a very bad situation but focused public attention on it, with the result that much improvement was effected.

Checking Equipment and Court Facilities

Checking equipment and the court is a requirement which must be carried out by specific stipulation of the rules (Rule 2, section 2). These requirements include an inspection of the ball, the baskets, the backboards, and the markings and clearances on the court.

The rules give the manufacturer specifications for the ball. The official may or may not check these specifications with precision. He should, however, note the bounce and observe the general roundness. All schools should provide the official with the proper facilities for testing the bounce of the ball. A slight difference in pressure can cause the bounce of the molded ball to vary outside the limitations of the rule. Usually two balls are furnished. The official will choose the one which he thinks most nearly meets the specifications.

In any event, it is wise to ask about the ball at the very beginning because there have been many instances when the home team has inadvertently forgotten the ball.

The court markings must be observed carefully. There are often many markings on a gym floor. Those which are

Did you check the ball?

to govern the boundaries for the game must be pointed out to the opponents. The home team is familiar with them, but the opponents can easily be confused. If there are two 10-second lines, these should be identified.

The court markings which are most often neglected are those used for the dispersion of players along the free-throw lanes during the throwing of free throws. These markings save much confusion and delay. If they are absent, it is wise to mark them out in chalk. No provision in the rules has been more helpful to the players and officials.

Some courts still have only two feet of clearance from the face of the backboard to the end line. The officials should notice the end line distance. Limited space should be called to the attention of the opponents. Less than four feet means more out-of-bounds decisions, more crowding under the basket, and less opportunity to clear rebounds without contact.

The method used to hang and support the backboard must be studied. Can the ball hit on the edges, particularly the top of the backboard, without hitting a support? Are there wire supports or bracings which the ball may hit on shots or rebounds? Can the backboard be moved out of line when players run against the supports? Are the backboards protected from the spectators? These are questions which are of importance to the officials. No game should be started before these points are checked. Unsatisfactory conditions should be corrected, or provisions should be made by ground rules to cover any exigencies that may arise.

The basket itself should be checked. Several times every season, a basket breaks before or during a game. The nets are neglected and game time approaches with the condition of the nets unacceptable. They are not properly fastened, cords are broken, or they are too long or will not release the ball. The latter condition will interfere with fast-breaking offenses and should be corrected before play begins.

The clearance beyond the boundary lines is important. If it is less than three feet, then restraining lines must be established for the control of play from out-of-bounds. Inadequate clearance necessitates a check on the restraining line markings on the court. If these are not present, the players must be cautioned to keep ample distance from the player who has the ball out-of-bounds. If the lines are marked, the players must be notified whether or not they are to be used.

In general, the court and surroundings should be surveyed carefully for any obstructions or hazards that might interfere with the game or be dangerous to players. Nonstandard conditions should be corrected or precautions taken to protect the players and to insure playing conditions as normal as possible.

All of the above factors can be checked in less time than it takes to read about them here. They are, however, important. No official should neglect to go through this routine before each game. Considerable emphasis has been given to these details because officials are wont to be lax about them. It is hoped thereby to stimulate a more serious regard for these factors for the purpose of handling them before trouble comes, rather than after it occurs.

The most important piece of personal equipment to the official is his whistle. Without it he is impotent on the court. He should be sure that he has his whistle. Even better, it is wise to carry two whistles. A whistle with a rubber grip for the teeth is highly recommended.

Most officials carry their whistles between the teeth. This is a most dangerous practice. Even with the rubber grip, the danger of being hit on the mouth with the ball, or by an elbow or shoulder from a player when the official is observing play at close range or is tossing a ball for

Carry the whistle in your hand for safety

a jump, is too great. One accident may result in broken teeth or badly cut lips. (The author learned this fact the hard way.) Also, one may blow the whistle inadvertently while running with it between the teeth.

Because of the possibility of injury, it is recommended that the whistle be carried in the hand. As one anticipates the need for blowing it, the whistle can be raised close to the mouth in readiness for immediate use. In order that there be no danger of dropping the whistle, two methods of carrying it are in practice. It can be carried on a string which hangs around the neck, or a finger or hand device may be used. A metal ring large enough to slip over the ring finger may be inserted through the hole in the end of the whistle. This will prevent the official from dropping his whistle. It can be carried in the hand with the snout lying between the thumb and forefinger so that it can be put to instant use.

Another device for carrying the whistle is to fasten it to a heavy rubber band, by feeding one end of the band through the ring and then drawing one end of the band through the other. The hand may now be placed through the rubber band with the whistle next to the palm. The snout of the whistle again protrudes between the thumb and forefinger. Fig. 21, p. 196 shows various ways of carrying the whistle.

Those two devices are handy, inexpensive, homemade methods for carrying the whistle. Also, one may purchase whistles with either leather hand straps or metal finger straps attached.

SCORERS AND TIMERS

The rules stipulate that each game shall have six officials. The referee and umpire are usually the only two who are given any consideration. Even the referee and umpire tend to overlook the importance of their four assistants—the two scorers and two timers. It should be real-

Did you instruct the scorers?

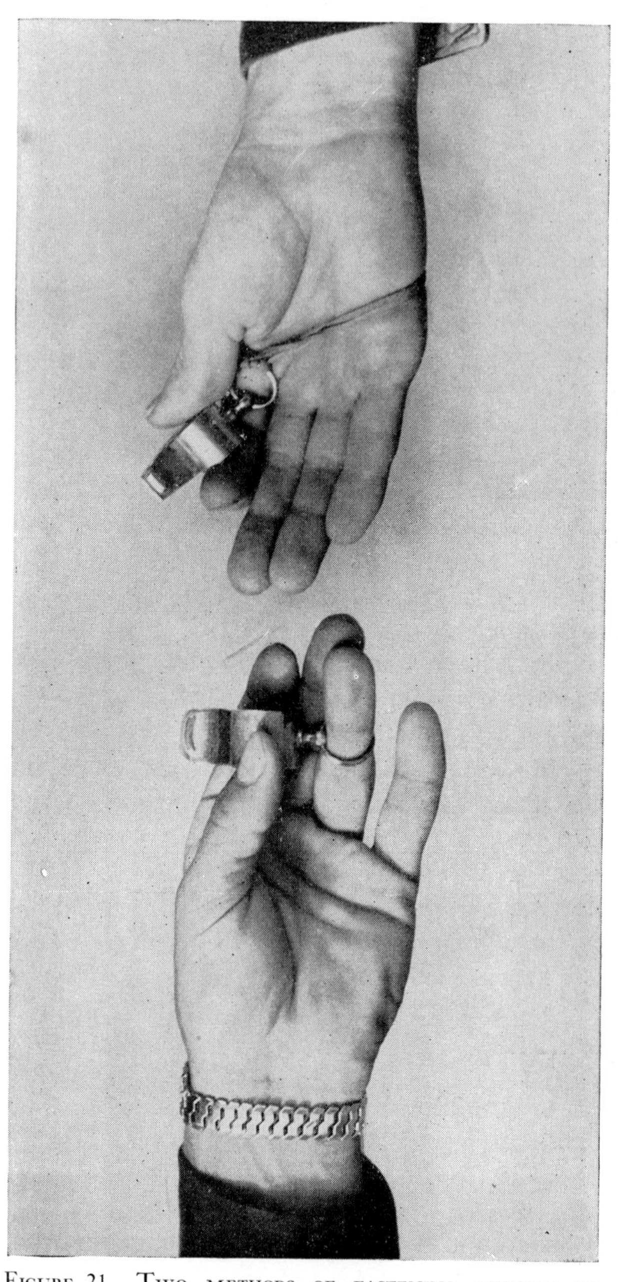

FIGURE 21. TWO METHODS OF FASTENING WHISTLE TO HAND FOR READY USE.

ized that either the scorers or timers may decide the outcome of ball games and that their decisions in specific instances become the official ones. For example, in controversies over the score or personal fouls, the record of the official book is final, unless the referee has information which permits him to rule otherwise. Likewise, at the end of the game or period, if the timer's signal is not heard, the testimony of the timers determines whether a score shall count or a foul shall be charged, unless the referee has information which would alter the situation.

The responsibility of the scorers and timers is so great that the referee and umpire must be certain to set up the closest understanding and co-operation with them. Many schools use faculty men or interested citizens to act in the capacities of scorer and timer. Others use student managers or other students with the idea that it is a part of the educational pattern. Whoever the scorers and timers may be, the referee and umpire should never take them for granted. They should be made to realize that they are not spectators, but that they are an important part of a game and that they must see to it that the game is run off smoothly and efficiently.

The following routine checks should be made before every game:

To the Scorers

1. Designate the official scorer.
2. Advise nonofficial scorer regarding checking every entry which is made in official book.
3. Order immediate action in case of any discrepancy in the record.
4. Caution to make no entry if in doubt, but to ask for official decision.
5. Arrange for plan of designating player who commits a foul.
6. Instruct concerning time to send substitute into game.

Do scorers know duties on substitutions?

7. Check signal devices for announcing substitutes or calling officials.

The rules provide that the home scorer shall be designated as the official scorer, unless the referee rules otherwise. Except in places where an official scorer is provided, such as in the sports arenas in large cities, the home scorer is practically always designated as the official scorer. Sometimes, however, where an electric timing device is recognized as the official timepiece, which must be operated by the home management, the referee may appoint the visiting scorekeeper as official. This divides the responsibilities between the representatives of the two teams.

The nonofficial scorer should check each entry with the official book at the time it is made. For example, each time a player scores a point, the scorers should announce to each other the name of the player scoring and then check on his total scores. Following this the total running score for the game should be changed and the total score for each team repeated. If an electric scoreboard is being operated, this score should also be checked. At the end of a half, the sum of the individual scores can be checked against the total running score which has been kept.

When a personal foul is committed, the name of the player who committed the foul should be repeated. A "P," with the proper numeral indicating the number of personal fouls charged against him, should be entered in the proper column opposite his name. The total number of fouls against this player should be repeated by the scorers, so that they have a check on this important record. If a multiple throw is awarded, a letter "M" can be used, so that later the total number of throws can be checked against the fouls which have been called and recorded.

As the rules suggest, when a player is awarded a free throw, a circle should be entered in the record opposite his name. If the throw is successful, an "X" should be marked inside the circle. If it is missed, the circle is left blank.

Scoring is accounting—do the books balance?

In this way, an accurate account can be made of the fouls and attempts. At the end of each half, a check should be made to see that the number of free-throw attempts indicated by "P" and "M" is equal to the number of circles.

The details of keeping score in this manner are recorded here in the interest of a uniform method of accurate bookkeeping and accounting. The referee will not explain all of these details.

The referee should insist upon two procedures in scorekeeping. First, if at any time the scorers find a discrepancy in their records, they should notify the referee the next time thereafter that the ball is dead. And second, they should make no entry in their books which is based on their own judgment. If they do not get the signal for decisions clearly concerning who is charged with a foul, they should sound their horn. The official should designate the violator for them, so that there can be no question about the accuracy of the records.

With respect to giving signals to indicate fouls and the player charged and the number of free throws, the following procedure is now in common practice and is highly recommended. When a foul is called, the official should pause momentarily to gain attention. Then he should indicate by the use of his fingers the number of the player. If teams follow the number plan of having no digit greater than 5, the fingers of the right hand are used for the first digit of a number and the fingers of the left hand for the second digit. Thus, if number fifteen committed the foul, five fingers would be raised on the left hand and one on the right.

Where this plan of numbering players is not followed, the number of fingers held up are added. If the number is more than ten, the fists will be closed after holding up all ten fingers, and following this, the additional number held up to make the total necessary. For example, if the foul was committed by number 18, ten fingers would be raised, then the fists closed, followed by the raising of eight more fingers. If the number were 28, ten fingers would be held up twice and then eight.

As a further check with the scorers, the official may point to the player, and the umpire may repeat the number as he goes by the scorers. As a last check, the official who handles the ball at the free-throw line should look to the scorers before placing the ball at the disposal of the free thrower and be ready to repeat the number of the player in case the decision is not clear to the scorers. If the scorers are advised concerning this procedure, they will withhold their horn and wait for the repeat of the information from the free-throw line.

To indicate a substitution, the scorers may sound their horn at any time when the ball is dead. The officials, however, should call to their attention the fact that when the ball is awarded to the free thrower at the free-throw line, it is considered to be in play. The scorers may sound their horn while the official has the ball in his possession, but when it is given to the free thrower, they should withhold their signal until the next time the ball becomes dead, in order to avoid disconcerting the free thrower. This point is emphasized because it is the one which is misunderstood, and thus violated, by scorers.

The officials should always make sure that the scorers have a signal by which they can announce substitutes or get their attention at any time the ball is dead. In spite of the emphasis in the rules, the officials should be sure that there is a horn, klaxon, or gong which is distinctly different from their own whistles.

To the Timers

The officials should follow a similar procedure with the timers. It is even more important that the timers be properly instructed, because their decisions officially end each period. Consequently, the actions of the timers are of tremendous significance.

1. Designate official watch.
2. Suggest method of co-operation for two timers.
3. Check signal devices for ending periods.
4. Check timing equipment.
5. Question concerning knowledge of time-in and time-out.

It is necessary to designate the official watch. If an electric timer is used, there is no problem; but if each timer has a watch, only one may be used as the official watch. If the referee should fail to designate an official watch and the game is close or tied, there is likely to be trouble. Each timer could claim his watch as the official one. The time of each would probably not be the same. Naturally, each would argue for his time if it were to the advantage of his team. It is easy to see that the results could be embarrassing. This is not a hypothetical situation. It has happened on numerous occasions. That is why it is so important for the official to assign one watch as the official one.

The official should also make sure that the signal devices for announcing the end of a period have sufficient volume and that they make a type of sound which will penetrate the noise of rooters. A signal which fails to sound or is difficult to hear when pandemonium reigns, places the officials in a position where they must accept the judgment of lay assistants.

In anticipation of such emergency, the referee should give the timers full instructions. However, if the signals are automatic and synchronized with an electric scoreboard and clock, there is little need for the following. Toward the end of a period, the timer who is operating the watch should count the last ten seconds aloud as he watches his timepiece. The other timer watches the action on the court and holds the gun or other signal. If play is stopped at any time during the last ten seconds, the timer watching the play calls time. As the ball is put in play again, he calls play. The other timer continues his count. As the time expires, he calls time and the other timer, who has picked up the cadence of the count, fires the gun or sounds the signal.

In anticipation of a shot or a foul at the end of a period and the fact that the signal may not go off or may not be heard, the referee should ask the timer who is watching the action to be able to tell him one thing: "Where was the ball when time expired?" On the basis of this information, the referee can make decisions concerning play at the end of a period.

This procedure is suggested because it tends to remove the element of suggestion which may be planted by other comments. The significance of this procedure is indicated by the rule (Rule 2, section 12), which states in part: "If the timer's signal fails to sound or is not heard, the timer shall go on the court or use other means to notify the referee immediately. If, in the meantime, a goal has been made or a foul has occurred, the referee shall consult the timers. If the timers agree that time was up before the ball was in the air on its way to the basket, or before the foul was committed, the referee shall rule that the goal does not count, or in case of a foul, that it shall be disregarded unless it is flagrant. But if they disagree, the goal shall count or the foul be penalized unless the referee has knowledge that would alter the ruling."

By focusing the attention of the timer on the position of the ball at the moment time expired, the referee tends to remove the power of decision with respect to a score or a foul from the timer. This decision is left for the referee who is the proper person to make such a decision. If a leading or suggestive question such as "Did the goal count?" or "Was the ball in the air?" is asked, one may get a reply which is influenced by the question. Also, if the timers

Decisions at the end of a period are vital

follow the procedure in which one watches the timepiece and counts off the last ten seconds and the other watches the ball, any possibility of disagreement over the position of the ball is avoided.

From the foregoing rather exhaustive discussion of the duties of the timers and scorers and their relation with the officials, the importance of attention to these assistants before the game starts should be quite evident. Mr. Lawrence C. Lobaugh has developed from the rules a list of instructions to scorers and timers which may be handed to them some time before the game. Some schools have adopted the practice of pasting these instructions in their scorebook so that they are available for ready reference and study. They have been found to be very helpful.

These instructions are reproduced herewith for the information of officials.

INSTRUCTIONS TO SCORERS

1. Consult referee as to signals used to designate fouls and time outs.
2. Write name, number, and position of each starting player at least two minutes before the start of the game.
3. Write name and number of each substitute who may participate in the game.
4. Record field goals made, free throws made and missed, running summary of points scored, personal and technical fouls on each player, and time outs.
5. Designate each goal and each foul thus:

    Field goal: X or 2
    Free throw attempts: O
    Free throw made: ⓧ
    Free throw waived: O w
    Free throw violation: O v
    Personal foul: P_1, P_2, P_3, P_4, P_5
    Technical foul: T
    Personal foul (multiple throw): P_{m1}, etc.

Do the time and the score affect your decisions?

Field goals scored in wrong basket are not credited to any player, but are credited to the team in a footnote. Points awarded for illegally touching ball or basket are credited to the thrower. When a live ball goes into a basket, the last player who touched it causes it to go there.

6. Notify referee the moment a player has five personal fouls. Also when a team has called its fifth time out, and time out in excess of the legal ones.

7. Check with fellow scorer on each entry in scorebook, such as score, fouls, substitutions, charged time outs, etc. If any discrepancy occurs, notify referee at once on next dead ball.

8. *Blow horn to stop game only when the ball is dead.*

9. *Substitutions.* When a substitute reports, signal as soon as ball is dead. Allow substitute to go on court only when official beckons. *Do not signal after ball has been placed at the disposal of a free thrower.* On a multiple throw or throw for a double foul, a substitution may be made between throws. If thrower is to be replaced, do not signal for substitution until the ball is dead after the throw. A player who is disqualified may not legally reenter the game either during the regular playing time or overtime.

10. Scorers should be equipped with a horn, siren, gong, buzzer, or other sounding device. It should be unlike that used by the official or the timers.

INSTRUCTION TO TIMERS

1. *Consult officials* as to signals used to indicate time out and resumption of time.

2. *Keep eyes on officials throughout game.*

3. *Check on duration of time outs, substitution, time of periods.* A separate watch should be available for measuring the length of time outs.

Did you check all signals?

4. Note position of ball when signal sounds to end any quarter, half, or extra period. The timekeeper's signal ends these periods.

During the last ten seconds of any period, one timer should watch the game clock and count aloud: 10-9-8-7-, etc. The other timer should watch the ball and note its position when time expires.

5. *Start watch after it has been stopped, when:*

a. The ball leaves the official's hand on a toss.

b. When it is touched in the court by another player after a pass in from out-of-bounds.

c. When the last throw on a free throw (except after a technical foul on a double foul) fails to score a goal. After a technical foul, the ball is thrown in from out-of-bounds. After a double foul, the ball is tossed at center.

6. *Stop watch when:*

a. Ordered to do so by signal from either the referee or umpire.

b. A foul is called.

c. An official blows his whistle to recognize a substitute.

d. A held ball is called, a period ends.

7. *Length of periods:*

a. High school games—8-minute quarters, 3-minute overtime periods.

b. College games—20-minute halves or 10-minute quarters, 5-minute overtime periods.

8. *Duration of time outs:*

a. Charged time out, 1 minute.

b. Substitutions—one minute, 30 seconds in case of injury if injured player is removed before end of one minute.

c. Two minutes between quarters.

Did you check the score and time at the end of each period?

d. Ten minutes between halves of a high school game (and also college game by mutual agreement) or fifteen minutes between halves of a college game.

e. Two minutes between end of game and beginning of extra period. Also two minutes before extra periods.

9. *The timers should have two watches*, one for timing the game and one for checking the duration of time outs. The timers should have a signal which will penetrate the sound of the crowd for the purpose of indicating the end of a period.

10. *If the timers' signal is not heard or fails to sound, the timers should immediately go on the floor* to notify the referee that the period is over and to tell him where the ball was at that time.

11. *The referee should designate one of the timers to operate the watch.*

MEETING COACHES AND CAPTAINS

The final act of the officials before starting the game is to meet the coaches and the captains. Many officials have formed the habit of never meeting the coaches before a game. This practice probably stems from professional circles. It has no place in amateur athletics. In the first place, the coaches are asked by many conferences and officials' associations to rate the officials. If it so happens that the coach has not met either official before (this is not an uncommon occurrence), it is a little difficult for him to distinguish between the two when he makes his report. And in the second place, there is usually the necessity of discussing special rules and interpretations or explaining special court conditions. The great variation in courts makes this latter point necessary. And third, an exchange of pleasantries is likely to establish much friendlier relations.

Did you inform the captains and coaches on special rules and regulations?

The meeting with the captains is partly social or sporting and partly for business pertaining to the game. The captains should know each other and the officials. The visiting captain has the privilege of choosing his goal for the first half. This is a pure formality because invariably he will choose the goal used for the warm-up. More particularly the meeting is for instruction purposes. Ground rules, court markings, and any special rules or interpretations as previously mentioned should be explained. Here is an opportunity for the captains to ask any questions or to make any requests in connection with the game or the practices of the officials which may have a bearing on the game. The officials may remind the captains that they are the official representatives of their respective teams in case any questions come up during the game.

It should be emphasized here that it is out of place for officials to caution the captains about rough play or playing clean. Neither should they warn them that they will call the game closely. It is to be expected that the game will be handled by competent men and played by well-trained sportsmen. The game itself will reveal the validity of both assumptions. No preliminary statement, challenge, or threat is likely to alter the outcome.

CENTER JUMP AND TOSSING THE BALL

At the beginning of the game the referee tosses the ball. He takes a position on the opposite side of the court from the scorers' and timers' table so that he may face these assistants. His primary responsibilities are to toss the ball correctly and to see that the two centers play in accordance with the rules governing the center jump. The art of tossing the ball for a jump is discussed below.

The umpire takes a position along the side line near the scorers' and timers' table and to the right of the center line of the court. It is his primary job to watch the players other than the jumpers. He should see that they do not

Are you a "held ball" addict?

push, crowd, or otherwise violate the rules before or after the ball is tossed. He is responsible for calling violations of the restraining circle by the eight players other than the jumpers.

If the umpire is fulfilling his duties in connection with the other eight players, he will not be able to make decisions with respect to the tossing of the ball or the action of the jumpers. A test of neglect of duty is to hear the umpire blow his whistle to call attention to a defective toss or a foul or violation by one of the jumpers at the center jump. His attention, if he is doing his job, will be focused on the other players.

Diagram 23 shows the positions of the referee and umpire before the toss. The umpire follows the play in whichever direction it goes. If the ball goes to his right, he goes right and then stations himself along the end line, with the referee following the play from behind and at the side of the court. If the play goes to the umpire's left, he follows it until the referee can get to his position at the end line (see topic on "Switching"). Thereafter, the umpire drops back to watch the play from behind and at the side line.

TOSSING THE BALL FOR A JUMP

A common fault among officials is to toss the ball without sufficient height. As a consequence the art of jumping to tip the ball has been lost. Instead, players maneuver to tip the ball as it is going up. It is necessary to do this in order to get a chance to play the ball at all. The rule prohibits a player from tipping the ball before it reaches its highest point. But the rules also require that the official toss the ball higher than either player can jump. Since he fails to throw the ball high enough, the players must jump as the ball leaves the official's hand in order to get a chance to tip it at all. If the players waited until the ball reached its highest point, and then jumped, they would reach above the ball and consequently there would be no contest in jumping and each would be thrown off stride. To avoid this, the jumper has, in self-protection, formed the habit of cheating by tipping the ball as it goes up. The contest then becomes one of jumping first, and not one of out-jumping an opponent. This is unfair to the better jumper.

This practice is so prevalent that when an official administers a toss correctly, the players will usually not tip

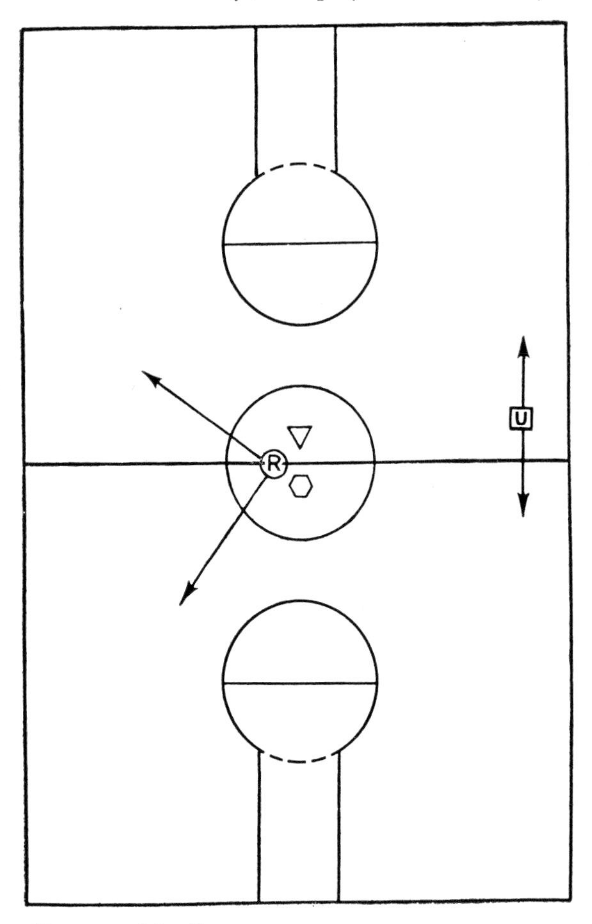

DIAGRAM 23. POSITIONS AND MOVEMENTS OF OFFICIALS AT THE CENTER JUMP.

Cover ten players, not two, on all jump balls

the ball at all. They jump too soon and thus are usually coming down from the height of their jump before the ball begins to descend. If the ball is tossed high enough and the jumper happens to tip the ball as it is ascending, the violation will become very apparent.

The best advice to give to the young official is to toss the ball too high rather than too low. Since the tendency is to undertoss, this emphasis will usually produce a toss which is the correct height. Tossing the ball midway between the two jumpers seems to be easier to control than regulating the height. The technique of tossing with one or two hands is largely dependent upon individual preference. Starting the toss from eye level [1] is sometimes advocated over a toss which begins with an arm swing from the chest or waist to prevent the player from tipping the ball as it ascends. Here, again, the exact method depends entirely on habits of the individual official. None of these will of themselves guarantee a legal toss or jump. If the proper height is emphasized, the method is unimportant.

Players occasionally become spirited as the result of aggressive play preceding a jump. An official can allay emotional flare-up and prevent fouls by calmness, a slight delay, and even a fixed stare at the jumpers before tossing the ball. In cases where the players are crowding each other, they may be separated by stepping between them and spreading the arms. Such a maneuver is more effective than verbal directions. An excited or intense person seems to act more quickly as a result of physical contact. Likewise, players who are too far apart before the jump can be placed properly by pulling one into position.

When tossing the ball, an official should avoid two hazards. He should not hold his whistle in the mouth. He is so close to the jumpers that there is danger of having the whistle knocked out of his mouth by a swinging arm of a jumper. Grave dental injury may result.

[1] Pacific Coast Conference, *Basketball Rules Interpretation*, 1947–48.

A pause may calm the ruffled spirit

He should not move back, away from the jumpers, after making the toss. To do so invites collision with a player who is charging for the ball. Officials have received serious injuries by stepping back into the path of a rapidly running player.

Of course, the official should always stand with his back to the nearer side line when administering a jump ball. So important is the technique of properly tossing the ball that officials should spend time in practicing it so that they become proficient and consistent at it. Since the height and ability to jump vary from player to player, one must develop expert judgment in order to make accurate tosses.

Figure 22 shows an official making a proper toss. It should be noticed that the ball is above the height that either player can jump. Also, the official has not moved back but is holding his position until after the ball clears.

To repeat, it is better to toss the ball too high than not high enough.

FRONT COURT PLAY

It is customary for each official to take certain positions on the court when the ball is in play and the players are moving in and out of the defense at one end of the court. The referee takes a position along the end line which is to his right as he faces the scorers' and timers' table when the ball is at that end of the court. The umpire takes a position along the opposite end line when the ball is in play at the opposite end of the court.

When the referee is at the end of the court, the umpire will be on the opposite side of the court but out toward the center line. The officials will reverse their positions when the ball is at the opposite basket. These relative positions always place one official ahead, or in front, of the play and the other behind, or alongside of, the play.

Both officials should move so that they have a clear view

Surround the play—one official in front, one in back

FIGURE 22. TOSSING THE BALL FOR THE CENTER JUMP. NOTE HEIGHT OF BALL.

Don't move back after tossing the ball

at all times of the ball and the players contesting for the ball. Thus, the official working along the end line would move from a position behind the basket to the corner of the court farther from the other official. The other official would move along the side line for the most part, but at times he would find it necessary to move over into the court in order properly to cover the play which goes toward the side of the court opposite from him. He will move from the center line along the side line up to, and sometimes beyond, the free-throw line extended as the ball penetrates the defense and moves toward the goal.

The positions of the officials are always predicated upon an uninterrupted close observation of the play, and noninterference with the free quick movement of players.

Diagram 24 illustrates the positions and movements of the officials when the ball is in play at one end of the court.

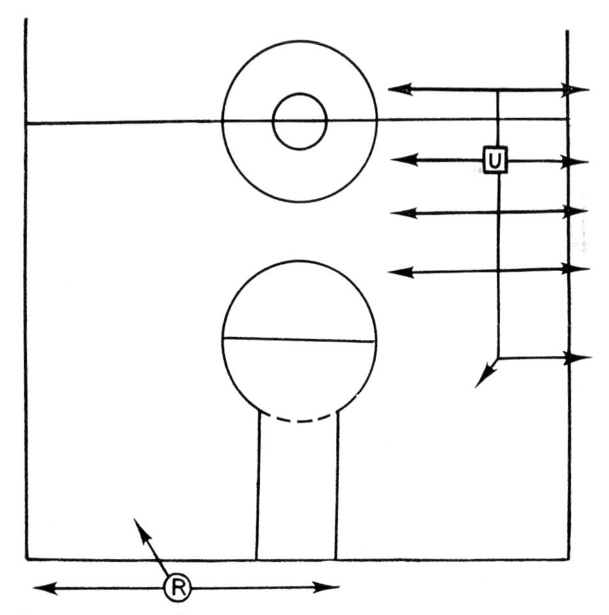

DIAGRAM 24. POSITIONS AND MOVEMENTS OF THE UMPIRE AND REFEREE WHEN THE BALL IS IN PLAY AT ONE END OF THE COURT.

Be sure that no area is left unsupervised at any time

Diagram 25 shows their movements when the possession of the ball changes and play moves to the opposite end of the court. The movements and positions of the referee and umpire are now reversed. The umpire has preceded the play to the opposite end while the referee has trailed it.

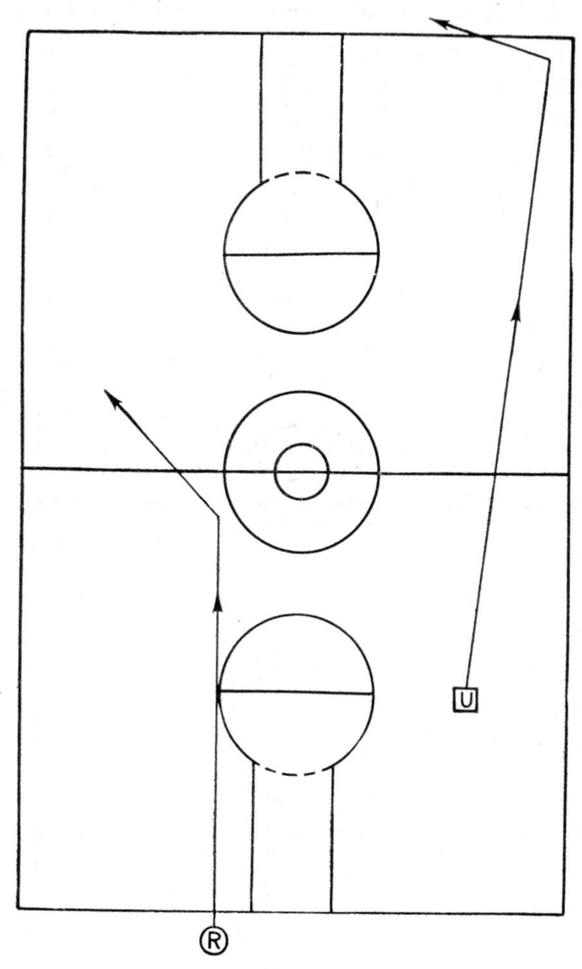

DIAGRAM 25. MOVEMENTS AND INITIAL POSITIONS OF REFEREE AND UMPIRE WHEN THE BALL GOES FROM ONE END OF THE COURT TO THE OTHER. THE UMPIRE LEADS THE PLAY. THE REFEREE TRAILS IT.

Erase ideas of sacred court areas for each official

This pattern of movement permits the officials to surround the play at close quarters from the front side and back side when it becomes congested around the goal, where decisions are difficult to make and yet where they are most important. This technique removes any semblance of a practice in which the end official makes all the decisions at the goal at his end of the court. It eliminates any possibility of unequal calls at the two goals. Both officials will be on top of the play at each end and both will usually be making the same decisions at both ends.

There will be no such thing as a zone of influence or responsibility for each official. The reason for having two officials is that two can do everything done formerly by one official, and do it better. The assignment of two officials was not for the purpose of dividing the responsibilities. Rather it was for the purpose of having a double check on the play. It must also be remembered that in spite of efforts to the contrary, an official occasionally has his line of sight blocked. Because this happens, each official should call everything (note exceptions in jump balls and out-of-bounds plays) which he sees at any time. To do this effectively for under basket play requires that he be close to the play.

Shaded diagrams have been developed to show the working area or positions of officials. Unfortunately, these have been misinterpreted. From them, many officials have drawn the erroneous idea that they were responsible for calling plays in these areas. It is readily seen that if one official was more technical than the other or if he placed a different interpretation on certain plays, there would be quite different officiating in each area.

Some conferences and some officials' associations are now adopting the practice of having the officials change ends after every ten minutes of play in order to compensate for the above tendency. It is the author's opinion that this practice merely distributes or divides the aforementioned fundamental error in mechanics. It does not correct the fault. For this reason, the foregoing emphasis was placed on developing a technique which will eliminate bad practice and produce more effective game administration.

When the ball has been tipped after a center jump, the umpire follows the play closely, regardless of the direction, until the referee is able to assume his normal position. (Switching is described later in the text.) After the referee moves to his normal position, the umpire moves back to his regular spot if the initial move of the ball at the tip-off has required him to cover momentarily for the referee. This kind of team work guarantees that the play will always be covered closely by at least one official. This movement is indicated in diagram 23.

As the officials maneuver with the play at one end of the court, they must be ready to handle fast breaks to the opposite end as a result of interceptions and recoveries. When situations of this kind occur, the official who was behind the play before the interception, now must keep in front of it as it speeds to the other basket. The official who was working along the end line follows the play from behind. Diagram 25 illustrates this movement. Usually the official who is back and to the side of the play can anticipate these reverses by seeing the situation develop. By means of his alertness he is able to move out ahead of the play without difficulty. There are times, however, when the situation changes so unexpectedly that he will be left behind momentarily. This fact should not discourage him from penetrating deeply to the front court to assist in handling the action around the goal.

JUMP BALL

Experience has decreed that officials shall be assigned specific duties in a few cases. Tossing the ball for jumps is one of the instances in which the duties for each official are designated.

Anticipate the movement of the ball

The official who does not toss the ball will stand in the court near the side line along which he is normally working. The responsibilities of each will be the same as described under the "center jump."

The official who does not make the toss must be ready to cover fast break movements to the opposite end of the court. If the end to which the play goes is not the end where he normally works, he will substitute for his fellow official until that official can take over his normal position.

If the ball is to be tossed at the free-throw line, the trailing official makes the toss. This practice permits the official who normally works along the end line in that half of the court (the leading official) to be ready to freely cover the scoring plays which may develop close to the basket as a result of the jump. He is not delayed by the duties which are required of the official who tosses the ball. He must, however, move to the side line opposite the jumpers until after the toss in order to be able to support his colleague should the play go to the opposite basket after the tip.

Diagram 26 illustrates the positions of the officials on a held ball at the free-throw line. When a jump ball is administered at the center circle, the position and duties of the officials are the same as during the center jump at the beginning of the game.

The preceding is the generally accepted practice at the present time. However, some officials and some associations adhere to the opposite assignments for tosses at the free-throw line. The reasoning which this group presents is a logical one. They say that if the official who is working the end line tosses the ball, the other official is free to cover a fast break. This movement would be his normal movement and, therefore, the one for which he was conditioned. No switching would be necessary.

If the play continues at the end where the ball was tossed, both officials are at that end to cover the play. The official who has not made the toss is along the side line and up to the free-throw line where he should be in order to cover close basket play. The other official, while momentarily not at the end line, quickly works to this position, so that the officials have the play between them. Even if the first procedure is followed, the end official is not at the end line on the tip. He must move to that position after the tip.

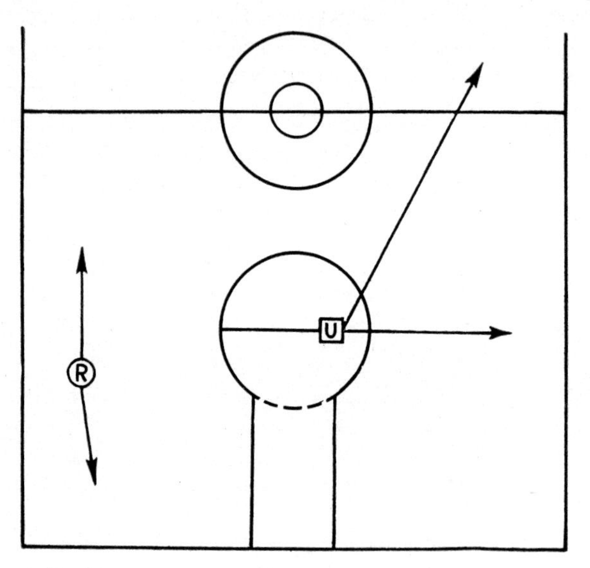

DIAGRAM 26. POSITIONS OF THE REFEREE AND UMPIRE ON A JUMP BALL AT FREE-THROW LINE. POSITIONS ARE REVERSED AT OPPOSITE FREE-THROW LINE.

The author much prefers this latter technique because it places both officials more nearly in their normal positions, obviates any necessity for a switch, and protects against a fast break. In the present-day game the fast break is the more difficult play to cover. Diagrams 27 & 28 show the position of the officials for this technique.

Recently, a new technique has developed for administering jump balls. This has come about since all held balls have been taken to one of the three circles for the jump.

The referee, (the official facing the scorers and timers) tosses the ball. There are two advantages to this procedure. The same official tosses all balls during at least one half of

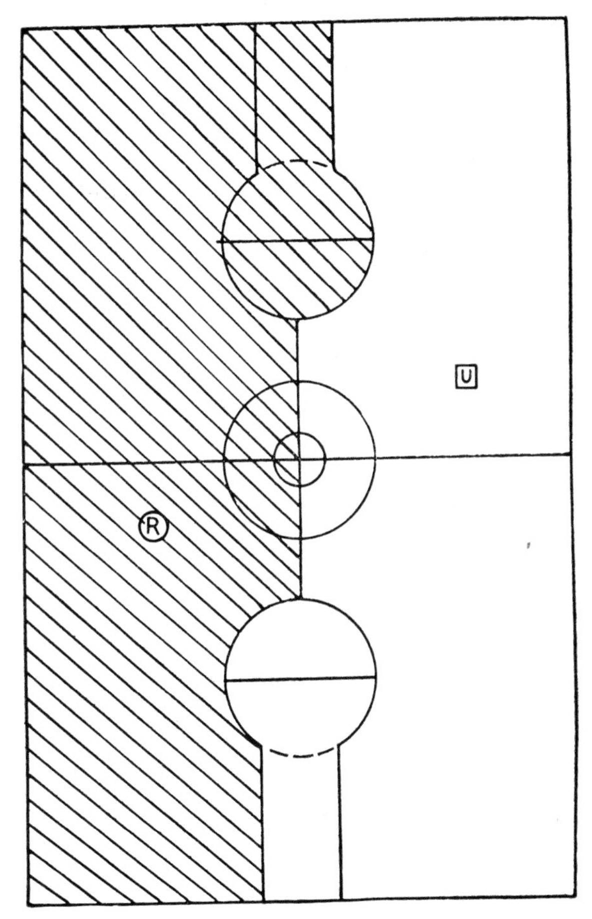

Diagram 27. Area for tossing jump balls. Referee tosses all held balls in shaded areas. Umpire makes toss in unshaded area.

each game. This would tend to develop greater consistency in the art of the toss. In addition, the official who makes the toss is always facing the scorers' and timers' table.

Are non-jumpers always observed?

Thus, he is in a better position to handle substitutions. The objections are those that have already been discussed.

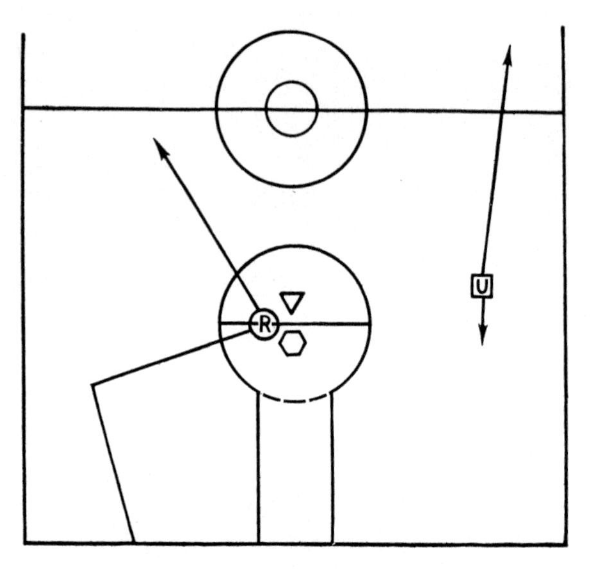

DIAGRAM 28. POSITIONS AND MOVEMENTS USED BY OFFICIALS IN SOME ASSOCIATIONS FOR HELD BALL AT FREE THROW LINE.

OUT-OF-BOUNDS

In order to call out-of-bounds plays correctly, it is necessary for the official to be close to the play, to be able to sight along the boundary line, and to be between the player and the boundary line. It is difficult to see the ball or a player in relation to a boundary line if the official has the player between him and the line. Shadows or the perspective from such a position may deceive the official and cause him to call a boundary violation when none has occurred. If one is not close to the play, it is difficult for him to see accurately and to tell who last touched, or who was last touched by, the ball before it went out-of-bounds.

Spectators are certainly not reliable judges in delicate

Call out-of-bounds at your end and side line only

out-of-bounds situations. This is evident when they are heard to voice their disapproval of boundary decisions where the ball has grazed a shoulder or a finger without being perceptibly deflected from its course. But for the fact that the official who made the decision was right on the play, he too might have been in error.

It is because experience has shown officials that the one who is across the court from a boundary line play is not a reliable judge, that a definite practice is now universally followed. Only the official who is working along a side line or an end line makes boundary line decisions on balls or plays which cross that side line or end line. The other official does not even blow his whistle. He does not even make a decision unless he is called upon to do so by his fellow official. The line of responsibility for each official is shown is diagram 29.

The assumption here is that the decision of the official along the side line or end line is more reliable than that of his colleague. Therefore, it is better to have a few mistakes in the one case than many in the other. Also, it is bad practice for officials to be opposing each other in their decisions. Both would invariably make decisions on out-of-bounds plays, unless specific authority was delegated to each. It is especially bad for the official who is out of position, not near the boundary line and twenty or more feet away from the play, to make a contrary decision to the official who is in an advantageous position to determine with greater accuracy what has actually occurred. Here is one instance where spectators raise justifiable objections.

It is recognized that there may be cases where a ball is last touched by a player in the center of the court and then rolls out-of-bounds and that the official along the boundary line which the ball crosses does not know who last touched the ball. It is also acknowledged that there are times when the official who is delegated to make a boundary line decision does not know who should be awarded the ball. He

Co-operate—don't oppose

should in such instances look toward his colleague, who should be ready to assist. If the colleague saw the play, he should without hesitation announce the team which is

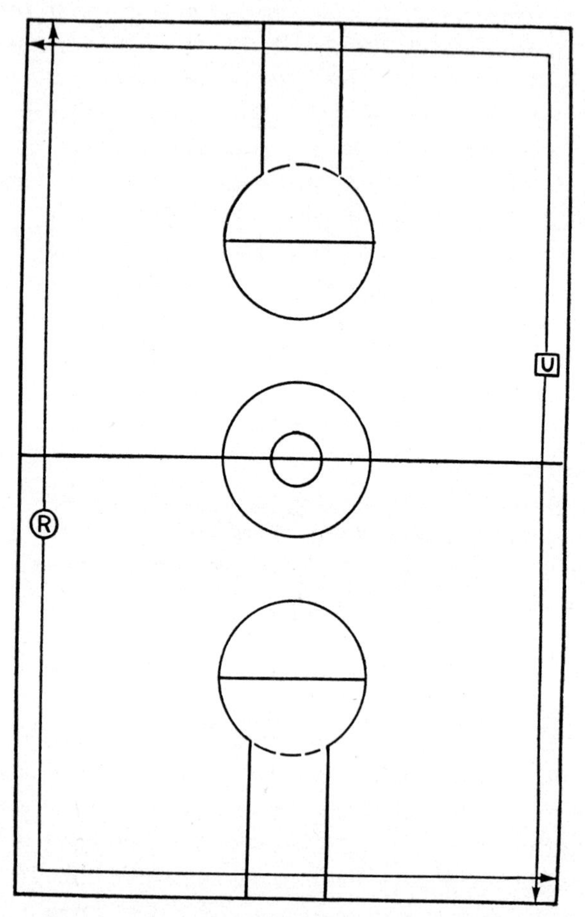

DIAGRAM 29. LINES BETWEEN THE ARROWS SHOW THE BOUNDARY LINE OVER WHICH EACH OFFICIAL HAS JURISDICTION FOR OUT-OF-BOUND BALLS.

to play the ball. If he is in doubt or did not see, he should immediately indicate a jump ball.

This type of co-operation between the officials on

Have you developed habit patterns for all play situations?

boundary decisions is preferable to dual responsibility. It is one of the exceptions mentioned previously.

In the administration of out-of-bounds play the rules admonish officials to make their decisions clearly evident to both teams. (Note to officials following Rule 7, section 1.) If there is any confusion, the official should obtain possession of the ball and withhold play until both teams have had a chance to recover their positions.

Two procedures are customarily followed for purposes of clarity. The official indicates the team to which the ball has been awarded by calling out the color of the jersey that team is wearing, for example, "red-play," and at the same time pointing in the direction of the goal of that team. If the out-of-bounds play is in the front court, the official must, by rule, hand the ball to the player to whom it has been awarded.

There are times when an official must leave his normal position for covering the court in order to retrieve or handle the ball on an out-of-bounds play.

Two examples will demonstrate this situation. An out-of-bounds play occurs in the extreme left hand corner of the court to the umpire. The umpire must hand the ball to the front court team. If an interception should occur on the play, the umpire would be at a disadvantage to cover the play.

If, on the other hand, an out-of-bounds ball should occur at the extreme left corner for the referee and the ball is awarded to the team in its back court and if it is necessary for the referee to retrieve the ball or handle it in order to make his decision clear, he is forced into a position which is at the opposite end of the court from where he should be to cover the play as it comes up the court. When circumstances of this kind arise, it is necessary for the other official who normally would follow the play to precede it. This maneuver is called switching. The same tactics are employed after a jump ball. In this case, the official who does

Make your decisions crystal clear

not make the toss precedes the play regardless of the direction.

SWITCHING

There are two techniques practiced in connection with switching. In the one, the officials maintain their switched positions until there is a convenient time after a dead ball for them to switch back to their normal positions. A convenient time would occur after a foul, a held ball, or a substitution. It might occur after an out-of-bounds ball. It would not be convenient to switch back after a score.

In the other technique, the switch is only a momentary one. It lasts only so long as it is necessary for the official who was forced out of position by reason of a toss or out-of-bounds play to move into his normal position. As he moves to his end line, the other official simultaneously moves out to his normal position. This switch back is done without confusion or relaxation of vigilance.

This latter method is advocated by the author because it tends to hold the officials in their normal working positions to which they are conditioned. It is used prevalently throughout the country, except in the east.

FREE THROW

After a foul is called, the following routine should be carried out before the ball is placed at the disposal of the free thrower:

1. Designate the player who has committed the foul. On preceding pages the methods of relaying this information and of repeating it to the scorer by means of the fingers have been explained.

2. The umpire takes possession of the ball when the throw is to be attempted at the free-throw line to his left, while the referee takes possession of the ball when it is to be attempted at the free-throw line to his left.

3. The official who is to handle the ball should get pos-

How do you switch?

session of it. He should go to the free-throw line immediately in order to avoid delay in putting the ball in play. His first duty after reaching the free-throw line is to check with the scorer to make sure that he has correct information concerning the foul.

4. The official with the ball should stand between the free-throw line and the basket until all is in readiness for the try for goal. He should see that the players are properly distributed along the lanes. If the court is properly marked, there will be little difficulty on this point. If it is not properly marked, he should assign positions at the first try and ask the players to assume the same relative positions thereafter. This will save time as well as difficulty

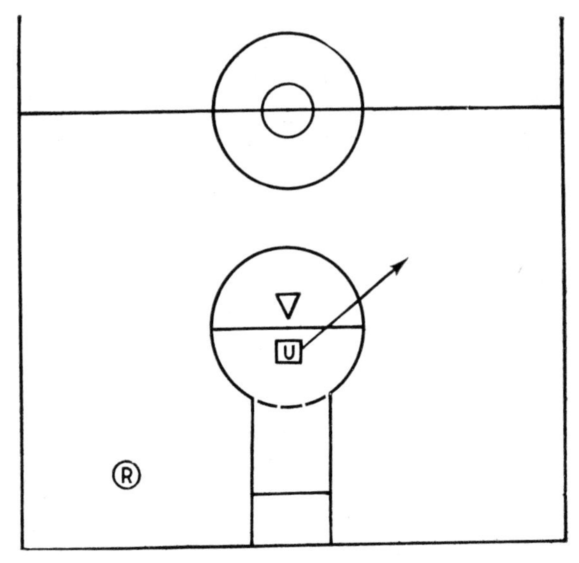

DIAGRAM 30. POSITION OF OFFICIALS ON FREE THROW. THEIR POSITIONS ARE REVERSED WHEN FREE THROW IS AT OPPOSITE GOAL.

later in the game. Diagram 30 shows the position of the officials before and during the try. Their responsibilities are reversed when the free throw is at the opposite goal.

Check all before awarding the ball

5. It is always necessary to indicate the number of free throws which have been awarded. Regardless of where the foul occurred, the official will be asked the number of throws unless he announces the number each time.

6. Finally, he turns and hands the ball to the free thrower or places it at his disposal at the free-throw line and steps out of the free-throw circle, back and to the side of the thrower, so that he is out of the visual field of the free thrower. As he moves to this position he indicates to the timers the number of throws, so that the timers will know how to operate the watch.

This routine which consumes a small amount of time is sufficient delay to permit the team to decide whether or not it prefers to waive the free throw or try for a point.

7. It is the duty of the official who handles the ball at the free-throw line (the trailing official) to see that the free thrower abides by the rules while he is in the act of shooting for goal and until the ball has touched the basket. He must also be ready to rule on the ball in case a legal throw has not been made.

8. The official at the end line should take a position so that he may watch the players along the free-throw lane lines. He should not stand behind the backboard because this may disconcert the free thrower. As a rule, he can observe play more effectively if he stands in the court a few feet from the end line and about midway between the free-throw lane and the side line.

If a multiple throw is awarded, the end line official should quickly retrieve the ball after each throw except the last and pass it to his colleague at the free-throw line. The official handling the ball at the free-throw line will again hesitate momentarily to see that all is in order and to permit the team which is free throwing for a goal a chance to waive the free throw if it chooses to do so.

In the case of a technical foul where the ball is to be awarded to the team throwing for a goal at mid-court after

How many shots?

the throw, the opposite technique to that described above is followed. See diagram 31. The end line official assumes possession of the ball and clears the opponents from the area between the free-throw line extended and the end

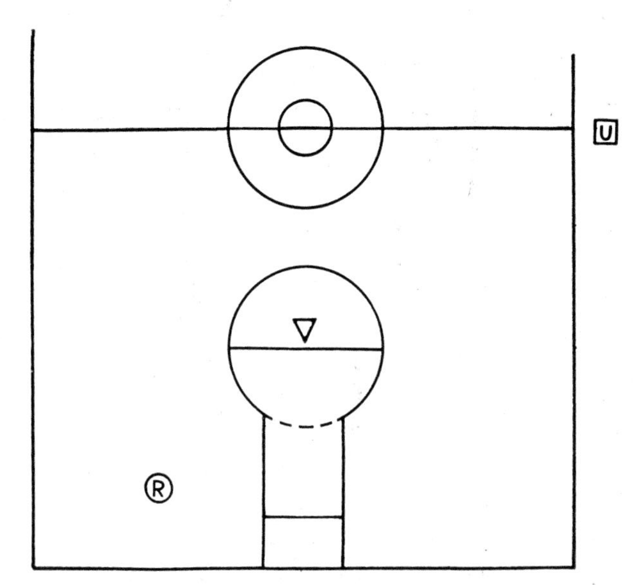

DIAGRAM 31. POSITIONS OF OFFICIALS ON A TECHNICAL FOUL.

line. The trailing official goes to mid-court where he is ready to hand the ball to the team which was awarded the free throw for technical foul, to play in from out-of-bounds. The end line official will throw the ball to him after the try.

If a double foul has been committed, each end line official will handle the ball at his end of the court. This official also clears the area at his goal and rules on the legality of the play. The referee usually makes the toss at center after the last throw. In some sections, however, the official who administers the first free throw goes to the center circle to receive the ball from his fellow official after the last free throw. The purpose of this latter procedure is to avoid delay. The former method, however, permits the referee to check with the timer and scorer before the toss. It is consistent with the procedure at the start of each half and is recommended.

TRY FOR GOAL

When a team shoots for goal from a distance of fifteen feet or more from the basket, it is usually necessary for the officials to concentrate momentarily on different areas before the ball reaches the basket. The official who has been behind and to the side of the play (the trailing official) should focus his gaze on the shooter and the player guarding him. He must be sure that neither of these players interferes illegally with the other to the disadvantage of either. The shooter should not be permitted to charge, push, or jump into the guard. The guard should not illegally interfere with the shooter either before, during, or after the shot leaves his hand. He must not block the shooter so he cannot rebound. The fact that the players are aware that the trailing official has not followed the flight of the ball but is watching them is a powerful deterrent (the potential of presence). Figure 23 shows the trailing official watching the shooter and his guard after the shot has been made. Note also that the end official is concentrating on the players near the goal.

After the trailing official has assured himself that all is well between the shooter and his guard, he turns his gaze upon the basket. He must time this change of focus so that he can watch the ball as it approaches the basket. The trailing official is primarily responsible for enforcing the two goal tending rules. He also rules on the ball and determines whether or not it has scored a goal or hit a support or the back of the backboard. Figure 24 shows the change of focus of the trailing official as the ball nears the basket.

The trailing official administers the goal tending rules

If, in addition to these duties, he can help to cover the play about the basket, he should do so. On long or medium long shots, he will not be able to assist in the under basket play as effectively as on short and lay-up shots. In

FIGURE 23. A SHOT FROM OUT IN COURT. TRAILING OFFICIAL HAS EYES ON SHOOTER AND HIS GUARD. THE END OFFICIAL WATCHES THE TWO PLAYERS AT THE PIVOT POSITION.

the case of long or medium long shots there is not usually so much congestion under the basket, so that attention of both officials is not so necessary as it is on rebounding for the ball or on short shots. However, the trailing official will move in toward the goal after a shot from the floor, so

Trailing official—move toward the goal after a shot

that he will be in a position to assist in any rebound play which may be subsequent to the original shot.

The end line official will devote himself to the maneuvering of the players close to the basket immediately following a floor shot. He must be sure that there is no blocking, tripping, holding, charging, or pushing as the players jockey for favorable positions in preparation for rebound-

FIGURE 24. OFFICIALS COVER END OF SHOT CORRECTLY. TRAILING OFFICIAL NOTES BALL AS IT ENTERS BASKET. END LINE OFFICIAL FOCUSES ATTENTION ON PLAYERS ABOUT BASKET. THIS IS THE SECOND STAGE OF FIGURE 23.

End officials—where are you looking?

ing the ball in case the shot is missed. (See figures 23 and 24.)

Whereas, the trailing official lingers with the players in the area of the shot, the end official turns his gaze from the area of the shot to concentrate on the players in the vicinity of the goal. As the players converge on the goal, the attention of the two officials is again brought together. By this method of co-operation, the total court area is well covered for all important action.

Some officials have developed the bad habit of following the flight of the ball when a shot for goal is made. Except in cases where there may be overhead obstructions, no good purpose can be served by focusing attention on the ball. The ball will come down without human help. Newton has guaranteed this fact. The trailing official must see the ball as it approaches the basket, and both officials will naturally keep it in their visual field on rebounds. To watch the ball at any other time in its flight is evidence of poor technique. Such practice invites players to indulge in illegal tactics. Players are quick to sense when officials' eyes are raised in the air and not directed at the players. Figure 25 shows the end official, with eyes turned upward, watching the ball instead of the players.

A study of pictures taken of games will reveal the fact that this habit is a common one, the rule rather than the exception. For this reason, officials should make deliberate efforts to develop correct court tactics in this respect.

As previously stated, the trailing official must see the ball as it approaches the basket. He is primarily responsible for determining a score. If there is interference by the defense (violation of the goal tending rule), he must be in position to rule on it. If a foul is called on a shot, he must be ready to rule on whether the goal made counts or whether the goal was made by a rebound by the same or another player. But the trailing official does not have to follow the ball through its entire flight to administer these duties. Only

No need to watch a ball in flight—watch the players

as the ball approaches the basket is it necessary for him to focus his attention on the ball. If he develops a wide

FIGURE 25. OFFICIAL AT END LINE HAS EYES FOCUSED ON BALL INSTEAD OF ON PLAYERS AROUND BASKET. NOTE PUSHING AND VAULTING THAT HE HAS OVERLOOKED.

Don't be timid—blow your whistle sharply

vision, he will also be able to watch the players around the basket.

RESPONSIBILITY FOR 3- AND 10-SECOND RULE

The official who is working along the end line or the official who is in front of the play, by reason of his position on the court, is in the most logical position to govern the area of the court affected by the 3-second rule. He is so close to this area that he can easily see and evaluate the movements of the players in this area, while, at the same time, he is watching the movement of the ball in the front court. By the same reasoning, the official who trails the play takes the primary responsibility for the 10-second-rule violations. This same official is the logical one to rule on center line violations. This official is closer to the play which is near the center line and is, therefore, better situated for observing violations of this phase of the rules.

Specific duties or responsibilities have been assigned to each official for the court situations described in this chapter. This is done because it is felt that the position of the official in each case gives him a particular advantage which should permit him to see more easily and therefore to rule more equitably on the action incident to the situation. It is intended to show a way for co-operative effort, so that more effective administration of a game may be attained.

It is not intended, however, to infer that the other official may not make decisions on any of these play situations. In all these cases, except the two specifically mentioned, both officials are to feel that they are at liberty to make any decision on any of these play situations which they can see.

TIME OUT

During time out, the officials have three responsibilities. They should, first of all, administer to the wants of either team and be ready to recognize substitutes. They should

Are you a literal second counter?

also use the opportunity to check with the scorers and timers on any points that may be pertinent, such as the amount of time left to play, checking score, and reiterating instructions concerning failure of signals to sound at end of period. Such precautions often avoid problems in close, exciting contests.

During time out, the officials should confer on any phases of the game which are questionable. If they are not in tune, a brief conference may clear up moot points so that they will work more smoothly together.

SIGNALS

No treatise on officiating would be complete which did not include a presentation of the signals which are used to interpret for the spectators, coaches, and players the decisions of the officials. The signals, reproduced here for this reason, have been adopted by all associations and are included as an official part of the rules. Every official should learn these signals. Each is obligated to use them as a means of relaying his rulings.

The voice, if the official has a strong one, may be used to supplement his body signals. It must be pointed out, however, that the use of the voice alone can be adequate only when the audience is quiet.

The official must have a sense of timing and the art of an actor to get across either by use of voice, pantomime, or both, his decisions to the public. There is always noise attendant upon exciting play near the basket or for that matter anywhere else on the court. Quite often the official's whistle evokes a response from the crowd. Consequently, a moment's pause before announcing a decision tends to create a hush of expectancy and draws attention to the official. At that point the official should go into action to tell his story and explain by pantomime the reason for his action. This is the surest way to satisfy a crowd and win their agreement even though they are partisan.

Do you have a sense of timing?

It must be repeated here that there is no place in basketball for the official who has the attitude that the game was created for him to perform and show off. Since the "grandstand" official is in the minority, the author has no

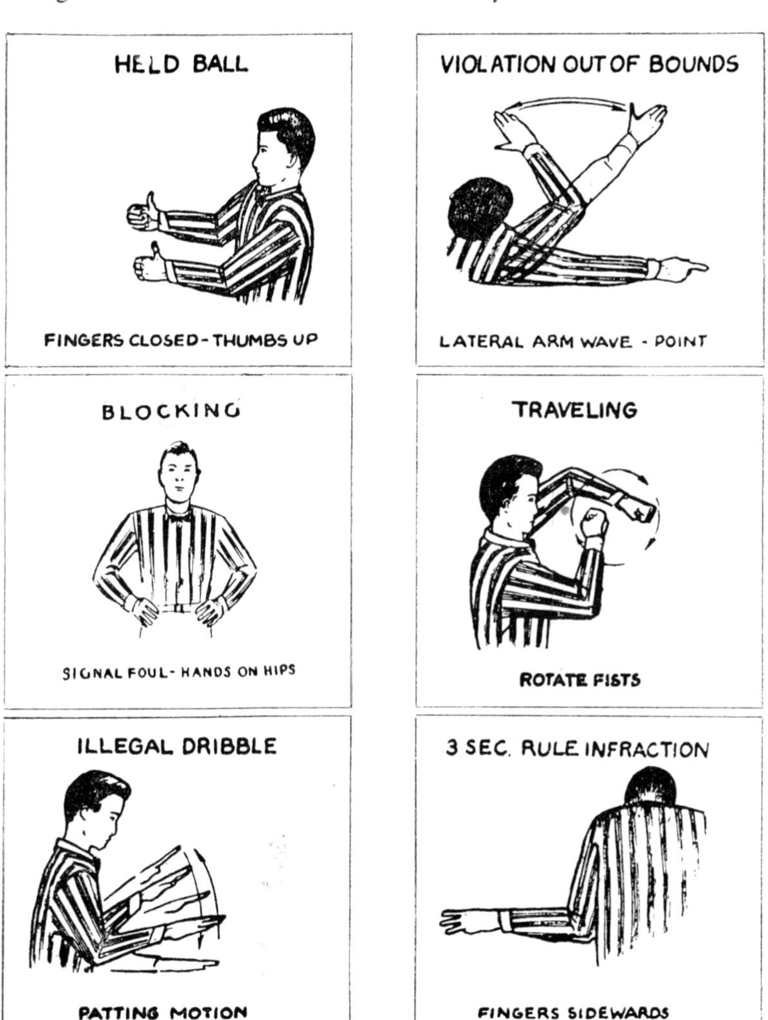

Reprinted by permission from N.B.C. Official Basketball Guide.

FIGURE 26 (A). BASKETBALL SIGNALS.

Be dramatic but not a show-off

eing misunderstood when he emphasizes the neces-
conveying decisions clearly to the crowd. The
entitled to this consideration. It is a way of edu-
m in the technical aspects of the game. Too

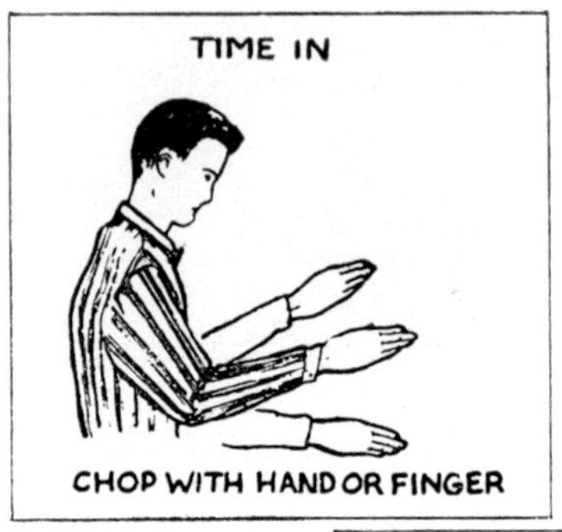

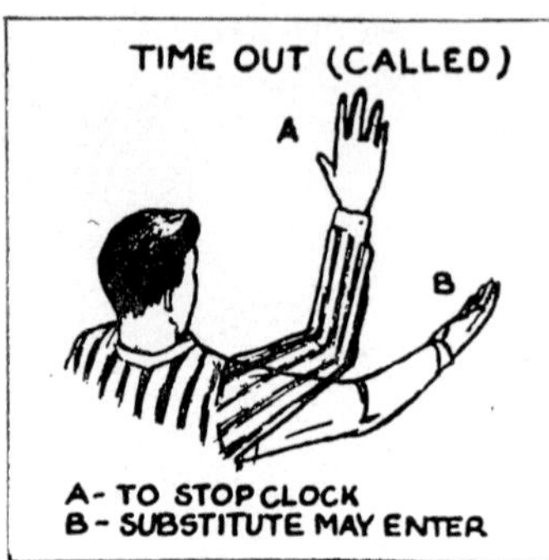

TIME OUT (WITH FOUL)
FOR DOUBLE FOUL ALSO
POINT AT EACH BASKET

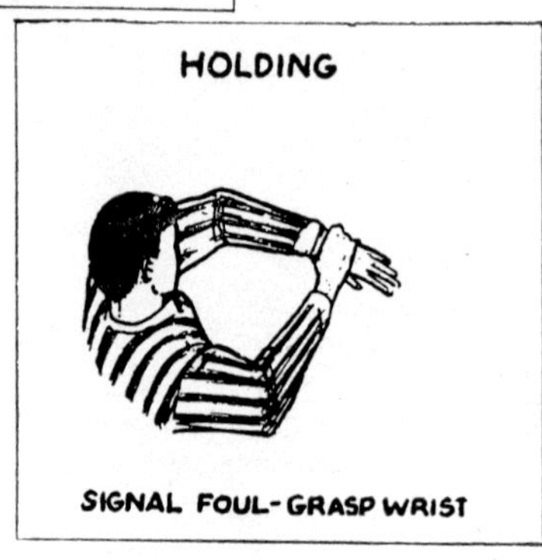

FIGURE 26 (B).

Clear signals educate the spectators

many officials through timidity or fear of being conspicuous, neglect this part of their job. By such neglect they weaken their effectiveness as officials. (See figures 26A, 26B, and 26C.)

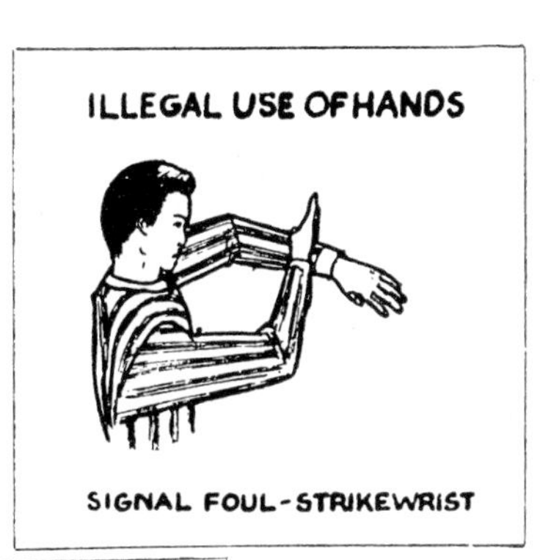

ILLEGAL USE OF HANDS
SIGNAL FOUL-STRIKE WRIST

TO DESIGNATE OFFENDER
HOLD UP NUMBER OF PLAYER

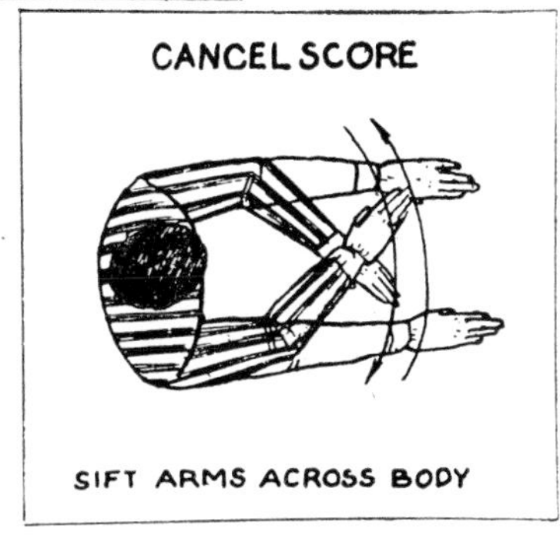

FIGURE 26 (C).

Timidity weakens the effectiveness of the official

18

Basketball—Guide to Contact Problems

THE PURPOSE OF THIS CHAPTER IS TO LAY THE GROUNDwork which will help officials, coaches, and players to develop a pattern by which more consistent play and decisions on play may develop. The end in view is to reduce game interruptions and also to eliminate, at least to minimize, as many incorrect and unnecessary decisions by officials as possible.

GUIDES TO CONTACT PROBLEMS

The decisions of officials which govern personal fouls are subject to more vitriolics on the part of the coaches, players, and spectators than decisions on any other part of the game. This is because such decisions have a more tangible effect upon the game. There may be just as many inconsistencies in the administration of other rules, but the calling of a personal foul gives a team a chance to score one or more points. Too many fouls against the same individual eliminate that player from further participation in a game. Therefore, it is important that there be a common understanding of those rules which pertain to personal fouls. It is also important that officials adjust their practices on the court to concur with this common understanding.

Groundwork for a common understanding

Seven guide posts will serve to lay a foundation upon which to develop judgments for common court situations where personal contact is involved. These have been taken directly from the rules or they have been deduced as a result of official interpretations of the rules. They represent a logical sequence for a clear understanding and administration of movements which cause contact.

1. *Judgments with respect to situations where personal contact occurs or is likely to occur should be based upon the action surrounding that particular situation and the result of that action. Such judgments should not be based on intent or suspicion. This conception may require a change of focus on the part of many officials.*

Screening and blocking maneuvers may be used to illustrate this point. A player may move to a spot on the court with the avowed intent of preventing an opponent from reaching a desired position. Rule 10, section 7, the third paragraph, indicates that he may take such a position. A player may sneak up behind his opponent. He may move away from the ball to a spot on the opposite side of the court. He may pass the ball to a teammate and run toward the opponent who is guarding this teammate. These movements in themselves do not constitute grounds for calling a personal foul, even though the intent of such a player to impede the progress of his opponent is expressed before he starts to move. On the contrary, the decision of the official must be based on the results of those movements in the light of the following criteria. *Intent or suspicious movement does not in itself constitute a foul.* The laws of our land do not penalize for intent. There must be an overt act.

2. *A player must make or cause personal contact to commit a personal foul (Rule 4, section 7d).*

At one time the rules prohibited a player from turning his back on the ball, completely disregarding it, facing his opponent, and moving as his opponent moved. This was a personal foul. No personal contact was necessary. Now that this rule has long since been deleted from the book, no situation exists whereby a personal foul may be called unless there is personal contact. Even though a player takes an illegal position which may cause contact, no foul can occur unless personal contact results therefrom. A screening position so close to an opponent that, in the opinion of the official, the opponent had no chance to avoid contact, is an example of this situation.

3. *Contact may occur, even violent contact, without a personal foul being committed.*

This statement implies that the official must not only see the end result of movement which causes contact but that he must see the action which leads up to the contact. As a matter of fact, his decision will be based largely on the movement of the players, their relative positions, and the direction of their movement, rather than upon the fact of contact. The comments on the rules which refer to personal contact state and imply this principle.

There are several situations which may be used to illustrate this. Two players are charging for a loose ball. They come from different directions. Each has an unimpeded path to the ball. They reach the ball at the same time and collide with terrific impact. If both have played the ball but, in spite of this fact, contact occurs, neither is guilty of committing a foul. Players 1, 2, 3, and 4 in diagram 32 represent this case very clearly.

If, on the other hand, one player was between his opponent and the ball and this opponent charges into the player from behind as he dives for the ball, a different situation prevails. In this case, a foul has been committed. Also, even though both players are approaching from opposite directions, if one dives beyond the ball and into his opponent so that he blocks his opponent from the ball, a foul has been committed. In this case, the player is not playing the ball but rather is blocking his opponent. Players 5, 6, 7, and 8 in diagram 32 indicate movements which produce illegal contact.

These diverse examples are given so that the conclusion will not be drawn that in all cases of loose balls, there is no possibility of committing a foul. Guidepost number 1 must not be forgotten. Judgments must be based on the

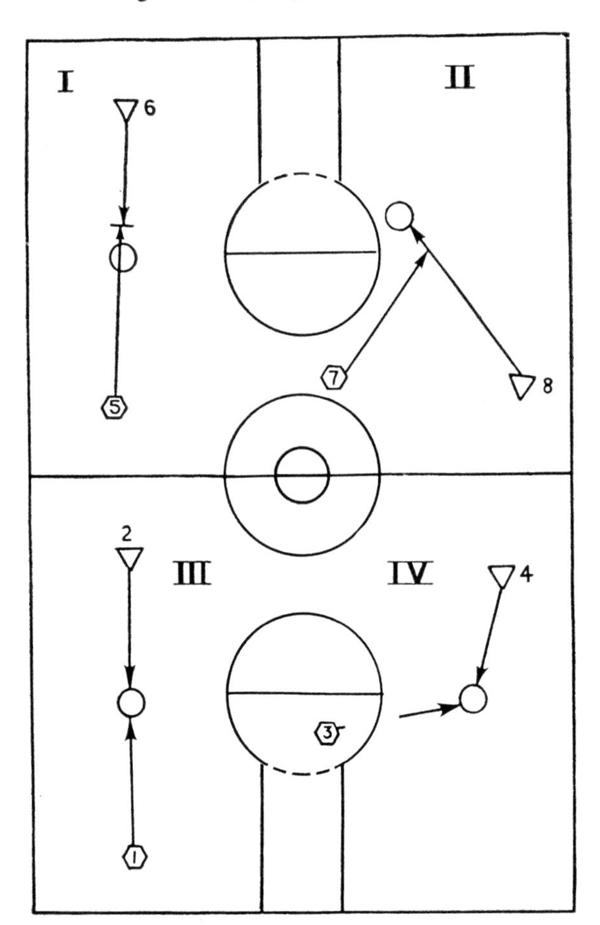

DIAGRAM 32. LEGAL AND ILLEGAL CONTACT IN CONTEST FOR A LOOSE BALL. I AND II SHOW ILLEGAL MOVEMENTS, PLAYERS 5 AND 7 ARE NOT PLAYING BALL. III AND IV ARE LEGAL.

There is no penalty for intent or suspicion

action. The accompanying diagrams will help to clarify these loose-ball descriptions.

Occasionally a player will attempt to dribble between two opponents when there is not sufficient space to permit free movement or he may attempt to dribble between an opponent and a boundary line. As a result of his efforts, he trips over the legs of an opponent. The assumption here is that the opponents are in a legal position. No foot has been extended nor movement made by the opponents to impede the progress of the dribbler. While the dribbler may take a terrific spill, it could not be charged that the defensive player has committed a foul in this instance. The dribbler actually suffered from his own folly.

4. *Blocking applies only to a player who does not have the ball.*

By definition, blocking is personal contact which impedes the progress of an opponent who has not the ball (Rule 4, section 1). Conversely, it should be remembered that in no case may a defensive player block the player who has the ball. If the defensive player can get directly between the player with the ball (usually a dribbler) and the goal in a normal guarding position (Rule 10, section 7) he cannot commit a foul for blocking. The only possible way he could foul would be to charge, after assuming a legal position, or he could fail to get into position and thus charge from the side, impede the progress of the player with the ball by contact, by means of an extended arm, hip, shoulder, knee, or foot, or by leaning into his path with his bended body. While it is not possible to block the player who has the ball, this player should not be assessed a foul for charging if the defensive player takes a position in front of him so quickly that he is unable to avoid contact.

Failure of officials to realize the full import of guide number 4 often causes the defensive player to suffer unjustly. The four examples which follow are typical. These are singled out because they represent situations in

There may be contact and yet no foul

which the innocent player is penalized too frequently.

A player with the ball is dribbling toward the goal. An opponent places himself directly in the path of the dribbler. The dribbler catches the ball, jumps into the air to shoot. Either before or after shooting, he charges into the guard, who has not moved toward the dribbler, but who may have retreated slightly, jumped into the air in an attempt to block the shot, held his position, or ducked to avoid injury. Without question, the responsible person for the contact here is the shooter.

Under no circumstances could the guard be guilty of an illegal act under the conditions as described above. The shooter may receive a jarring fall as a result of his own overaggressive advance. The guard would still be blameless because he has first placed himself directly in the path of the shooter before the shot and he has not charged, pushed, held, or committed any other illegal act.

Many times it is necessary for defensive players to shift from one opponent to another. To illustrate: One player has the ball and a teammate cuts around this player to receive a pass and to displace his guard. The guard who originally guarded the player who first had the ball, now shifts to guard the player who received the ball. As a result of this shift, he places himself directly in the path of the player who has the ball and is charged by him. If a foul has been committed it is committed by the player who has possession of the ball, and not by the guard. The assumption here is that no other factors are involved except those described above.

A player gains possession of the ball as a result of a successful rebound attempt. As he returns to the floor after his jump, he turns and dribbles toward the side line. An opponent places himself directly in the path of the dribbler who makes contact with the body (torso) of the opponent. No other factors are involved. It is assumed that the opponent does not place himself in front of the dribbler

It is not possible to block the player who has the ball

so quickly that he cannot deviate his course to avoid contact. If a foul has occurred here, it has been committed by the dribbler. The guard could not block because he is playing the man who has the ball.

A similar movement occurs when a player receives the ball with his back to his goal. He may be in mid-court, in the back court, at the free-throw line, anywhere. An opponent places himself directly behind this player. The player with the ball turns to move toward his goal and crashes into the body of his opponent. Here again no other factors are involved. This situation should not be confused with the guarding from the rear which is covered completely in the next section of the chapter. If a foul has occurred, then the player with the ball is responsible. The guard could not be charged with blocking because he was impeding the progress of the man with the ball.

5. *When players are moving in exactly the same direction, the responsibility for contact rests on the player who is behind.*

It is legal for a player to move in front of and in the same direction as an opponent for the purpose of impeding his progress. If the opponent runs into such a player, there is no foul for blocking. If any illegal act has been committed, it would be for charging by the opponent who is behind. The player who is in front may even slacken his pace or stop. This occurs in play where a player is running interference for a teammate who has the ball. In order to prevent an opponent who is approaching from the rear from overtaking his teammate, the player slows up or stops and thus causes the opponent to run into him. The responsibility is placed on the opponent who comes up from the rear.

It must be borne in mind that any deviation from the path which is in the same direction as the opponent is taking, introduces an entirely new set of conditions. Action under these circumstances must be judged and administered

Progress may be deliberately impeded legally

in terms of the criteria governing these new conditions (see 6 or 7).

Diagram 33 illustrates these two situations. Players 1 and 2 are offensive players. A is on defense. A and 1 are moving in exactly the same direction. 1 lets A run into him so that 2 may go to the basket unguarded. In the other part of the diagram, 3 and 4 are offensive players. B is on defense. 3 is not

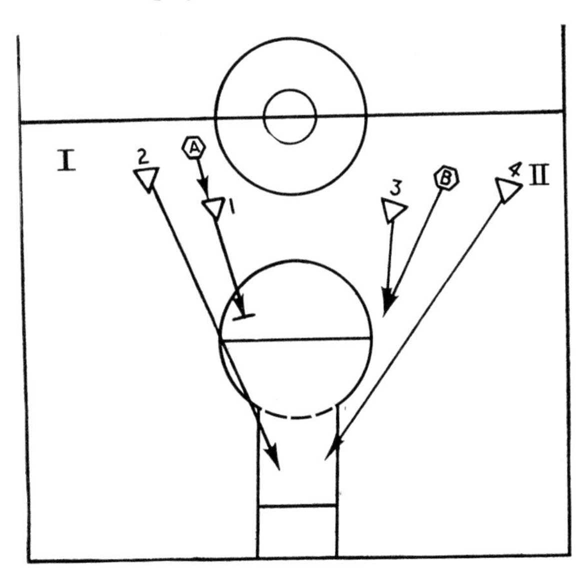

DIAGRAM 33. LEGAL AND ILLEGAL SCREENING MOVEMENTS. I. LEGAL: A AND 1 ARE MOVING IN EXACTLY THE SAME DIRECTION. II. ILLEGAL: 3 IS NOT MOVING IN SAME DIRECTION AS B; B CANNOT DEVIATE FROM COURSE.

moving in the same direction as B. Here 3 has the greater responsibility, if contact occurs. Whether or not a foul occurs must be judged in the light of the principles stated under 6 and 7 which follow.

6. *When players are moving in different directions or even opposite directions, the greater responsibility for con-*

Blocking or screening? It depends on relative position, timing, speed, direction of movement tact rests on that player whose team has possession of the ball.

If, as stated under 6, both players are moving so that their paths cross or if they are moving directly toward each other (see diagram 34) and they continue in motion, then it behooves the player whose team has possession of the ball to

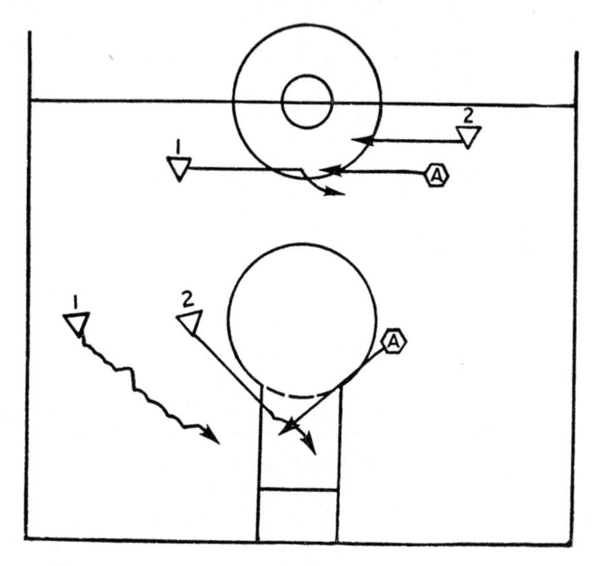

DIAGRAM 34. OFFENSE MOVING IN DIFFERENT OR OPPOSITE DIRECTION TO DEFENSE. OFFENSE 1 AND 2 MUST AVOID CONTACT AS SHOWN WHEN PASSING A.

avoid a collision. The defensive player will usually be following an opponent or cutting to intercept a play. The offensive player under these circumstances has no right to impede his progress. If he does, then he is guilty of blocking. This is in accordance with Rule 10, section 7, and with comments on blocking on page 32 of the official Basketball Guide for 1949.

Principles 5 and 6 are applied to some clever but complicated screening maneuvers which to be legal require per-

If it is a questionable blocking situation, the offense has the greater responsibility

fect timing between teammates. The term "roll screens" is used to denote these maneuvers. A typical play is shown in diagram 35.

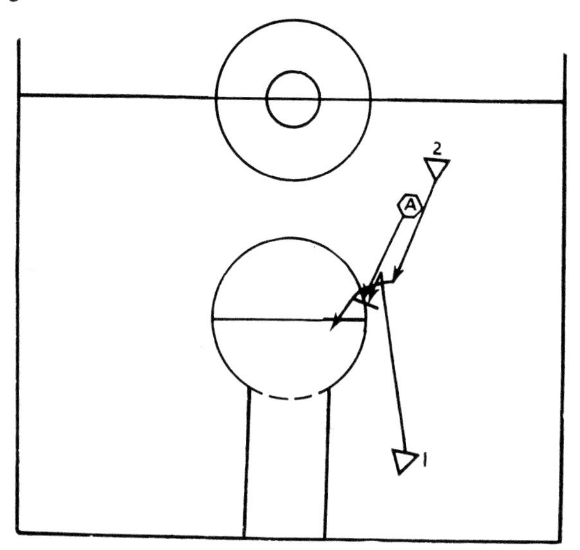

DIAGRAM 35. ROLL SCREEN MOVEMENT. 1 HAS CHANGED DIRECTION AND IS MOVING IN SAME DIRECTION AS A AT TIME OF CONTACT. 1 REVERSES IN TIME TO PERMIT A TO DEVIATE FROM COURSE IF HE CHOOSES TO DO SO.

In the diagram, player 1 (the team in possession of the ball) has moved up behind player A. Just as 2 starts to break by A, 1 reverses his direction. A runs into 2 when both are moving in the same direction. As described in principle 5 above, this is a legal movement. The important factor here is timing. 1 must time his reversal so that he is moving in exactly the same direction as A when contact is made. If 1 is going in the opposite direction to A when they collide, then of course, he is blocking. It would be the responsibility of 1 in this instance to avoid contact. If, on the other hand, 1 is stationary when A runs into him, then principle 7, which follows, applies.

An opponent must be given an opportunity to deviate his course of movement

7. *A player may assume a stationary position anywhere on the court providing that, if this position is taken in the path of an opponent, it is taken in time to permit an opponent to deviate from his course of movement.* (Page 32—comments on blocking.)

This statement implies that the opponent may not change his course and, therefore, may cause contact. If, however, in the judgment of the official, it would have been possible for him to avoid contact had he seen the trap which was set for him or had he not been maneuvered into the trap, then the player who has set the screen has effected a legal act. The principle applies to a moving opponent and to a stationary one, alike.

This principle applies to many situations which create by far the bulk of the problems which pertain to blocking. It is difficult to administer because of the difficulty in determining whether or not the opponent for whom the screen is set has an opportunity to avoid contact. It is also difficult because of the lack of clarification of what constitutes "normal bodily movements" as used in the explanation of blocking in the comments or the rules. It is true that a distance factor (approximately three feet) is used to guide the official. But even the use of the yardstick is a bit confusing.

In addition to the distance between two opponents when a screen is set, the element of timing and the speed of movement of one or both of the players are also involved. The following three diagrams are representative of the types of situations covered by this principle. They should give the official a definite guide upon which to base his judgment on this phase of the game.

In diagram 36, 1 has approached defensive player A from behind and has taken a position less than three feet back of him. 2 and A are both stationary. After 1 stops, 2 moves forward to force A into 1. Then, 2 runs quickly by player A who is stopped mo-

Eighteen inches may be sufficient space in which to deviate

mentarily when he runs into 1. 1 is stationary after taking his position behind A except as he is forced to move by the pressure from the contact by A.

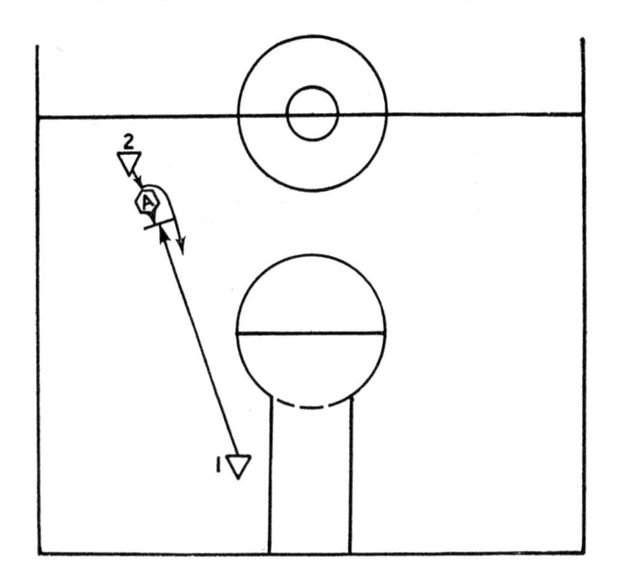

DIAGRAM 36. LEGAL SCREENING MOVEMENT. 1 TAKES POSITION BEHIND A AND STOPS BEFORE 2 STARTS IN MOTION. 1 IS FAR ENOUGH AWAY TO PERMIT A TO STEP BACK.

In this case, 1 has executed a legal play. A ran into 1 either because he did not know that 1 was there or because 2 maneuvered him into the contact. A, had he been aware that 1 was behind him, could have moved to the left or right of 1 in order to follow 2 whom he was guarding. A should not be penalized for colliding with 1 unless the contact is more than incidental (that is, appears to be deliberate and excessively forceful). It is the intent and hope of 1 and 2 that they can force A to contact 1.

The approach from the rear was used because it represents the most difficult play of this type. The same reasoning would apply if 1 were to approach from the side, at an angle, or from in front. The important points here are that:

1. 1 leaves sufficient space for A to take a step toward him. In actual demonstrations under authoritative observation, a distance of a foot and a half was sufficient to permit A to take a step. It should be mentioned here that the comments on the rules, as referred to above, used the word "approximately" when speaking of space between opponents. This word was deliberately inserted to indicate that in some situations (to wit above) the distance could be less than three feet, whereas, in other situations, the distance would have to be greater than three feet to permit a player to avoid contact.

2. 1 must be stationary before 2 starts in motion for the purpose of causing A to move into 1. If there is any doubt about the stopping of 1 before 2 moves, then 1 should be held responsible for any contact that results.

3. 1 must remain stationary until he is bumped by A or until 2 has gone by him. Any moving of the hips, shoulders, arms, or legs by 1 which impedes the progress of A by causing A to charge him should be construed as blocking.

4. A should not be penalized for crashing into 1 unless such contact is violent. 1 and 2 have planned to cause this contact within the rules.

In diagram 37 all three players are moving rapidly. 2 is slightly in front of A. 1 does not avoid A as under principle 6. Rather he hopes to cause A to run into him. If A deviates from his path to avoid contact, then 1 hopes he will be delayed sufficiently to permit 2 to evade him. Since the players are moving rapidly, it is necessary for 1 to stop (since he plans to screen A), at a much greater distance than one foot and a half as in diagram 36 or even three feet in order to give A an opportunity to avoid contact. It may be as much as five feet.

Have you a closed mind or are you willing to improve?

It is important to notice here that the distance of 1 from A when 1 stops is dependent upon the speed at which A and 1 are moving. The faster they are moving, the greater must be the distance in order to permit A to avoid contact.

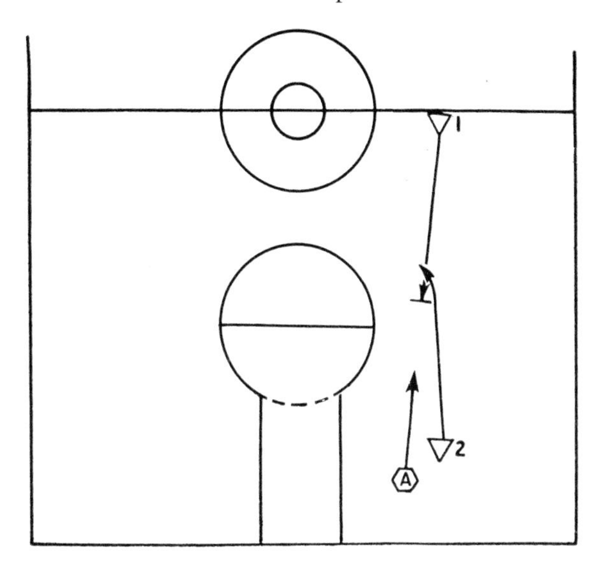

DIAGRAM 37. LEGAL SCREENING MOVEMENT. ALL THREE PLAYERS ARE MOVING RAPIDLY. 1 STOPS FIVE OR SIX FEET FROM A SO THAT A MAY DEVIATE COURSE.

In diagram 38, a slightly different type of maneuver is used to illustrate the third type of play to which principle 7 applies. Here, 2 and A are stationary. 1 is running toward them. Just as 1 comes abreast of A, he steps in front of 1 who charges into him. A has taken his position so quickly that 1 does not have a chance to avoid contact. A is blocking.

This illustration is presented because it is a common form of blocking indulged in by the defense. Unfortunately, officials are so block minded in terms of the offense, that invariably the offense, in this case 1, is penalized. This is really a type of drawing a foul by taking advantage of a common officiating weakness.

Fast moving players may need five feet or more in which to deviate their course of movement

This same tactic is used on players who are executing a weave or figure of eight movement out in front of the defense. Screening out on rebounding is also a common place for this third type of movement. In this case, if the

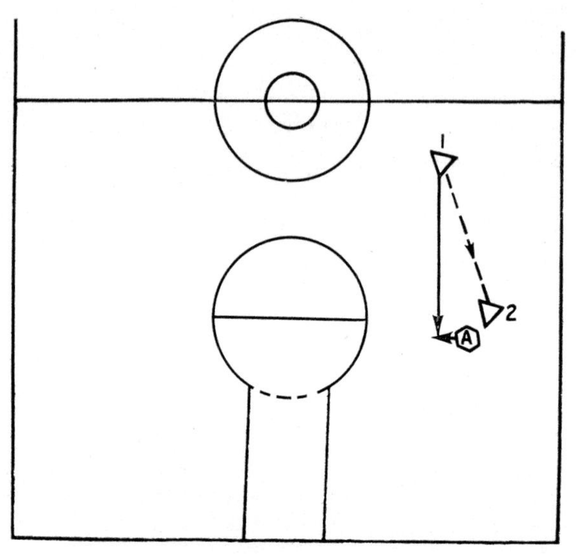

Diagram 38. Blocking by the defense. A steps in front of 1 so quickly that 1 may not deviate his course to avoid contact.

player who is between his opponent and the basket, takes his position between his opponent and the basket just as the opponent reaches him and so that the opponent has no opportunity to avoid contact, then blocking has occurred. Diagram 39 illustrates this situation.

On the other hand, if A takes his position at a point where he expects the rebound from the backboard or takes a position which is desired by an opponent and takes it in time to permit his opponent to go around him, then no blocking foul can occur. If contact occurs in this instance, it occurs because the opponent desires the same posi-

The defense may be guilty of blocking

tion in order to get the ball and not because A jumped in front of him too quickly for him to avoid contact.

Principle 7 is admittedly the most difficult to administer equitably. The official is required to make judgments on the basis of space between players relative to the speed of

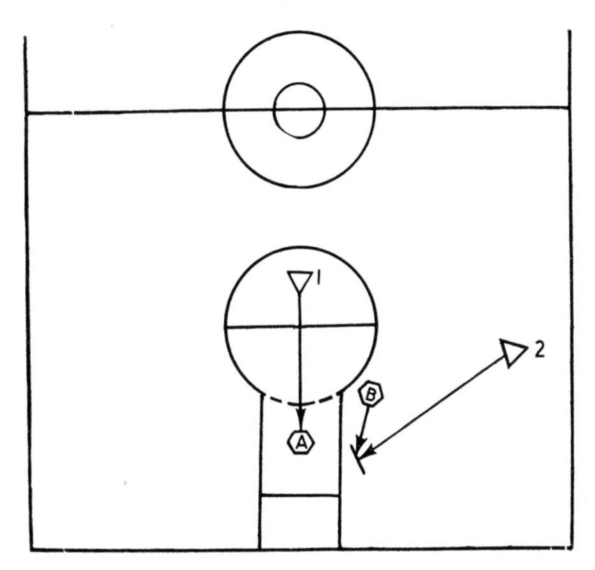

DIAGRAM 39. SCREENING ON REBOUNDS. A HAS TAKEN LEGAL POSITION IN PATH OF 1 WHO HAS HAD TIME TO DEVIATE FROM HIS COURSE. B HAS STEPPED IN FRONT OF 2 JUST AS 2 REACHES HIM. B, THEREFORE, IS GUILTY OF BLOCKING.

the players and the time that a player takes his screening position. The three illustrations above with the rather extensive discussions have been presented with the hope that definite patterns would help to clarify actual court situations. If the official has these definite guides, his judgment should be the more consistent.

Certainly, it should point to the fact that every time there is contact in screening situations, there is not necessarily a

The man behind does not always commit the foul

foul. Also, that even though there is a foul, it is not necessarily the offense which commits it. There can be defensive blocking. The judgment and comprehensive vision of the official must be acute enough to make these discriminating distinctions.

SPECIFIC PLAY SITUATIONS—PERSONAL CONTACT

The importance of official rulings on noncontact tactics are usually depreciated in comparison to those which involve personal contact. Actually the only difference is the fact that fouls for personal contact eventually disqualify a player. The opportunity to score by the free-throw method is balanced by the discovery through the research of Coach Howard Hobson [1] of Yale who found that every time a team loses possession of the ball, it in effect scores a point for the opponents.

It is not intended, therefore, to place any more emphasis on personal contact by this discussion than should be given to the noncontact cases. The job of the official is no different, and the basic philosophy should be applied exactly as in the case of noncontact situations by determining the effect on the play.

The situations which are described below are those which have evoked the greatest amount of discussion and whose administration by officials has produced the widest range of judgments. They are always present in some degree. It is, therefore, pertinent to include them in any discussion of officiating.

Guarding from the Rear

The note following Rule 4, section 11, lays particular stress on the hazards involved from attempts to guard from the rear. There are really two factors to consider. The first has to do with the unfavorable position of the player

[1] Proceedings National Association of Basketball Coaches, 1948. Also Howard Hobson, *Scientific Basketball*, (New York: Prentice-Hall, 1949).

Skilled players seldom foul out of games

who is in the rear. He is in this position usually because of clever court tactics on the part of his opponent. The player with the ball realizes the advantage of having his body between his guard and the ball, so when the guard attacks him, he pivots or turns so that the ball is protected by his body. Because of this advantage it would be highly undesirable to permit the player in the rear to offset such advantage by illegal tactics—contact.

In this case slight contact makes considerable difference. Consequently, it is better to stop the temptation to try for the ball from the rear by penalizing the guard for even slight contact. This recommendation may seem to contradict some earlier statements with respect to our basic philosophy. However, since a modicum of contact places the player with the ball at considerable disadvantage because it throws him off balance and limits his freedom of movement, there is justification for such a strict stand.

The second factor gives even stronger reason for a strict interpretation of the rule. Contact from the rear seems to invite reprisals. The player being contacted from the rear tends to rise up, to pivot, to resort to quick feinting movements. These invariably aggravate the contact already made and create a situation which becomes difficult if not impossible to administer equitably if the initial contact is ignored. The result is similar to that which developed before the 3-second rule was inserted into the rules.

Again we refer to the Pacific Conference.[2] This group sensed the significance of strict interpretation of this rule when it instructed its officials as follows:

> Strict interpretation of this rule (guarding from the rear) should be adhered to. No contact whatsoever should be allowed by the guard who is attempting to guard from the rear.

---

[2] Pacific Coast Conference, *Basketball Rules Interpretation*, 1947–48.

The player behind is at a disadvantage

This statement recognizes that the guard is out of position to try for the ball without great hazard. It seems to say that a little of this kind of play leads to trouble, so it is discouraged altogether.

There has been and still is rather wide variation in the administration of this rule. It has been noted that the Northwest has ruled with strictness; the East, particularly New York City, with greatest of liberality; while the Midwest has been in the middle of the road. On one occasion, an official asked by a captain concerning contact from the rear (the guard had locked the arms of the player with the ball so he could not pass and, of course, made other body contact in addition) said that the guard had his hands on the ball. This fact seemed to make the play legal in his mind.

Fortunately, this does not represent the general attitude. The weight of experience strongly recommends a strict enforcement of the spirit and intent of this rule.

Blocking Shots

There is no play in basketball which requires closer scrutiny, observation from closer range, or more delicate discrimination than that between a guard and a player who is shooting for goal. The shooter must be protected. Contact which would throw him off balance or which would deflect the path of the ball to the slightest degree must not be permitted. On the other hand, the actions of a guard who has clearly blocked the ball, after a herculean effort, must not be misjudged. Neither must incidental contact which occurs after the work of blocking the shot has been completed be interpreted as causal. Nor should contact which has been caused by the movement of the shooter be attributed to the guard.

Reference is here made to those shots within a short radius (6 feet) of the goal, where the guard may be between the goal and the shooter who is stationary or moving

Was the contact on the shooter causal?

in or up. Or the guard may be rushing in from the side or rear and leaping in an attempt to block the shot. There are many such shots during a game.

It is not possible to lay down any hard and fast rules to guide the official in this situation. It is important, however, that he:

1. be close to the play,
2. have a clear uninterrupted view of both players,
3. be able to observe the effect of the action of each player upon the other.

Here definitely his judgment must be guided by our basic philosophy.

Underhand Shot

The underhand shot which is used to reach under the outstretched arms of the guard creates a special type of situation, although closely akin to the previous discussion. The shot is usually made after a pivot in an attempt to evade a guard. There is some disposition to place the ruling for this type of play in the same category as blocking, which is described in the comments on the rules following Rule 10, section 7.

This statement reads: "It is legal for a player to extend his arms or elbows in taking a defensive position but the arms or elbows should be lowered when an opponent attempts to go by, otherwise blocking or holding by the defensive player usually occurs."

There are, however, two real distinctions between the above and the underhanded pivot shot. In the first place, the player with the ball is not attempting to go by. He does not dribble. Rather he pivots, sometimes jumps into the air, and shoots. And in the second place, his movements are designed, as a rule, to trick his opponent into a foul. He hopes to draw a foul by his movement of reaching under the arm of the guard and then moving his arms up in making his shot so that contact results.

Be sure the underhand shot is not designed to draw a foul

In the light of the foregoing and in conformity with the attempt to set up practical guides for court decisions, the following procedure would seem to be the most logical. If the guard who always starts in the rear on this play is not guilty of making contact by guarding from the rear, has his arm extended and as the shooter reaches under his arm, holds it in the same position or moves upward, he would be considered to be in a legal position. If contact occurs under these circumstances, it would be the responsibility of the shooter. The movement of his arms has actually caused the contact. There would not, however, be a foul on the shooter. He is only placed at a disadvantage. Again the instructions of the Pacific Coast Conference,[3] which follows this pattern of reasoning, are cited.

On the other hand, if the guard moves his arm downward and cracks across the arms of the shooter, then, even though the movement of the arms of the shooter is upward, the guard would have committed an illegal act. A foul should be charged against him.

Dribbling Around an Opponent

The second paragraph of Rule 10, section 7, holds the dribbler responsible for avoiding contact in passing an opponent, if the opponent is directly in his path as the dribbler approaches. At one time the statement read that "the dribbler must go clearly around the guard."

Emphasis is laid on this point because the general tendency is to penalize the defensive player. For some reason or other, considerable immunity accompanies possession of the ball. The theory that the player with the ball is king and that the king can do no wrong seems too often to be the practice.

Actually, there should be little if any difficulty in administering this rule. Three simple, easily observed guides

---

[3] Pacific Coast Conference, *Basketball Rules Interpretation,* 1947–48.

The dribbler is primarily responsible for avoiding contact

should, if followed conscientiously, bring about little or no variations.

1. If the guard is directly in the path of the dribbler in time for the dribbler to avoid him and the dribbler charges into the body (not the arms) of the guard, the dribbler is responsible for the contact.
2. If the dribbler in attempting to go around his guard, gets his head and shoulder by the guard without contact, does not turn back into the guard, and is charged from the side by the guard, the responsibility for the contact is with the guard.
3. If the guard is directly in the path of the dribbler and is moving toward him and they meet head on, they are equally responsible for any contact. If both are going the same speed and the guard plays the ball, there is probably no foul. If the guard, on the other hand, appears to be the aggressor and crashes the dribbler, then the guard is at fault. If the dribbler is the one who crashes, then he is the offender. The official must see the action and the result.

If the officials will follow these three simple guides, few inconsistencies are likely to occur.

Charging by the Shooter

Closely akin to the above is the situation in which a player who is shooting for goal charges into his guard who is directly in his path. As a matter of fact, the play is exactly the same as that above which applied to the dribbler, except that the player with the ball is shooting (usually at the end of a dribble) and not attempting to dribble around. The same three rules should be applied in exactly the same fashion.

There are, however, two other factors involved by reason of the fact that the player with the ball is in the act of shooting and is jumping into the air. Since the player is shooting, the official must be sure that the guard does not interfere with the shot illegally when he attempts to block

The shooter is not king

it. Since the shooter jumps into the air, the official should note whether he jumps forward toward the guard or whether he stops and moves only in a vertical direction.

If the shooter moves forward while the guard is stationary or is retreating slightly and there is contact, then the shooter is probably the violator. In this connection, there is a tendency to penalize the defensive player for dodging or ducking to avoid injury even though the offensive player comes down on top of him with his elbows and knees and, sometimes, feet. In making the decision in this way, the official is confusing the meaning of that part of Rule 10, section 7, which refers to a normal position of the body. There is a similar reference to normal body position in play situations, number 290.[4]

Both of these references, however, are concerned with blocking or impeding the progress of an opponent. It must be remembered that it is not possible to block or impede the progress of a player who has the ball. The reader should again turn to the definition of blocking in Rule 4, section 1.

For a fair adjudication of this situation, the official need only observe whether or not the guard is directly in the path of the shooter. If the guard is in this position, then the fact that he turns his back, covers his face, or ducks to protect himself against the crash of the shooter should in no way excuse the acts of the shooter. There is no question but that the shooter is charging and should be penalized accordingly.

On the other hand, if the guard crashes into the shooter by moving toward him or if the guard comes at the shooter from the side or at an angle, then the guard would be, almost without exception, the guilty person, if there is contact.

---

[4] *Basketball Play Situations* (Nat. Fed. State High School Ath. Associations, 1947–48).

The player with the ball does not have the right-of-way

Contact on the Pivot Play

In the discussion of the 3-second rule, some of the problems incident to officiating the pivot play were mentioned. Also in Chapter 4, the center pivot play was used as an example when the principle of "seeing the total action" was under consideration. Actually, if the official has observed the position and the beginning of movement of players before contact occurs in connection with the pivot play, the problem of adjudication is a relatively simple one.

The common positions of the players are for one to be behind the other and both to have their backs to the goal. In the maneuvering before receiving the ball one must observe which player moves into the other. If the player in front moves back and contact results, then he is responsible. Contrariwise, if the player behind moves up to the player who is in front of him and causes contact, then he is liable.

Sometimes the defensive player takes a position at the side of his opponent. This in no way changes the situation and the same tests are applied.

After the offensive player gains possession of the ball, the conditions which were discussed under "guarding from the rear," "the underhanded shot," "blocking a shot," and "dribbling around" apply. The player with the ball may pivot back into the guard in order to dislodge him before turning toward the goal to shoot or dribble. If contact occurs therefrom and the guard is placed at a disadvantage thereby, the offensive player should be penalized.

There are really no new factors introduced in this play so that if the official sees the total action, he should have no difficulty.

It should be called to the attention of the official that if the defensive player is playing in front of the offensive player as is done often in cases where the offensive player is within ten feet of the goal, the defensive player is attempting to avoid contact. It is necessary for him to avoid con-

See the start and finish of the pivot play—then the ruling is simplified

tact in order to prevent the opponents from successfully passing the ball over his head. If the defensive player permits contact with his opponent, he permits the opponent to screen him from a high lob pass which if timed correctly is almost certain to result in a goal.

Rebounds

From the officials' point of view the factors which govern play in connection with rebounding are first those which pertain to blocking (as described earlier in this chapter) and then those which involve charging and pushing. Prior to rebounding the players contested for position. The advantageous position is the one which places a player between his opponent and the basket. The plan is to secure this position so that the opponent will be screened out from free access to the ball as it bounds from the backboard.

To get this position, players step in front of, and turn their backs on, their opponents. Sometimes the players bend their knees and spread their feet apart as wide as possible. It can be seen immediately that the test of legality or illegality of movement depends upon principles 5, 6, and 7 which were established in the discussion on blocking.

If the player who is between the goal and his opponent takes his position in time to permit his opponent to deviate his course of movement and if the player does not extend his arms so that he blocks his opponent's attempts to go around, the tactic is perfectly legal. Both players will usually be moving toward the basket, so that if they are moving in exactly the same direction, the player in front may stop or slow his pace with impunity. The player in front hopes that the player behind will contact him. This makes the screen more effective. If a foul occurs under these circumstances, the player behind is responsible. The foul will be for either charging or pushing. Pushing occurs as a rule when the rebound comes back over the heads

Possession of the ball is no guarantee of immunity from fouls

of the two players. The man behind (often unconsciously) uses his opponent as a take-off post to help him change his direction and get a quick start. One must be sure in this case that the player in front has not first moved back into his opponent.

Charging usually occurs when the player who is behind his opponent is several feet away from him and comes toward the basket rapidly, jumps high into the air, and either knocks his opponent forward or lands on his back. The fact that this player secures possession of the ball in no way changes the aspect of the situation.

The player who sets the screen may not back up to cause the contact; nor may he, if he approaches from an angle, take his position so quickly that he throws his hips or buttocks into his opponent or so that his opponent has no opportunity to change his course of movement.

Backboard play is a spectacular part of basketball, so that when both players are in favorable positions to rebound there may be contact, and yet the situations under which fouls would be called are not present. Here again the official must view this phase of play in a realistic fashion and he should not interrupt the play by overtechnical decisions. What are the players trying to do? How are they going about the job of doing it? What are the results? These are pertinent questions which an official might be continually asking himself.

For example, let us suppose that both players are jumping for the ball and that the player behind has jumped into his opponent so that contact occurs. But the opponent secures possession of the ball and without losing balance and without delay clears the ball from the backboard. There would be no reason for stopping the play.

Again, let us assume that, as both players jump for the ball, both get possession. As they regain their positions on the floor one player is directly behind the other. The player in front is able to pull the ball forward so that his

Understand the basic philosophy

opponent is on his back. If the opponent immediately releases the ball, as he is obligated to do (he is in the unfavorable position as he is guarding from the rear), so that the other player obtains full possession of the ball and is able to move into subsequent play, the fact of momentary contact may well be overlooked. Only the player who made the contact has been placed at a disadvantage. Therefore, why penalize him doubly by calling a foul on him?

The reader may think of many other contact situations. A sufficient variety of samples of play have been presented to illustrate the technique of analyzing each in terms of the basic philosophy and principles which have been established. If the official will approach these and other court problems in exactly this fashion, he will be rewarded in the end by the favorable reaction of players, coaches, and spectators. A better game and one more pleasing to watch will inevitably evolve.

19

Soccer

SOCCER OFFICIATING SINCE 1930 HAS SHOWN MARKED improvement, but probably it lags behind the other sports insofar as officials' organizations are concerned. Since 1945 great advances have been made in attempts to standardize officiating procedures among the soccer officials. This has been carried on by soccer officials' organizations, the United States Football Association, and college and high school coaches' groups.

These groups have been conducting annual clinics. At the clinics, outstanding authorities have been secured to conduct interpretation meetings. Demonstrations of proper techniques in officiating have been given. Exhibition games have been played for the purpose of illustrating game situations which require the officials' attention. Examinations have been prepared for the purpose of testing and rating officials. A sample of such an examination is shown in form VIII, pages 266, 267, 268. To further upgrade the caliber of officiating, reports are made on the work of the official after each contest. The forms for these reports are IX and X as shown on pages 269 and 270.

Present indications are that soccer officiating in the near future will be comparable to that in any of our other sports. Probably in no other sport is the demand for properly trained officials as great as in the field of soccer. It is a strenuous, fascinating job even though the official's life is full of grief. There are many responsibilities. In soccer to date, the emphasis on the part of the official has been on service, rather than on the financial remuneration that goes with this work.

FORM VIII

United States Football Association

Series of Questions Based on the Laws of the Game

1. What are the dimensions of the playing field?
2. What are the height and width of the goals?
3. What are the required markings of a playing field?
4. What is the duration of a game?
5. Where must the players stand at a penalty kick?
6. If time is up just as the whistle is blown for a kick, would you allow time for the kick to be taken?
7. If at any time during the game the ball should strike the referee or linesman would you allow the game to continue?
8. How far must the ball travel from a goal kick before it can be played by another player?
9. Can a goal be scored direct from a corner kick?
10. If a corner kick is taken and the ball rebounds from the goal post to the kicker who again plays the ball, what would be your decision?
11. Can the goalkeeper be penalized for handling the ball at any time?
12. When may a goalkeeper be charged?
13. How far can a goalkeeper carry the ball?
14. Can a player be charged from behind?
15. For what offenses can a free kick be awarded and a goal scored direct?
16. For what offenses can a free kick be awarded and NO goal scored direct?
17. What other kick is there from which a goal cannot be scored?
18. Would you allow a goalkeeper to come out of his goal or jump about on the goal line while a penalty is being taken?
19. Can a goalkeeper be charged during the game?
20. If the referee sends a player off the field, is he permitted to allow the player to return?
21. If at the time of taking a free kick, a player or players refuse to retire to the proper distance from the ball, what action should the referee take?

FORM VIII (*Continued*)

United States Football Association

Series of Questions Based on the Laws of the Game

22. When may a player, having been permitted to leave the field of play for shoe repairs or other cause, return to the game?
23. If a player who has been permitted to leave the field of play, plays the ball, before reporting to the referee, what action should be taken?
24. If a captain wins the toss must he choose the end of the field his team will defend?
25. If the boots of a player were, in your opinion, dangerous and likely to cause injury to other players what action would you take?
26. Is it permissible for the goalkeeper to have the ball played or kicked into his hands by another player when taking a goal kick?
27. If the goalkeeper is penalized for carrying the ball, can a goal be scored direct from the free kick?
28. If during the taking of a penalty kick when a goal is scored, one of the defenders walks into the penalty area, would you order the kick to be taken or allow a goal?
29. If a player is in an offside position but not interfering with the play, would you stop the game?
30. How must the throw-in from touch be made?
31. When play has been temporarily stopped and the referee drops the ball to restart the game, and the ball is intentionally handled, what would be your decision?
32. Can a player be offside from a throw-in?
33. When a player has been ordered from the field, what action should be taken?
34. Has the referee power to allow for time wasted?
35. If a player has been slightly injured would you stop the game?
36. If a player is standing in an offside position in the penalty area and not interfering with the play and is deliberately tripped by an opponent, what would be your decision?
37. If two competing teams arrive on the field in the same colors what action would you take?
38. If the goalkeeper has been changed during the game without notice to the referee and he handles the ball inside the penalty area, what would be your decision?
39. Can the player who kicks off to commence the game play the ball a second time before another player has touched it?

FORM VIII (*Continued*)

United States Football Association

Series of Questions Based on the Laws of the Game

40. Can a player remove a corner flag when taking a corner kick?
41. When would you award a corner kick?
42. When can a player who has only one opponent between him and the goal not be ruled offside?
43. What is the minimum height of the corner flags?
44. If a player was struck by an opponent, what action should be taken?
45. If a defending player strikes an opponent in the penalty area what decision would you give?
46. What is a place kick?
47. What is a free kick?
48. What is the circumference of the ball?
49. What is the weight of the ball?
50. If an attacking player stands directly in line with the full-backs and has only the goalkeeper in front of him, is he offside?
51. If a defending player is penalized for dangerous play inside the penalty area would you award a penalty kick or a free kick?
52. What kind of boots may a player wear?
53. What is meant by holding?
54. What action should be taken by the referee if he had a neutral linesman who was not acting in an impartial manner?
55. If a player used abusive language to a referee, what action would you take?
56. Is a player allowed to shout "Right" or "Let it go" to an opponent?
57. If a referee has blown his whistle for an offense and the offending player commits a more serious offense after the play has stopped, which offense would you punish?
58. Would you allow a player to stand less than 10 yards from the ball at a corner kick?
59. Can a goalkeeper be charged in the goal area at any time?
60. If at any time the ball is played against or strikes a player's hand or arm should he be penalized?

Probably the prime factor for success in soccer officiating is judgment which aids the official in discriminating between legal and illegal play.

Generally accepted qualifications of soccer officials include the following: a complete knowledge of the rules, frequent diligent study of them, and attendance at all interpretation meetings.

The Intercollegiate Soccer Football Association of America

TIME OF PERIODS
1st Period
2nd Period
3rd Period
4th Period
Extras

SEND THIS BLANK WITHIN 2 DAYS AFTER GAME TO
Lawrence E. Briggs
Univ. of Mass.
Amherst, Mass.

Date
Where Played

Name of Home Team | Name of Visiting Team

PLAYERS' NAMES			LINE UP	PLAYERS' NAMES		
Subs	Subs	Starting Line-Up		Starting Line-Up	Subs	Subs
			G			
			RF			
			LF			
			RH			
			CH			
			LH			
			OR			
			IR			
			CF			
			IL			
			OL			

(*) Indicate Re-Substitution in this manner.

Home Team					SCORE	Visiting Team			
GOALS SCORED BY					GOALS SCORED BY				
1st Period	2nd Period	3rd Period	4th Period	Ex. Period	1st Period	2nd Period	3rd Period	4th Period	Ex. Period

OFFICIALS

Linesmen __________ __________

Referee __________

This Report Completed by: __________ (Name of College or University)

__________ (Manager)

RECORD ALL REMARKS ON REVERSE SIDE OF THIS SHEET

FORM IX

Further, it is impossible to do a good job unless the official is in good physical condition so that he is alert and ahead of the play, and can follow the ball closely.

REFEREE REPORT BLANK

The Intercollegiate Soccer Football Association of America

DATE OF GAME			FINAL SCORE
	CONTESTANTS	GOALS SCORED	
HOME TEAM			
VISITING TEAM			
Please forward within 5 days after game is played to: E. C. Waters, S.T.C., West Chester, Pa.		1 2 3 4 Over time PERIOD	

REPORT ON OFFICIALS

NAME OF REFEREE	NAME OF REFEREE
Last Name First	Last Name First
CONTROL OF GAME AND PLAYERS	CONTROL OF GAME AND PLAYERS
Excellent Good Fair Poor	Excellent Good Fair Poor
ABILITY TO KEEP UP WITH PLAY	ABILITY TO KEEP UP WITH PLAY
Excellent Good Fair Poor	Excellent Good Fair Poor
PROPER ENFORCEMENT OF RULES	PROPER ENFORCEMENT OF RULES
Excellent Good Fair Poor	Excellent Good Fair Poor

DID HE FAVOR EITHER TEAM	WOULD YOU WANT HIM AGAIN	DID HE FAVOR EITHER TEAM	WOULD YOU WANT HIM AGAIN
☐ No	☐ Yes	☐ No	☐ Yes
☐ Doubtful	☐ Do Not Care	☐ Doubtful	☐ Do Not Care
☐ Yes	☐ No	☐ Yes	☐ No

Submitted by:
Graduate Manager
Coach

College or University

FORM X

Also, it is essential to be consistent and absolutely impartial in interpretation and decisions. The decisions must be clean-cut, decisive, and with no misunderstanding possible.

Mr. Referee, what is your popularity rating?

Personal appearance must be neat. The referee must control the game at all times, and it is certainly advantageous if he has an agreeable disposition and an even temperament.

PREGAME DUTIES

The official should acknowledge immediately all official assignments. The week of the game he should send a card announcing his arrival, in order to give assurance to the home management. It is customary to arrive at the place of the contest one-half hour before game time and appear on the field ready to work at least ten minutes before the scheduled time of the game. He should inspect the field of play; check with the timekeeper and the scorer as to the time out, the length of playing periods, and any signals to be used; instruct the linesmen; secure the game ball and see if it conforms with the rules; meet with the captain of each team; and discuss with the other referee procedures and any other items that will tend to improve the officiating. They should be sure to select the working areas so that neither referee will in any way interfere with the players of the teams.

THE DOUBLE REFEREE SYSTEM

One definite improvement in collegiate soccer officiating since 1946 has been the introduction of the double referee system. This has not been mandatory, but its success has been so pronounced that today most college games employ two officials. From the knowledge of the duties of an official and from the experience of coaches the following method of covering the field has seemed to be most beneficial. First of all, it is absolutely necessary that the officials themselves have a clear understanding with each other as to which section of the field each will handle and the extent to which they will co-operate in covering the play.

Agree on the working area with your colleague

The success of double officiating is absolutely dependent on each official calling a consistent, uniform game. If consistency is not attained, the officials will fail to work a satisfactory game. Actual work on the field under capable supervision is the only practical solution to the development of consistency as well as co-operation.

Dividing the field diagonally as indicated in diagram 40 seems to be most effective. The shaded area is to be

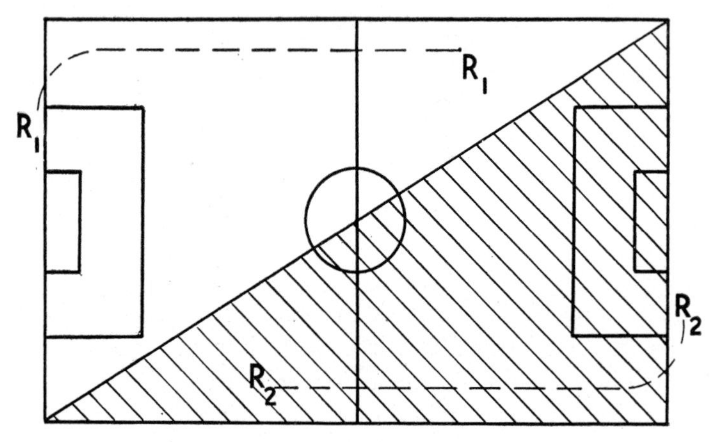

DIAGRAM 40. AREA COVERED BY EACH REFEREE IN A SOCCER GAME. ONE OFFICIAL LEADS AND THE OTHER TRAILS PLAY AT ALL TIMES WHEN THE BALL IS IN PLAY.

covered by one referee. He works as near the side lines as possible and he always works toward his right. The unshaded area is the section of the field covered by the other referee, who should work as outlined above. The two should never be opposite each other.

On the center kickoff, the referee should take his stance facing the timers' table. He should signal the captains of each team, other referee, timers, and scorer, that he is ready to start the game. Both referees should station themselves so that they will not interfere with the formation play of either team. (See diagram 41.)

Consistency through officiating under supervision

As the play of one of the teams carries the ball up the field toward its own goal, the official on the right side of the field as he faces that goal must always be ahead of the ball. As the play nears the goal, this referee should be working along his goal line always being as near the ball as possible. He should shift his position as the play on the field shifts. The other referee should trail the ball up the

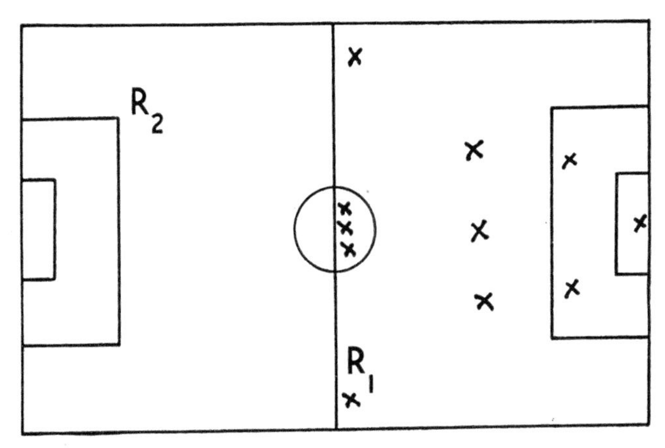

DIAGRAM 41. POSITIONS OF THE REFEREES AT THE KICKOFF IN SOCCER. IF THE KICKOFF WAS IN THE OPPOSITE DIRECTION, THE OFFICIALS WOULD REVERSE THEIR POSITIONS.

field watching, in particular, all backfield play. This referee should work up the field to a point ten and even twenty yards beyond the center line. This position will give him a clear view of the backfield. Diagram 42 illustrates the positions of the officials in this situation.

Generally speaking, the trailing referee should allow the official ahead of the ball to give the decision on the play as his position will give him a better view as the play comes toward him. The trailing referee should be alert to cover the play when shifting players screen the view of the other official.

The leading official usually makes the decision

PENALTIES

After a penalty has been called, the referee should secure the ball and place it on the proper spot. The referee ahead of the play should take his position outside the goal line, out of the direct vision of the kicker. (See diagram 42.)

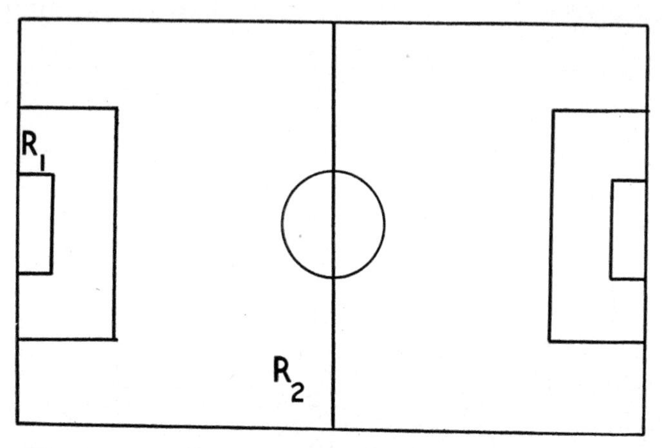

DIAGRAM 42. POSITION OF REFEREES ON PENALTY KICKS.

On corner kicks the front official generally stations himself on the far corner post so that the play will be in front of him. On the other hand there are times when the referee may wish to station himself near the near goal post. (See diagram 43.)

THE DUTIES OF A REFEREE DURING PROGRESS OF PLAY

The general routine duties of the referee are listed below: [1]

1. To enforce the laws and decide any disputed points.
2. To keep a record of the game.

---

[1] National Collegiate Athletic Association, *Official Soccer Guide* (New York: A. S. Barnes and Co., 1949).

On corner kicks the leading official is at the goal post farther from the kicker

3. To act as timekeeper (if there are no official timekeepers present) and allow the full time or agreed time and all time lost through accidental or other causes.

4. To stop the game for any infringement of law, or if any player is seriously injured.

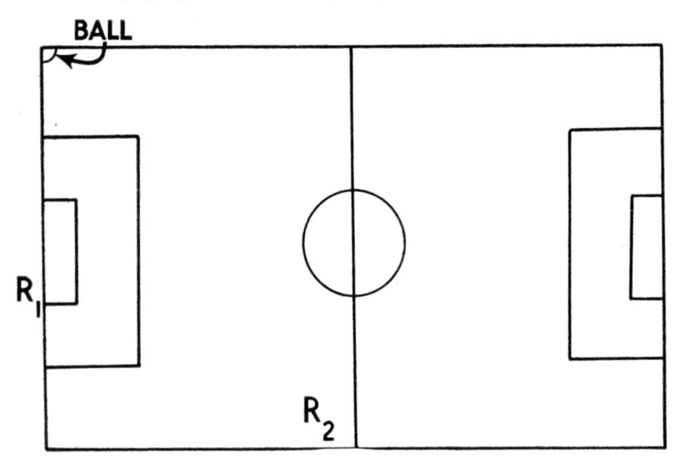

DIAGRAM 43. POSITIONS OF REFEREES IN KICKS FROM CORNER INDICATED BY ARC OF CIRCLE.

5. To suspend or terminate the game when he deems such action necessary.

6. To caution a player guilty of misconduct or ungentlemanly behavior.

7. To suspend a player from further participation if guilty of violent conduct, or if he persists in misconduct or ungentlemanly behavior.

8. To stop any personnel other than the players and linesmen from entering the field of play without his permission.

9. To signal for recommencement of the game after all stoppages.

GUIDES TO PLAY SITUATIONS

The soccer rules provide the referee with discretionary powers in making his decisions in the administration of the game. For example, violations which would not operate to

The referee may keep time

the detriment of the offended team may and should be ignored. The following points are offered as guides to the referee in the intelligent use of his judgment on situations of this type.

1. The referee's decision on point of fact connected with play is final, insofar as the result of the game is concerned.

2. The referee has discretionary powers from the time he enters the field of play. His powers of penalizing extend to offenses committed when play has been temporarily suspended, or when the ball is out of play.

3. If a player leaves the field before a game actually begins, another player may take his place, but the kickoff must not be delayed.

4. The referee should refrain from penalizing in cases where he is satisfied that by doing so, he will be giving the advantage to the offended team. For example: an attacking player, intentionally tripped, may recover to press home his attack. Should the referee penalize the intentional trip, the attacking move would be halted and the offending side have time to cover up in defense (thereby gaining an advantage again); the referee should allow the team awarded a free kick for an infringement all the advantage of the situation. Delaying the free kick may give time for the defending team to recover and thus gain advantage. Provided conditions of the law are fulfilled, a quick restart of the game would give the advantage to the right team. Where a player of the offending team deliberately and repeatedly stands nearer than ten yards from the ball to delay the free kick and allow time for his colleagues to recover, he should be cautioned for ungentlemanly conduct.

5. The referee is entitled to add time to the play on account of:

a. Time which is deliberately wasted by a player. Such a player should be cautioned.

Do not penalize if penalty hurts offended team

b. Time lost to allow a player who is seriously injured to be removed from the field of play; for a player only slightly injured, play shall not be stopped until the ball is out of play. The player who is able to go to the goal line or touch line for attention of any kind, must not be treated on the field of play.

c. A penalty kick at the end of any period.

6. It is not necessary for the referee to blow his whistle in signaling for recommencement of the game after the stoppages. He may, if he wishes, signal with a wave of the hand. The referee should, if possible, avoid waste of time in restarting the game.

7. When suspending or terminating the game by reason of weather or interference by spectators or other causes, the referee should report the matter to the Association under whose jurisdiction the game was played, as soon as possible. Referees should only terminate or suspend a match on account of the weather after very careful consideration.

8. When cautioning a player, the referee should call him by, or inquire, his name, and plainly state that if he is again considered to be guilty of ungentlemanly behavior, he will be ordered off the field.

GENERAL SUGGESTIONS

In general, the game should be kept running smoothly. Good judgment should be used in calling penalties (don't anticipate penalties) and "call them as you see them." Never touch a player.

A smart official will always check the scorebook at half time and at the end of the game. He will instruct the timer to notify the coaches and captains three minutes before the second half starts. He will check any changes in the line-up before the second half gets under way.

No good official will be influenced in any way by the spectators. The good official is not noticed in the course of the game and at its conclusion, like the Arab, he "folds his tent and silently steals away."

In many respects, the official can determine the level of sportsmanship. He is a guardian of the sport. Soccer will be just as good as he makes it. He should join his local officials' board, be businesslike and reliable in all dealings. He should never cancel one assignment to accept another but hold to his original agreement. He should not fraternize with coaches and players. He should never solicit games nor forget that he is hired as an official and not as a scout. It is not good ethics to knock brother officials.

Every official has his ups and downs and it takes years of conscientious study, practice, and effort to reach the top. Good officials today have given many hours and have worked countless games for no other fee than that of experience.

If, when a mistake is made, it is analyzed so that it will not be repeated, the official will profit by the experience. Remember that everyone can't be pleased. If there is anything that can be done to make the job easier, do it and keep out of trouble.

CONSTRUCTIVE HINTS SUMMARIZED FOR SOCCER OFFICIALS

HUSTLE HUSTLE HUSTLE

Run the game and be the boss. Show the players you mean what you say at all times.

Know the rules, but don't be too technical.

Be on top of all the plays. Then you can call them. That's the only way they can be called RIGHT.

Do not guess on any fouls. If you are not in a position to see fouls plainly, and if there is any doubt in your mind whether they are fouls, don't call them.

Every game is important; there are no crucial ones.

Never second guess your partner. When he calls a play, that's just what it is. Always.

Make your decisions at a dead stop. They look different when you are on the run.

Lost time is made up

Never turn your head until the play is completed.

Look right at the player when you call a penalty.

Call your own plays. Never let the coaches or players call them for you.

Never criticize any official. There will be days when you can't miss 'em and there will be days when you can't call 'em right even if your very life depends on it.

A smile and a pleasant look will go a long way toward your success anywhere at any time.

Do not let your voice or your tone be antagonistic.

When the game is over, go up to your fellow official and walk off the field together.

There is nothing worse than to call a play too quickly. You will look a lot better out there if you take just a little more time, and call it right the first time.

Remember to

HUSTLE HUSTLE HUSTLE

DUTIES OF THE LINESMEN

Two linesmen are required. One operates along each side of the field. It is their job to follow along the side line with the ball as it moves from one end of the field to the other.

The linesmen are usually lay officials who receive no remuneration for their services. They are appointed by the home management, but they are under the direct supervision of the referee. He should instruct them in their duties before the game.

It is desirable that the linesmen have a working knowledge of the rules. However, their specific duties are to indicate when the ball is out-of-bounds and to determine the team which is entitled to corner kick, goal kick, or throw-in.

The linesman should make his decisions instantly when the ball has crossed the touch line. He must not be influenced by suggestions from the coaches or players on the bench or by the spectators. If he is uncertain which team touched the ball last, he may turn to the referee for assistance.

The linesmen are provided with flags which they wave to indicate when the ball has passed over the touch line. In some cases, a flag is attached to each end of the flagpole. These two flags are of different colors. One color represents one team, while the other color is for the other team. The linesmen display the proper color to indicate which team is to put the ball in play.

It must be remembered that the referee has authority to overrule the decisions of the linesmen. In other words, the decisions of the referee take precedence over those of the linesman.

DUTIES OF THE TIMEKEEPER

There are two timekeepers. A representative from each team shall be responsible for keeping the record of the playing time. The rules recommend that the referee be relieved of the responsibility of keeping time. While the timekeepers should know the rules pertaining to timing a game, the referee should be sure to instruct them thoroughly in their duties. Since the sounding of the timekeepers' signal stops play and is the controlling factor in case a question arises, it is quite important that the timekeepers work in close co-operation with the referee and that they know the position of the ball when time expires.

GUIDES FOR THE OFFICIAL ON THE INTERPRETATION OF THE RULES

The Field

The size of the playing field may have an important bearing on play. Because of difficulty in obtaining adequate playing spaces the laws of the game allow considerable variation in dimensions, always providing the length is greater than the breadth.

Clubs should try to obtain a field which conforms to the average dimension, that is, 110 to 120 yards by 70 to 80 yards. The field should be free from anything which may cause injury to players or result in a low standard of play.

Ten Yards Center Circle and the Arcs of a Circle

Restraining circles with radii of ten yards from the penalty spot provide practical indications of the law that "for all forms of free kicks, whether direct or indirect, the players of the opposing side shall be at least ten yards from the ball and shall not approach within ten yards until the kick has been taken." The purpose is clearly to prevent interference with the free kick. These kicks include all free kicks, place kicks, goal kicks, and corner kicks.

> Note: The rule—ten yards away from the ball—applies to opposing players standing behind the ball as well as those in front of it, except in two cases: one variant, and one exception.
>
> *Variant:* In the case of a penalty kick, all players, other than the goalkeeper and the player taking the kick, must be outside the penalty area on the field of play and ten yards from the ball at the time the kick is taken. The goalkeeper must stand on the goal line between the goal posts.
>
> *Exception:* When an indirect kick is awarded in the penalty area but less than ten yards from the goal line, players of the defending side are allowed to stand on the goal line between the goal posts.

The Halfway Line

The halfway line indicates a division of the field into two equal halves for the purpose of: (a) *kickoff*—when all the players must stand in their own half of the field until the place kick has been taken; (b) *offside*—a player cannot be offside in his own half of the field.

The linesmen are usually lay officials

Touch Lines

The touch lines mark length boundaries of the field. When the whole of the ball passes out of play over either of these lines a throw-in is taken by a player of the side opposed to that of the player who last touched it. (See page 300.)

Goal Lines

Goal lines are at each end of the field, joining at right angles to the touch lines. When the whole of the ball passes over the goal line (except between the goal posts and under the crossbar) either on the ground or in the air, the ball is out of play and the game is restarted by: (a) a *goal kick*—when the ball has last been played by an attacking player; (b) a *corner kick*—when the ball has last been played by a defending player; (c) the goal line between the posts serves to show that when the whole of the ball has passed over this line, and under the crossbar, a goal has been scored, unless otherwise provided by the laws.

Goal Area

The goal area has two purposes: (1) to indicate the only area in which the goalkeeper can be charged fairly when in possession of the ball (see special note for college games on page 300); (2) to limit the area in which the ball is placed for goal kick. For a goal kick the ball can be placed anywhere in that half of the goal area nearer to where it crossed the goal line.

Many goalkeepers place the ball near the forward corner of the goal area because such position adds a few yards to their kick or allows them a convenient run. If the ball were placed a little away from the extreme corners it might afford better footing at the time the kick is made and also enable the goalkeeper to cover his goal in case of a mis-kick which goes immediately to an attacker within shooting range.

Charging is limited in college games

The Goals

Width and depth of goal posts and crossbar shall not exceed 5 inches. It is recommended that posts and crossbar be painted white to help players to see them clearly even when the light is not good.

No regulation in laws of the game says that nets must be part of the equipment, but their use is advised. They should not interfere with goalkeeper, should be whole and properly pegged down, and should be securely fastened to the back of the goal posts and crossbars.

Flag Posts

Flag posts must be firmly fixed but not too rigid or they may cause injury to a player colliding with them. They may not be moved or inclined to assist a player to take a kick. *Corner flag posts* must not be less than 5 feet high with a nonpointed top. Flag posts mark the corners and assist the officials in deciding whether the ball passing close to the corner has gone over the goal line or the touch line. *Halfway flag posts* are not essential, but if used, must be opposite the halfway line not less than one yard, outside the touch line.

Players

1. A game of soccer is played between two teams of eleven players; one of each team must be the goalkeeper.
2. A player may change roles with the goalkeeper during the game, provided he notifies the referee. If this change is made without notifying the referee and a player who has changed to a goalkeeper handles the ball in the penalty area, then a penalty is awarded.
3. Substitutes may be allowed to replace players during a game, subject to agreement before the match. In many competitions substitutes are regulated by the rules of that competition and they must be carried out to that effect.

Unlimited substitutions are permitted by some groups

4. Any player leaving the field during a game, except through normal movement of play without the consent of the referee, is guilty of ungentlemanly conduct. The decision in such a case is a matter for the referee.

Equipment

Boots are the most important part of the player's equipment. They must conform to the following standards:

1. Studs and bars must be made of leather or rubber.
2. Nails must be driven in level with the leather or rubber.
3. Bars must be transversed and flat (not less than a half-inch in width) extending the whole width of the shoe, and be rounded at the corners. No bars or studs may be more than a half-inch in depth. Combined studs and bars may be worn.

Metal plates, even though covered with leather or rubber, must not be worn. The usual equipment of a player consists of jersey or shirt, shorts, stockings, shin guards, and shoes. A player should not wear anything such as a watch or ring which may cause injury to another player. He may wear spectacles at his own risk.

Colors used should make it easy to distinguish between two opposing teams or sides. The goalkeeper's jersey should be distinct in color from that of other players.

If a player is found to have any article of personal equipment not conforming to the above requirements he shall be sent off the field, and shall not return without first reporting to the referee, who shall satisfy himself that the player's uniform is in order. The player shall only enter the game at a moment when the ball has ceased to be in play.

The *ball* must have a leather outer case. Nothing may be used that might cause injury to players. It must be 27–28 inches in circumference, and weigh 14–16 ounces at the start of the game. For schoolboys a No. 4 ball is

Check the shoes of the players

recommended, (must be 25–26 inches and weigh 12–13 ounces at start of game).

THE OFFICIALS

There are three officials responsible for a game of soccer —a referee and two linesmen. In intercollegiate games four officials are used—two referees and two linesmen.

LAWS OF PLAY

Start of Play

It is customary for the captains of the two teams to shake hands with the referee and each other before the game starts, and then for the referee to toss a coin, giving the visiting captain the call. The captain winning the toss may elect: (a) to kickoff or (b) which end of the field his team will defend. If he elects (a), the other captain has choice of ends, and vice versa.

For the kickoff the ball is placed in a stationary position on the center spot. The referee gives the signal for the kickoff and a player of the team kicking off then takes a place kick.

The Kickoff

1. Every player must remain in his own half of the field until the ball has been played. Players opposing the team which is kicking off must be at least 10 yards from the ball until it is kicked.
2. The ball must be kicked into the opponent's half of the field.
3. The ball must travel the distance of its circumference to be in play.
4. The kicker must not play the ball a second time until it has been played or touched by another player.
5. A goal cannot be scored direct from a kickoff. In case of an infringement of the immediately preceding rule,

an indirect free kick is awarded to the opposing team. When a goal is scored the game is restarted in a like manner by the team losing the goal.

After ends are changed at the end of each period, the game is restarted by the opponent of the team which started the period. But after the second period (or half time as it is called), the game is restarted by the opponent of the team which started the game.

When extra time is necessary, the captains should again toss for kickoff or choice of ends, because it is the start of another game, although of shorter duration. This procedure is legal in soccer.

Ball In and Out of Play

1. It is possible for the ball to be out of play when a player plays it or goalkeeper catches it, even though he is standing in the playing area.

2. A player running outside the playing area may still keep the ball in play. The ball is not out of play when it rebounds off the goal post, crossbar, or corner flag into the field of play. Play should not cease until the referee gives a signal for stoppage. The ball is then "out of play."

3. If a goalkeeper, even though he is standing in the penalty area, handles a ball which is outside the penalty area, a direct free kick is awarded to the opposing team.

4. A ball may pass out of play during its flight, but swerve or be blown so that it falls in the field of play. It should be declared out of play. The ball is not out of play when it rebounds off referee or linesmen when they are on the field of play, and play proceeds normally. For example, even though the ball may strike the referee direct from a throw-in, the thrower may not play it again until another player has touched it.

A player outside the playing area may play the ball

Scoring a Goal

Scoring goals is the object of soccer football—the side scoring the greater number wins the game. As results may often be decided by the odd goal, regulations concerning the method of scoring should be clearly understood.

Conditions Relating to the Scoring of a Goal

1. The whole of the ball must pass over the goal line between the posts and under the crossbar.
2. The ball must not be thrown, carried, or propelled by the arm of a player of the attacking side.
3. If the crossbar has been displaced, the referee must judge whether or not the ball has passed the goal line between the posts and below where the crossbar should be.
4. The team scoring the most goals is the winner of the match. If an equal number, or no goals, are scored, the game is termed a draw. In condition 2 of this section only the attacking side is mentioned; however, if a defending player handles the ball, and it passes over the goal line into the goal, a goal is scored; should a goal be prevented by a defending player handling the ball, other than the goalkeeper, a direct free kick is awarded to the attacking side—or if the offense occurred in the penalty area, a penalty kick is awarded. Although conditions 1 and 2 of this section are fulfilled, a goal cannot be scored from an indirect free kick unless the ball has been kicked or touched by a second player, other than the kicker, before passing into the goal.

If an attacking player kicks an indirect free kick directly into goal, a goal kick is awarded to the defending team. If a defensive player kicks either an indirect free kick or a direct free kick into his own goal, a corner kick is awarded the attacking team.

The whole ball must be within the goal for a score

Duration of the Game

In college and school soccer, a game is divided into four equal parts or periods (in college games four 22-minute periods; in high school games four 15-minute periods; in junior high school games four 12-minute periods), unless otherwise mutually agreed upon by both teams taking part. The half time period is 10 minutes, with 1 minute between the first and second periods and between the third and fourth periods.

The referee only has the power to extend the time of the intermission at half time. In certain competitions the rules specify the time to be played and also extra time which may be necessary in case of a drawn game. The referee and players must abide by these rules and regulations.

In all games a referee is empowered to:

1. Make allowance in either half of the game for time lost through accident or other cause. The amount of time added to make up for time lost is a matter for the discretion of the referee.

2. Extend time to permit a penalty kick to be taken at or after the expiration of the normal period of time in any period of the game.

Suspension of Play

If play is stopped for an infringement of the laws, the game is restarted by an appropriate free kick. In certain cases play may be suspended for a cause not mentioned in the laws. Provided the ball has not passed out of play immediately prior to the suspension, the referee restarts the game by dropping the ball at the place where it was when play was suspended. If a player touches the ball before it reaches the ground it must be redropped.

Examples of games restarted by dropping the ball:

1. When the ball becomes lodged between two players and the situation may cause injury.

The referee may extend the intermission

2. After play has been suspended because of injury to player or official.

3. Interference by spectators causing the game to be stopped.

4. When the ball bursts, or a player is caught in an embarrassing position. If the ball has passed out of play immediately prior to suspension, the game is restarted by a goal kick, throw-in, or corner kick. Players and officials should keep the time lost through stoppages to a minimum.

Penalty Area

The penalty area is a rectangle 44 yards wide with two lines joining the goal line 18 yards from each goal post. It serves the following purposes:

1. Indicates that part of the field of play in which a penalty kick is awarded for any of the following offenses committed *intentionally* by a defending player:

   a. Charging opponent violently or dangerously.
   b. Charging opponent from behind.
   c. Handling the ball.
   d. Holding an opponent.
   e. Striking an opponent.
   f. Pushing an opponent.
   g. Tripping an opponent.
   h. Kicking or attempting to kick an opponent.
   i. Jumping at an opponent.

2. Limits the part of the field where the goalkeeper may handle the ball.

3. Indicates the distance the ball must be kicked from goal area when a goal kick is taken, before it is deemed in play (that is, before it can be played by another player).

4. When a penalty kick is awarded, indicates area outside which *all* players must stand on the field of play, other than the goalkeeper and the player taking the penalty kick, or when a free kick is taken by the defending side

The goal keeper may handle the ball in the penalty area only

from within its own penalty area. The penalty arc is not part of the penalty area; it is only the marking to show the distance of 10 yards away from the penalty spot.

Should any of the foregoing infringements take place outside the penalty area, a free kick is awarded against the offending side. Goal may be scored directly from such a free kick.

Free Kicks

Free kicks may be divided into three groups:

1. Kicks for starting the game, or restarting the game after a goal has been scored, or when the ball has gone over the goal line outside the goal posts.
2. Free kicks for technical offenses (that is, when regulations concerning method of play are broken).
3. Free kicks for "penal" offenses (that is, when intentional acts are committed which contravene the spirit of the game, or are likely to cause injury to an opponent).

Kicks used for group 1 in this section and free kicks for group 2 are indirect free kicks from which a goal cannot be scored directly. The exception is the corner kick from which a goal may be scored directly. Free kicks awarded for group 3 are direct free kicks from which a goal can be scored directly. If the offense is committed in the penalty area by the defending side, a penalty kick is awarded.

Indirect Free Kicks

(See special note for college games on page 300.)

A goal cannot be scored directly from an indirect free kick. The exception is the corner kick from which a goal may be scored directly. Indirect free kicks are awarded in the following situations:

1. Infringement of the offside law.
2. Against the goalkeeper for carrying the ball more than four paces without bouncing it on the ground.

Remember—there are three kinds of free kicks

3. Against attacker charging the goalkeeper fairly inside the goal area when the latter is not holding the ball, or obstructing an opponent.

4. Against a player for playing the ball a second time when taking any form of free kick, before it has been played by a second player, provided the game is suspended while the ball is still in play.

5. Against a player for dangerous play (attempting to kick the ball when held by the goalkeeper, or other form of play which the referee may deem dangerous).

6. Against a player for ungentlemanly conduct which includes:

    a. Persistent infringements of the law.
    b. Showing by word or action dissent from the decisions of the referee.

Direct Free Kicks

Direct free kicks are awarded for the following penal offenses when committed *intentionally:*

1. Handling the ball.
2. Holding opponent.
3. Striking or attempting to strike opponent.
4. Pushing opponent.
5. Tripping opponent.
6. Kicking or attempting to kick opponent.
7. Jumping at opponent.
8. Charging opponent violently.
9. Charging opponent from behind.

A penalty kick is awarded if any of the above penal offenses is committed intentionally by a defending player in the penalty area.

Points in Common Concerning All Free Kicks

1. Opponents of the player taking the kick must be at least 10 yards from the ball (except when a free kick is

Know when each kind of kick should be awarded

awarded to the attacking side nearer than 10 yards from the goal line. When this occurs, the opponent may stand on the goal line between the goal posts). For infringement the player must be cautioned.

2. The player taking the kick must not play the ball a second time before it has been touched by another player. For infringement an indirect free kick is given to the opposing side.

3. The ball must travel the distance of its circumference (27 inches) before the kick is deemed to have been taken.

4. The ball must be stationary when the kick is taken. For infringements of points 3 and 4 of this section the kick is retaken.

Additional Rulings Concerning Certain Free Kicks

1. When a goal kick or any other free kick is taken by the defending side within its own penalty area, the ball must be kicked outside the penalty area before it is deemed in play. Should this not happen the kick is retaken.

2. From a place kick (that is, the kickoff) the ball must be kicked into the opponent's half of the field.

3. Players cannot be offside during a goal kick or a corner kick.

4. From a penalty spot kick the ball must be kicked forward.

Charging

Players may charge if the charge is made fairly and when the ball is within reasonable playing distance of the players concerned. The players must be definitely attempting to play the ball in order to gain possession or to retain possession of the ball when challenged by an opponent.

A fair charge is one in which the player fairly "shoulders" his opponent. It is a shoulder-to-shoulder charge which is not violent or dangerous, has at least one foot in contact with the ground, and does not utilize the arms as a means of pushing. The law states that the player shall be penalized by a direct free kick if he charges in a violent or dangerous manner, or charges an opponent from behind, unless the latter be deliberately obstructing. If a goalkeeper deliberately obstructs an opponent it is permissible to charge him even when he is not in possession of the ball and is within his goal area.

Handling the Ball

A player has "handled" the ball if he has intentionally carried, struck, or propelled it with his hand or arm. Sometimes it may be impossible for a player to avoid "handling" the ball, having no time to withdraw his hand or arm before the ball strikes him. Even though the player may thus gain an advantage, because of the ball being directed along a different path, if it is not intentional the referee should not penalize it.

This is important in the penalty area, where a player unable to beat an opponent may deliberately kick the ball directly at him, hoping to strike his hand or arm with the ball and thus get a penalty.

Pushing

Body contact games are likely to cause the use of hands and arms to maintain balance or protection.

A player must under no circumstances use his hands or arms to hold an opponent back or push him away from the ball. This offense often occurs when the arms of players become interlocked; it may appear "accidental" but is really intentional.

Tripping

There is a difference between an intentional trip and a trip resulting from normal play. It is possible for a player to be tripped or kicked accidentally. In tackling for the ball, for example, it may happen that even though the ball

Handling must be intentional to be a violation

is played, the approaching player is tripped unintentionally. It is also possible for a player to feign a trip in order to gain a free kick, even though his opponent does not intentionally trip him.

The referee may decide that a player has not been deliberately kicked or tripped and award an indirect free kick against him for being guilty of dangerous play.

Jumping

A player is penalized for jumping at an opponent. This does not mean that when a player, jumping to head the ball, makes contact with an opponent, he has committed an offense. Jumping for the ball should not be confused with jumping at an opponent.

A sliding tackle done fairly is not dangerous to either player and should therefore not be penalized, but to jump with both feet at the ball, when it is being played by an opponent can result in injury and is therefore penalized.

Offside

In most field games where the main purpose is to score through the opponent's goal, some restrictions are applied to prevent the direct but uninteresting mode of attack, which consists of a player or players waiting in close proximity to the goal, ready to score from short range.

This restricting ruling in soccer football is known as the offside law, and provides notable technical features of the game. As the infringement of this law results in an immediate breakdown of the attack, it is essential that the issue of the law should be clearly grasped in all its details.

Stated in full the law says that "a player is offside if he is in advance of the ball at the moment the ball is played, unless:

a. He is in his own half of the field of play.

b. There are two of his opponents nearer to their own goal.

Don't confuse jumping for the ball with jumping at an opponent

c. The ball last touched an opponent or was last played by him.

d. He received the ball direct from a goal kick, a corner kick, a throw-in, or when it is dropped by the referee.

A player in an offside position shall not be penalized unless, in the opinion of the referee, he interfered with the play or with an opponent, or is seeking to gain an advantage by being in an offside position.

For infringement of this law, an indirect free kick shall be taken by a player of the opposing side from the place where the infringement occurred. Players should remember that if they are ahead of the ball they are liable to be penalized for being offside, but if they are behind the ball they cannot be offside, even though there may be no opponents between them and their opponent's goal line when it is last played by one of their own side. Players should remember if they are caught in an offside position that they must keep out of play and can only be put onside by the conditions explained above.

Penalty

The penalty kick can only be awarded for the following nine offenses, intentionally committed by a player of the defending side, within the penalty area:

Two offenses with the body: charging an opponent violently or dangerously; charging an opponent from behind (unless he is intentionally obstructing).

Four offenses with the hands: handling the ball; striking or attempting to strike an opponent; holding an opponent; pushing an opponent.

Three offenses with the feet: tripping an opponent; jumping at an opponent; kicking or attempting to kick an opponent.

If necessary, time of play shall be extended at quarter time, half time, or full time to allow the penalty to be taken.

The penalty kick is taken from the penalty spot or mark,

Grasp the purpose of the offside rule

12 yards from the midpoint of the goal line between the goal posts. When a penalty kick is being taken all the players other than the goalkeeper and the player taking the kick must be:

a. On the field of play.
b. Outside the penalty area.
c. At least ten yards from the ball, until the kick is taken.

Note: Players may stand along the side lines of the penalty area if they so wish.

The goalkeeper must stand (without moving his feet) on his goal line between the goal post until the ball has been kicked by the player taking the penalty.

The player taking the kick must kick the ball forward, and shall not play the ball a second time until it has been touched or played by another player.

The ball is in play directly it is kicked (that is, traveled the distance of its circumference).

A goal may be scored from such a kick.

If the ball touches the goalkeeper before passing between the posts, even though it is after the expiration of quarter, half, or full time, the goal counts.

For any infringements by the defending team of the above laws: if a goal is scored—goal allowed; if a goal has not been scored—kick retaken.

For any infringements by the attacking team, other than the player taking the kick: if a goal has been scored—kick retaken; if a goal has not been scored—penalty kick ended.

For any infringement by the player taking the kick, a player of the opposing team shall take an indirect free kick from the spot where the infringement occurred.

Questions and Answers on the Penalty Law

Q. "A" of the attacking side takes the kick, but as it enters goal, "D," also of the attacking side, runs into the penalty area.

A penalty kick is awarded for nine offenses—learn them

A. A goal. "D" did not move before the ball was kicked by "A," and if a goal had been scored the goal would be allowed.

Q. "A_1" of the attacking side kicks the ball which strikes the upright and rebounds into the penalty area, "A_2" of the same side runs and scores.

A. A goal. "A_2" is not offside and did not move forward into penalty area until "A_1" had taken the penalty kick. But if "A_1" were in front of "A_2" when the latter shoots, the referee might adjudge him to be interfering with the play and give him offside.

Q. Additional time is being allowed for the penalty kick to be taken. "A" takes the kick which is punched out by the goalkeeper. "A" kicks the ball into goal.

A. No goal. Additional time is allowed for the penalty kick only. As the goalkeeper has saved the kick, the referee should signal for full time.

Q. "A_1" of the attacking side is moving forward to take the kick, but before he reaches the ball, "A_2" runs over the 10-yard arc line.

A. "A_2," an attacking player, has infringed the law. Therefore, if "A_1" scores from the penalty, the referee orders the kick to be retaken; if "A_1" does not score, the kick is not retaken.

The Throw-In

(See special note for college games on page 300.)

When the whole of the ball passes over either touch line out of play, on the ground or in the air, it shall be "thrown-in" from the point where it crossed the line, as follows:

a. The throw-in is taken by an opponent of the player who last touched it before it passed over the touch line.

b. At the moment of delivering the ball, part of each foot shall be either on or outside the touch line.

An indirect free kick is given instead of a throw-in in college games

c. The thrower must use both hands.

d. The thrower must deliver the ball from in back of and over his head.

e. The ball is in play immediately it is thrown.

f. The thrower must not play the ball until it has been touched or played by another player.

g. A goal cannot be scored directly from a throw-in.

h. If the ball is improperly thrown in, the throw-in is taken by a player of the opposing team.

i. If the thrower plays the ball before it has been touched or played by another player of either team, an indirect free kick is taken by a player of the opposing team from the spot where the infringement occurred.

j. A player cannot be offside from a throw-in.

k. At the moment of delivering the ball the thrower must face the field of play.

Goal Kick

The goal kick must be taken by a member of the defending side from a point within that half of the goal area nearest to where it crossed the line. The ball is not in play until it has passed beyond the limit of the penalty area. Should it not be kicked directly beyond this limit, the kick is retaken.

Should any player other than the kicker contact the ball inside the penalty area, the kick is retaken.

The kicker may not pass the ball back to the goalkeeper.

The kicker may not play the ball again until another player has touched it after it has passed outside the penalty area. Should he do so, an indirect free kick is awarded to the opponents at the place where the infringement occurred.

A goal may not be scored directly from a goal kick.

Opposing players must remain outside the penalty area until the goal kick is taken.

Avoid delay—hustle, hustle, hustle

To encourage a rapid restart of the game the defender should be allowed to take the kick as soon as possible.

Corner Kick

A corner kick is awarded to the attacking team when the whole of the ball, having been last played by one of the defending team, passes over the goal line either on the ground or in the air, except when it passes into the goal.

The corner kick is taken by a player of the attacking team, within the quarter circle at the corner flag post nearer to the place where the ball passed over the line.

The corner flag must not be removed while the kick is being taken.

A goal may be scored directly from a corner kick.

Players of the opposing team shall not approach within ten yards of the ball until it is in play (that is, it has traveled the distance of its circumference).

The player taking the corner kick must not play the ball a second time until it has been played or touched by another player. Should he do so, an indirect free kick shall be taken by a player of the opposing team from the place where the infringement took place.

CONTROL OF THE GAME

Referee

Although the referee has two linesmen to assist him, the control of the game is entirely his responsibility. He must know all the laws of the game and should be capable of making assessments of play in respect of these laws. Quite often decision rests upon the referee's opinion. For instance: Was the handling of the ball intentional or unintentional? Will stopping the game give an advantage to the offending side? Is the player who is offside interfering with play?

The fact that in certain instances the referee has to use

A corner kick may score a goal

his own judgment shows that various interpretations are possible. It is important that, as far as possible, referees should be uniform in their interpretation of the laws.

Last, but not least, do not try to officiate a really important game until you become thoroughly experienced.

SPECIAL NOTE FOR COLLEGE GAMES

Two NCAA rules for soccer which apply specifically to the college game require a slightly different procedure for officials.

1. There is no throw-in after the ball has gone out-of-bounds. Instead, the ball is put in play by an indirect free kick. In this instance, it is not possible for players to be offside on the kick.

In order for officials to handle this new plan of play after touch with dispatch, these procedures are recommended:

(a) Each linesman should carry an extra ball. When the ball goes over the side line, the linesman should place the ball in his possession on the side line at the spot where the ball in play crossed the line. He then retrieves the other ball.

(b) The referee should blow his whistle immediately when the ball goes over the line. These two procedures are to prevent unusual delay.

(c) One referee should check the spot from which the ball is to be kicked. The other referee should take a position so that he will be ahead of the play as it first develops after the kick.

2. The second change in college play covers charging. The goalie may not be charged under any conditions.

20

The Techniques and Art of Wrestling Officiating

BECAUSE OF THE FAST ACTION AND NATURE OF WRESTLING as a competitive sport and due to the closely confined area of a wrestling mat and the rapidly changing situations thereon, the work of a wrestling official is one of the most arduous tasks of all arbiters of sports rules and regulations. Decisions under such conditions must of necessity be instantaneous and without hesitation. Such exacting judgments and decisions can best be understood and made only by an official who is schooled and experienced through long and faithful grounding in the knowledge of the rules, the best of techniques, and the proper manner of carrying out and enforcing the regulations.

In order best to equip oneself for such a task, it is suggested that the prospective official should become thoroughly acquainted with the written rules as published in the Official Wrestling Guide.[1] This publication sets forth not only the rules and regulations for collegiate wrestling but is the official guide for high school wrestling as well. In fact, most amateur wrestling in the United States is now following the pattern and rules as set forth in this annual publication. Not only are rules contained therein, but

[1] National Collegiate Athletic Association, *Official Wrestling Guide* (New York: A. S. Barnes and Co., 1950).

Fast action + confined area = a most arduous task

summary reports and photographs on wrestling in the various districts of the United States, and suggestions for coaches, participants, and officials have been included in order to acquaint officials with the total situation and problems surrounding amateur wrestling as a sport. Greater uniformity in the interpretation and carrying out of these rules and regulations should culminate in the development of a wholesome competitive occasion which will be satisfactorily appreciated and enjoyed by spectators, participants, coaches, administrative organizations, and officials. Such a favorable situation can eliminate much of the degrading trend which all too often has been present in wrestling and can place this sport—one of the earliest of man's competitions—on the high pedestal upon which it should stand.

Satisfactory experience in competitive wrestling and in coaching, though not essential basically for the qualified official, by no means detracts from his better understanding of the sport and, in turn, his appreciation of the point of view of the other persons who are always concerned in spirited competition. The well-qualified official will seek every means to equip himself thoroughly to be the neutral arbiter between keen competitors. Suggestions from coaches, participants, fellow officials, the public, and even the all too often uncalled-for criticism of the press, should be noted and brought to use by the learning official. For the young and inexperienced but willing referee, many techniques can be learned (and included in his repertoire and officiating manner) by watching the work of well-qualified and recognized registered officials, and then adapting it, to meet his type and style, to the situations as they arise.

Before he continues too far in his officiating career, the young referee will come to see that the spirit as well as the letter of the rule must be his guide in carrying out and enforcing the rules and regulations as they are written and

Coaching and wrestling experience are assets to the official

interpreted. The good official must not only act the part but must look the part. To this extent he should be properly dressed to handle a wrestling meet. The wrestling official's uniform usually acceptable to most sections and officials consists of a white-collared shirt with rolled or short sleeves, white trousers and belt, and white sneakers.

Set forth in the forms, which are included at the close of the material contained herein, are the reports on the wrestling official's duties, qualifications, techniques, etc., which should be studied, understood, and followed by the wrestling referee prior to and during the progress of a meet and the various matches. The official guide contains many suggestions and requirements for the work of an official operating under the different rules, in addition to the specific duties listed in Rule 18.

PREMEET DUTIES OF THE REFEREE

Checking with Coaches and Participants

In due time, and with allowance before the meet for the coaches' instructions to their teams, the referee should visit the dressing quarters of each team and inspect the participants and their uniforms. After carefully inspecting the hands of the men for rings (which should be removed), and the nails (whether smooth and clipped short), one should check the ears, neck, and shoulders for oily rub by running a hand gently over these parts. The belt is observed for a rough clip or buckle, which should be covered if worn (in order to prevent chafing or gouging of an opponent); and the shoes should be noticed to be sure that they have eyelets and not hooks. Shirts without buttons at the shoulder and long trunks are also a regulation requirement. Inspection of contestants in championships is usually made at the time the men come to the mat to wrestle. At this time, the official should talk to the coach (or the coaches, together) to be certain that any new

Inspect the competitors with meticulous care

changes or interpretations of the rules are clearly understood by the participants before the meet begins.

Five or ten minutes before the meet is to start, the referee, upon entering the gymnasium or wrestling area, should walk about the mat to observe whether the protecting mats are loose or tied down, the mat properly marked with circle and arrow, and the general conditions under which he will have to officiate the matches.

In championships it is usually the duty of officials to check the weights of the contestants. If a beam-weight platform scale is used, it is best to set the beam slide at the desired weight, before the contestant steps on the scale for his check. This will eliminate the tendency to quibble over the point of the check. If an automatic swinging-arm spring-balance scale is used, the exact weight is shown for each contestant as he stands upon the scale and he can more readily read it himself. Weight maintenance, weight reduction, and exactness in weight check are troublesome problems in wrestling. The official can avoid some of the pitfalls surrounding these problems by maintaining an unwavering attitude and adhering to strict compliance with rules.

Instructions to Timekeepers and Scorers

A combined timers' and scorers' table large enough for them to work at should be placed at one side and sufficiently away from the protecting mats not to interfere with freedom of movement during the matches. The referee sees to the placement of the men in accordance with the regulations in the guide and in the instruction digest (shown on page 322). The referee should also make clear the signals to be used and each man's duty as provided by regulations.

Just before the meet is to begin, if a dual meet, the referee calls the two captains to the mat and tosses a coin for choice of advantage position in split matches. For

Check the mats

championship matches, the toss is made following the first period of wrestling, if no fall occurs before that time.

Instructions to Wrestlers

At the time the match is to start, the contestants are called to the center circle on the mat cover, where they shake hands and are given brief instructions to do as much of their wrestling as possible in or toward the circle, and not to stop wrestling until the referee blows his whistle. They then step back to opposite sides of the circle and await the signal to wrestle. Rule 18, section 3, makes this method clear.

DUTIES OF REFEREE DURING MEET

Techniques While Contestants Are Wrestling on Their Feet

When the match is to begin, the referee starts the men by the hand and whistle signals as illustrated and described under "Wrestling Officials' Code of Signals" on page 329.

While the men are on their feet, the official should be constantly on the move in order to get the best view from the side of both wrestlers, and at sufficient distance not to interfere with their progress, but close enough to control any undue situation which might arise. As a wrestling official works alone on a mat, he should shift from one side to the other of the contestants occasionally, unless they, in maneuvering, bring a view from the other side to him. This should be done in order that one may get a view of the hand behind the neck, while the wrestlers are in the closed or contact position. This position is usually taken by wrestlers on their feet while working for control and an opening or a take-down. The hand of the other wrestler, usually partly blocked from view, can better be seen at this time to be sure that no illegal use of hands is being made by either contestant.

Keep the wrestlers in the center of the mat

Things to observe while the men are on their feet are their tendencies to "play the edge of the mat" or "intentionally go off the mat." These are common practices of a man who is pitted against a strong opponent. He does this in order to be able "to run off or back off" the mat to prevent his opponent from going behind and getting an advantage. The rules are clear as to punishment in such a situation. After one warning, the offender is placed in the "referee's position on the mat" and has two points scored against him for a "take-down."

FIGURE 27. POSITIONS OF WRESTLERS AND REFEREES FOR STARTING OR RESUMING A BOUT FROM STANDING POSITION. THE CONTESTANTS BEGIN WRESTLING WHEN THE WHISTLE SOUNDS.

An effective technique for officials to use in coping with the above situation is to ask the men "to work to the center," or "keep in the center circle." One excursion "off the mat" could hardly be interpreted as deliberate. However, repeated retreats of this kind should be handled with strict enforcement. Failure to act creates an unfair advantage. It is within the regulations and the best judgment of an official to make decisions as to whether a man is being

Keep to the side of wrestlers on their feet

"pushed off" or "intentionally leaves the mat." Either man can be at fault, and the referee should then bring the men back to center, and advise and warn them of what is taking place, and mention the penalty for such an offense. Most men, it is found, will pay heed to minor suggestions made to them in the spirit of fair play and good sportsmanship—the others are to be penalized. Contestants and coaches should know the rules.

"Stalling" while on the feet, or making no attempt "to wrestle aggressively" is another offense which must be met promptly and within the letter and spirit of the rules. "Warnings" are provided for in the rules. Tired or indifferent attempts to wrestle while on the feet should be met with firm decision if wrestling is to attract interest and if officials are to help improve the sport.

A good technique for a referee to acquire early in his officiating is to pass between his men, whether they are brought back to center or not, after a flurry off the mat. This forestalls any attempt on the part of a wrestler to take advantage of his opponent before the men are ready to wrestle and the signal is given. Such a practice will save embarrassment to the wrestlers and to the official. It will avoid unnecessary delay.

Techniques While Men Are on the Mat

Many of the techniques which are used by the referee when the contestants are maneuvering for position and holds while in wrestling position also apply when the contestants are on their feet. However, when the men are on the mat, fast action and rapid changes require extreme alertness on the part of an official.

When starting a match from the "referee's position on the mat," the contestants take the official position as designated in the rules (Rule 10, section 3, page 66) for the start of a period or situation. In order for the referee properly to observe the stance and positions of the two

Fearlessly penalize the wrestler who is stalling

men, he should begin the match from this position by being "eight or ten feet in front of the wrestlers, facing the scorers' table in the squat position," as indicated under "Wrestling Officials' Code of Signals." (See figure 28.) He should raise his hand, indicating "ready," and blow

FIGURE 28. REFEREE'S POSITION TO "BEGIN WRESTLING ON MAT." HE SOUNDS HIS WHISTLE TO INDICATE THE START.

his whistle when both men are motionless and in the proper position for starting the match. He should observe such things as knee, hand, and body positions of both men, as indicated in the rules, and correct, with all fairness and calmness, the irregularities, until a fair starting position is taken. Moving before the whistle and hand starting signal, edging or tightening hold on waist or arm, and other advantages should be met with firmness, one's best judgment, and decision. Too many officials become "officious" at this point and are apt to enforce unduly some minutiae of the regulations. It would be better to handle situations of this kind quickly and without stress, so that the match is not delayed to the disgust of spectators and the disturbance of contestants. Much practice by the young and learning official during scrimmage sessions will quickly indicate the most satisfactory manner for handling these situations, which are really the lesser evils of wrestling. The spirit as well as the letter of rules must be applied with one's best maturity of judgment. Minor infringements which in no way create an advantage for either opponent should be overlooked. The official should ignore the criticisms of a coach who attempts to incite an official to recognize inconsequential technicalities and thus mar a creditable officiating performance.

While the participants are maneuvering around on the mat for holds and counters, the official should at all times be near enough to observe and quickly check illegal situations—like the hammerlock—which arise as a result of a quick move. Illegal holds can be blocked before they become dangerous, by a warning from the official while the holds are developing. It is when the wrestlers are on the mat that the official must be most alert. He must concentrate fully on the work at hand and he must permit no distractions. The alert referee will anticipate punishing holds or positions and act to prevent them and the possible injury which may result. (See figure 29.) Of course,

FIGURE 29. REFEREE IN POSITION TO CHECK A POSSIBLE HOLD TO PREVENT INJURY.

Permit no advantage before the whistle

when violations occur, the regulations must be enforced and the concomitant penalties applied.

A referee can avoid many undue skirmishes or flurries at the edge of the mat by standing at the edge of the mat toward which the men are progressing and by directing them to "stay on the mat" or "work toward the center." (See figure 30.) By this same tactic he can prevent them

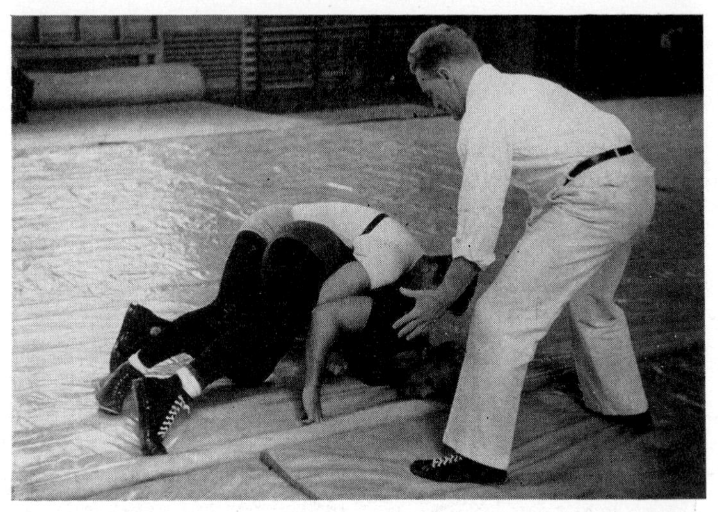

FIGURE 30. REFEREE'S POSITION WHEN MEN ARE ON EDGE OF MAT.

from going off the mat. He should not in any instance attempt to take hold of or push the men back onto the mat; neither should he be too quick to declare them off the mat. As long as "all supporting parts of one wrestler are on the wrestling mat proper" and both men not partly on the protecting mats, he should not declare them off the mat. (See figure 31.) This procedure holds true in similar manner for take-downs from the standing position. Figures 32 and 33, on the other hand, show the referee signaling to stop wrestling because all supporting parts of the wrestlers are not on the mat.

Be quick to check illegal holds

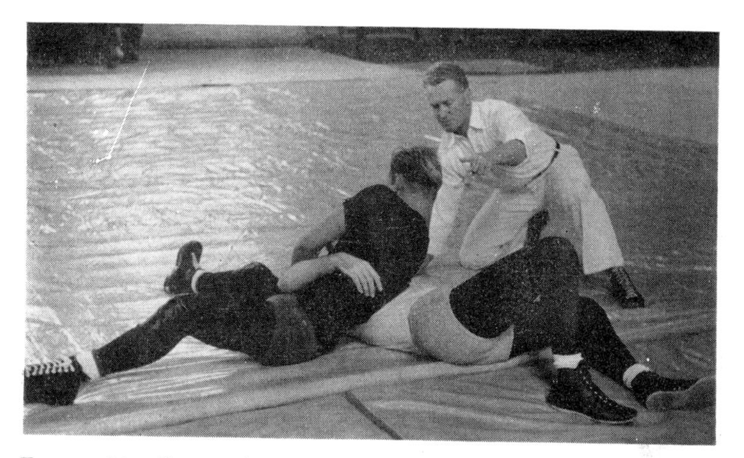

FIGURE 31. REFEREE'S SIGNAL TO INDICATE MAN WHO HAS THE ADVANTAGE.

FIGURE 32. REFEREE SIGNALING MEN TO STOP WRESTLING. IN ADDITION, HE BLOWS HIS WHISTLE.

Don't be too quick to declare wrestlers off the mat

Awarding Points

The man behind must have full control before a takedown is declared and before points are awarded for having earned a "position of advantage." This does not mean

FIGURE 33. REFEREE SIGNALING MEN TO STOP WRESTLING. HE BLOWS HIS WHISTLE AS AN ADDED SIGNAL. THIS SIGNAL ALSO INDICATES TIME OUT.

necessarily that a wrestler must be "behind" his opponent to receive such an award, but he must have him in a position where he has an advantage and distinct "control" of his man in the down position. Figures 34 and 35 show official awarding points. In like manner, an official should refrain from declaring "reversal of positions" until and unless a man has secured this control of his opponent. There are many brief flashes, both on the mat and when

There must be distinct control before points are awarded

coming to the feet, when a contestant has not lost control of his opponent, nor has his opponent gained freedom from the previous advantage. These instances must be met

FIGURE 34. REFEREE INDICATING AWARDING OF POINTS.

FIGURE 35. REFEREE INDICATING WRESTLER RECEIVING ADVANTAGE.

often, and in all their varied types, before one can always be sure that an advantage has been gained or an opponent has "escaped" to a "*neutral position.*" Figures 36 and 37 show an official indicating a neutral position.

Brief flurries do not necessarily mean an escape or reversal

FIGURE 36. NEUTRAL POSITION ON MAT SHOWING NO ADVANTAGE.

FIGURE 37. NEUTRAL POSITION STANDING.

If the man in the under position attempts to escape, comes to the feet, and earns the "neutral position" on the wrestling mat proper, he should be credited with an escape. However, if the men leave the mat proper while still locked together, the man who was in the "under position" must be placed in this same position in the "referee's position" in the center of the mat before wrestling is resumed.

It is in such situations as the foregoing ones that the skilled and qualified official shows his clarity of understanding of rules and his mature judgment which is based upon his wide experience with these situations. The well trained and qualified official will find that he fails or succeeds at this point in his officiating. These are the instances when points are earned or lost, and match decisions are fairly or improperly rendered. It should be repeated that alertness and keenness in judgment are most vital during the rapid changes which take place in ground wrestling.

Awarding Falls

In like manner, when declaring or awarding falls," the official can err or mark himself as a finished arbiter by the manner in which he handles himself and makes these close and important decisions. The official should not declare a fall unless he is in a position which enables him to see that both shoulders are distinctly down for the full elapsed time of two seconds. Wrestlers in such situations are often in such tangled and intertwined positions that an official will find it difficult to take a position, even with the side of the face down flat on the mat, where he can "positively" see both shoulders. This is particularly true if he is to one side of the men. An arm, an elbow, a hand, or head may block the view of the official so that he is unable to see whether or not both shoulders are down on the mat. In such instances there are two things the official can do. He can jump over from one side to the other to make sure the unobserved shoulder is distinctly touching the mat or the

The escape must be complete before leaving the mat

mat cover, and at the same time look across from above to see whether or not the other shoulder has raised from the mat. (See figures 38 and 39.) Or, better, he can go down to the feet position of one of the men and glance quickly

FIGURE 38. THE NEAR-FALL POSITION.

FIGURE 39. DECLARING A NEAR FALL.

from side to side in order to see if both shoulders are touching at the same time for the allotted count. (See figure 40.) These instances are among the most difficult

The test of the official—the quality of his discriminating judgment

the official has to face. It is here that matches, even meets, are won or lost. It is not considered the best of technique in such situations to slide the hand under the shoulder to feel if it is actually down, as this may be a warning to the contestant to raise his shoulder because a fall is pending.

FIGURE 40. REFEREE GETTING BEST VIEW OF SHOULDERS' POSITION BEFORE DECLARING A FALL.

Manner of Awarding and Declaring Points, Time Advantage, Time Outs, or Injury.

Rule 8, section 2, specifies the manner by which the referee shall "indicate orally and by pointing in such a manner that all present may know whenever a contestant has earned the position of advantage." The regulations also indicate the manner by which points shall be declared and advantage announced during the progress of the bout when the match reverts to the "no advantage" status. The "Wrestling Officials' Code of Signals" also specifies the types of signals and the word or phrase used to announce all situations, such as, "Neutral Position," "Stop Wrestling," "Advantage," or "Time Out." Rule 17, section 1, of the rule book also indicates a caution to the referee on signal to the timekeeper. (See illustrations of signals as shown throughout this chapter.)

The referee also makes sure by nod or glance at the table that the officials there have caught the awarded points and situation changes. Should any uncertainty arise as to the points awarded or the status at this instance, the referee or the head timekeeper should stop the match and straighten out the situation at once.

Likewise, the referee must make certain that the timers have observed his time-out signal. There are many brief flurries off the mat, when a wrestler's foot goes off or the contestant partly leaves the mat, with little or no time lost. In such instances the official does not ask for time out. It is only for lengthy periods or for conditions which require time to bring the participants back to the center circle to begin wrestling, either on the feet or on the mat, at the referee's signal of "Wrestle!" that time out should be taken.

During injuries, or for other delays, the referee will check with either the contestants, the officials at the table, and/or the coaches to see that all understand the situation. This provides an opportunity to care for the wrestlers, when these emergencies arise.

Declaring Falls and Near Falls

When the referee is in a position to see that both shoulders have been held in contact with the mat for the allotted two seconds of time, he declares and awards a fall by slapping the mat with the palm of his hand and at the same instant verbally announcing, "Fall!" as noted under "Code of Signals" of the Wrestling Officials' Signals. (See figure 41.)

In calling near falls, the referee must be in a position to observe that both shoulders are in contact with the mat for one full second but less than two seconds, or continuously within approximately two inches or less of the mat for two full seconds. Near falls shall be declared by "extending one arm vertically," but not until after the immediate situation is finished, no verbal announcement being given. (Code of Signals [8].) Figures 38 and 39 show the sequences in declaring near falls and awarding points for same.

FIGURE 41. REFEREE DECLARING A FALL BY STRIKING THE MAT WITH PALM OF ONE HAND.

Awarding a Decision or Declaring a Draw

At the termination of a match, when a fall has not occurred, the referee goes through the following routine:

1. He checks with the timers and scorers in order to obtain the point score for the match.
2. He then calls the contestants to the center of the mat.
3. He raises the left arm of the winner to a vertical position.
4. In case of a draw, he raises the left arm of both wrestlers.
5. If the match is terminated by a fall, he raises the arm of the winner.

This method of awarding decisions leaves the right arms free and permits the contestants to congratulate one another by the usual custom of shaking their right hands at this time.

Announce decisions—scorers acknowledge

It is recommended that the referee ask the contestants to shake hands as they approach him in the center of the mat. As they shake hands, he raises the arm of the winner. This technique tends to relieve any tension or embarrassment which the loser might otherwise experience. Referees who follow this procedure show consideration for the contestants. It is a means of fostering good sportsmanship.

FIGURE 42. REFEREE AWARDING A DECISION OR DECLARING A DRAW.

Provision for the awarding of decisions is provided for in the rules and is a part of the "Wrestling Officials' Code of Signals." (See figure 42.) The signals are shown in

The raised left arm permits a right hand shake

figures 41–45, 47, 48. There is some repetition here as they are grouped together for the convenience of the reader.

MECHANICS OF WORKING WITH THE TIMEKEEPERS AND SCORERS (THE TABLE)

At the beginning of the second and third periods and during the course of a match, whenever the wrestlers start from the down position, the referee shall be in a squat or kneeling position about 8 or 10 feet in front of the wrestlers and facing the scorers' and timers' table. (Figure 28.) This position permits him to see both the contestants and the officials. It assures the scorers and timers a clear view of his starting signals. The position stipulated for the wrestlers in the "referees' position on the mat" is discussed under Rule 10, section 3, and should be enforced by the referee, as presented. The uninitiated official should remember that while he should live up to the rules as written, there is also a spirit behind them which he should abide by. The picayune method of spending time on minute detail in getting men to take the proper position can be eliminated by making clear at the start of a match the position wanted, or punishing quickly for an illegal hold. It is more the duty of coaches to inform their men with regard to the legal and illegal holds and positions and for the contestants to see that they know such positions than it is for the official to instruct men who come to the mat to wrestle.

At all times during the course of a match, tne referee should make clear to the table by signal and word the progress and changes in the match. In case of any uncertainty he should stop the match and check with the officials at the timekeepers' table. The timekeepers and scorers in turn should carry out their duties as prescribed under the regulations of Rule 18, sections 13, 14, and 15. The suggestions and digested summary of "Instructions to and Duties of Timekeepers and Scorers" on Form XI,

In case of uncertainty, stop and check

may aid these officials in better understanding and carrying out their duties.

FORM XI

Instructions to and Duties of Timekeepers

General Instructions: There shall be no communication between the timekeepers or representatives at the timekeepers' table and coaches, contestants, or spectators; and the time advantage shall be kept a secret until the match is completed. This restriction is made to allow the timekeepers to give undivided attention to their duties. Timekeepers are directly responsible to the Referee.

I. *Head Timekeeper*
- A. Sit between the two assistant timekeepers, and keep a check on their work.
- B. Check stop watches to see if they are in good working order, etc.
- C. Must have pistol, gong, or horn.
- D. Record general time of the match.
- E. Notify the referee when the time limit of the bout has expired and when the time for intermissions has elapsed.
- F. Start watch at signal of referee when:
  1. "Starting or resuming a bout standing."
  2. "Begin wrestling on mat (referee's position)."
- G. Stop watch at signal of referee when:
  1. "Stop wrestling." (whistle)
  2. "Time out."
  3. "Declaring a fall."
- H. Call the number of minutes remaining to be wrestled in the following manner:
  1. Three-minute bouts:
     - a. 2 minutes! (at end of first minute of bout).
     - b. 1 minute! (at end of second minute of bout).
     - c. 30 seconds! (at end of 2 min., 30 sec., of bout).
     - d. 15 seconds! (at end of 2 min., 45 sec., of bout).
     - e. Sound gong or horn (at end of bout).
  2. Two-minute bouts:
     - a. 1 minute! (at end of first minute of bout).
     - b. 30 seconds! (at end of 1 min., 30 sec., of bout).
     - c. 15 seconds! (at end of 1 min., 45 sec., of bout).
     - d. Sound whistle (at end of bout).
- I. Should have two extra stop watches for recording "time out" in case of injury to the contestants.

FORM XI (*Continued*)

INSTRUCTIONS TO AND DUTIES OF TIMEKEEPERS

J. Should signal the referee immediately if any question arises between the timekeepers or scorers.
K. Should keep watches in plain view of all timekeepers.
L. Record time of each fall.
M. Record for referee the "choice of position" in each match.

II. *Two Assistant Timekeepers*
 A. "Home team" timekeeper.
  1. Sit to right of head timekeeper.
  2. Record accumulated time advantage of "visiting team" wrestler.
 B. "Visiting team" timekeeper.
  1. Sit to left of head timekeeper.
  2. Record the accumulated time of the "home team" wrestler.
 C. Report accumulated time advantage to referee at end of match.
 D. Start watch at signal of referee when:
  1. "Advantage" for wrestler whose advantage he keeps.
 E. Stop watch at signal of referee when:
  1. "Stop wrestling." (whistle)
  2. "Neutral position, standing" or "On mat."
  3. "Time out."
  4. "Declaring a fall."
 F. Should keep watches in plain view of all timekeepers.

INSTRUCTIONS TO AND DUTIES OF SCORERS

General Instruction: Scorers are directly responsible to the referee.

I. In all matches there shall be two scorers.
 A. "Home team" scorer.
  1. Record points awarded to wrestlers of visiting team.
 B. "Visiting team" scorer.
  1. Record points awarded to the wrestlers of the home team.
 C. Each scorer shall record the various points awarded by the referee to the contestant whose record he has been assigned to keep.
  1. Each "take down"–2 points.
  2. Each "escape" from defensive position on mat–1 point.
  3. Each "reversal of position" from defensive position on mat–2 points.

FORM XI (*Continued*)

INSTRUCTIONS TO AND DUTIES OF TIMEKEEPERS

4. Each "near fall"—2 points.
5. Points for accumulated time advantage at the end of match. No more than 2 points total.

D. Scorers should sit next to each other and check on the proper recording of scores in similar manner that the timekeepers check on each other.
E. Advise the head timekeeper immediately if there is a question about the score during any match.
F. Report total points of each contestant to the referee at end of match.

During the progress of a match, the head timekeeper shall call the minutes remaining and during the last minute the 30-second and 15-second intervals and signal with a small pistol, gong, or horn as time is up at the end of the match. The referee in turn will verbally convey the called times to the contestants, to keep them advised as to the time during the course of the match, and will stop the match with the "stop wrestling" and whistle signals, as indicated in the "Code of Signals."

Following this, the referee shall order the contestants to their corners, as indicated in Rule 18, section 12. Then he checks with each scorer on the total points for each man. Next, he checks the watches for the time advantage for each contestant. He subtracts these to find the net time advantage. The accrued advantage points and time advantage points are totaled to secure the points for the winner of the match. Advising the officials at the table of this, he then goes to the mat, has the opponents shake hands, and awards his decision as indicated under "Awarding a Decision or Declaring a Draw."

The preceding section, "Instructions To and Duties of Timekeepers and Scorers," indicates the conditions under which the referee and other officials shall check with one another during the course of a match. Specific duties for each official in a wrestling meet are also indicated on this form.

TECHNIQUES FOR OTHER SITUATIONS

There are many minor situations which the beginning official must learn to handle with dispatch and ease, in order not to draw undue attention nor detract from the smooth running of a wrestling meet. Time and experience will aid him in learning to solve disturbing problems.

Conferences with older and recognized registered officials on how to handle the many technical aspects of a match as well as the unusual situations will prove very helpful. For example, the learned referee turns a deaf ear to minor attempts of participants and coaches to aid a wrestler by comments, remarks, or exhortations. When these practices issue from the bench, they are called "sideline coaching" and are illegal under the rules. (Rule 12) Such situations can be deftly handled by the mere raising of a hand with the palm toward that team's bench to show those concerned that the official has taken note of their actions and that he disapproves. Procedures of this kind are effective and require no comments from the official. Should such conditions continue, it is within the right of the official to penalize the offenders by stopping the match and giving warning so that all may be aware of the situation. (See Rule 13, section 8.) The better thing to do, however, is to go quietly to the coach of the team concerned, at the first time out or between matches, and acquaint him with the rules and the spirit of good sportsmanship and advise him to supervise his bench and boys according to the rules. It is sometimes difficult to draw the line between sideline coaching and "encouragement" of wrestlers.

Another situation which can readily be handled by the referee without undue attention and delay is the occasional bulging of a mat cover upward when a wrestler is in a near fall or pinning position. As the official lies flat on the

Handle side line coaching with diplomacy

mat to observe the shoulders, he can pull upon the cover to flatten it and make the conditions proper in order to judge fairly a true fall or near fall. Of course, such bulging of covers can best be eliminated by the home management in seeing that the covers over the wrestling mats are tied or roped down to prevent slipping or bulging. A bulging or loose cover can also cause a contestant to trip or to slip. Rule 18, section 10 provides for the referee to handle this and other similar situations "in the spirit of good sportsmanship" so that undue advantage will not be permitted.

The official must provide himself with a whistle. While not required equipment, a stop watch may be found useful under many circumstances. Of course, the official always carries a silver dollar to use for the coin-toss choice. Other regular or unusual situations as they arise must be met and handled by the referee with the best of mature judgment.

TECHNIQUE AND ART IN OFFICIATING

The skilled and polished referee learns through practice and experience the manner by which he can best meet the requirements of his job. The job demands extreme physical and mental concentration. It requires tolerance for the unjust criticism which often accompanies officiating—even first-class work. However, if he is stimulated by the challenge offered, if he is interested in making a contribution to the sport, and if he is inspired to promote a true spirit of sportsmanship, he will surely receive great satisfaction from his efforts. He is most likely to attain the realm of the artist in his role as an official. Art in officiating, as in other things, takes the person beyond selfish motives and desires. It seeks to create a wholesome atmosphere in sports. Raising spirited competition to a high plane will make a real contribution to good citizenship. All connected with the sport—the participants, manage-

Tie or rope down the mat covers

ment, spectators, officials, coaches—are happier and better satisfied when the sport is conducted on this level.

CERTIFICATION

Wrestling associations and conference organizations have taken a great deal of interest in training and developing qualified wrestling officials. There is no national association of approved officials, as is the case with basketball officials. The job is being done on a local or district basis.

An excellent example of an efficiently organized group for this purpose is the New England District Committee for Approved Wrestling Officials. Organized since December 1940, the New England District has been testing and certifying approved wrestling officials. This organization is a part of the New England Intercollegiate Wrestling Association, which is a branch of the National Collegiate Athletic Association.

The following is a brief recitation of the procedures under which this body operates. Annually, prior to the opening of the wrestling season, in early December and at the meeting of the New England Intercollegiate Wrestling Association, the wrestling rules are interpreted. Coaches, officials, wrestlers, and college athletic officers gather to view films, discuss problems, interpret the new rules as they will be enforced in the district, and to examine new officials. The candidates are given a written test on the rules followed by a practical officiating test, at which time they officiate at a match. Three men must view and report on the outcome of the candidate's practical test. One member of the committee acts with a coach and registered official selected from those present. The prospective official must pass with a grade of 80 per cent on both the written and practical test to be approved for certification and included in the "Roster of Officials." (See Wrestling Guide.)

The form, "Report on Wrestling Official," included

Spirited competition kept on a high plane marks the official as an artist herein on page 329 is used as a check list for rating the performance of the new officials. The composite rating which the candidate receives forms the basis for his approval or rejection as a certified official. This check list can also be used in contests during the regular season. By this record, tangible information can be recorded for use in reporting the work of officials. The candidates are given copies of the check list prior to their examinations. In this way, they are able to learn the various factors which are used in the evaluation of their work. The check list also acts as a guide to the candidate in his preparation for his practical test. The results of the test are discussed with each candidate. This is done regardless of whether the candidate is approved or rejected. By this process, each official is informed concerning his strength and weakness. Some officials who are not approved but who show promise are placed on a probationary list. These men are recommended for officiating at freshman, junior varsity, practice sessions, high school, preparatory school, or other less rigorous competition. By this means, they are able to obtain further grounding and practice in the skill of officiating. This experience will be valuable to them when they present themselves for examination the following season.

RATING WORK OF OFFICIALS DURING THE SEASON

Form XII is used for the purpose of rating the work of an official during a regular match. These reports are mailed to a central office and form the basis for rating the officials as a group. The information on these forms is passed on to the official so that he may be advised concerning the caliber of his work. As indicated on pp. 331 and 332, the "Official's Check List" can be used during a regular contest for the purpose of facilitating the job of grading an official's work.

Organize for quality, have a plan

SIGNALS

See figures 27 to 42.

FORM XII

REPORT ON WRESTLING OFFICIAL

___________ vs. ___________ at ___________ Date ________

Score of meet (V) ______ (H) ______ Referee ___________

Remarks ____

____

____

Rating	Score	Coach's Numerical Score on Referee
Excellent	90–100	
Good	80–89	________________
Satisfactory	70–79	________________
Unsatisfactory	60–69	Coach's Signature

FORM XIII

WRESTLING OFFICIALS' CODE OF SIGNALS [1]

1. *Starting or Resuming a Bout Standing*–Extend *right arm* slightly above the horizontal to the front; verbally announce "Ready"——pause——quickly lower arm and at the same instant blow whistle.
2. *Stop Wrestling*–Blow whistle; at same instant extend arm slightly above horizontal to the front, palm outward.
3. *Neutral Position, Standing*–Upper arms front, horizontal; both forearms vertical, hands extended.
4. *Begin Wrestling on Mat (Referee's Position)*–Referee should be eight to ten feet in front of wrestlers, facing timers' table, squat position. Give signal for number 1 above.
5. *Advantage*–One arm and index finger extended pointing to wrestler receiving advantage. At the same instant verbally an-

[1] *Official Wrestling Guide 1950*, pp. 88–92

FORM XIII (*Continued*)

WRESTLING OFFICIALS' CODE OF SIGNALS

nounce "Advantage" and name the institution which offense represents.

6. *Neutral Position (No Advantage) on Mat*—Both arms extended sideward slightly below the horizontal, palms down; move hands back and forth with fingers spread and at the same instant verbally announce "No advantage."

7. *Time Out*—Give hand signal for number 2 above and blow whistle.

8. *Declaring Near Fall*—Extend one arm vertically; no verbal announcement. (Award of near fall should not be made until the immediate "situation" is finished, as indicated in last sentence of Note under Rule 15, section 5.)

9. *Declaring a Fall*—Quickly strike mat with palm of one hand and at the same instant verbally announce "Fall." Do not slap wrestler on the back. (See Rule 18, section 9.)

10. *Awarding a Decision or Declaring a Draw*—Referee shall call contestants to center of mat and raise the winner's left hand to a vertical position. In case of draw at end of match, referee shall raise left arms of both contestants to vertical position.

11. *Award of Points*—In connection with or immediately following the signal for change of position or advantage, the referee shall indicate award of points by pointing to the point scorer with the index finger of one hand and at the same time raise the opposite hand to or near a vertical position, extending one or two fingers of that hand to indicate the number of points awarded. Such signals must be clearly evident to the official scorekeeper and to the operator of the scoreboard (if such is used), and also so far as possible to coaches, contestants, and spectators.

FORM XIV

OFFICIAL'S CHECK LIST

_______ vs. _______ Place _______ Date ______ Time ______

Referee __________ Score ( )_______( )_______Reported by ________ Position __________

	Maximum Score	*Check**	*Total*
I. *PERSONALITY:* (15 points)			
A. Appearance			
1. Clean attractive attire	5	_____	
2. Well groomed	2	_____	
B. Poise and businesslike attitude	4	_____	
C. General—(Weak, antagonizing, uncertain, confident) (underline) ...	4	_____	_____
II. *INSPECTION AND INSTRUCTION:* (10 points)			
A. Before meet			
1. Wrestlers—(rings, nails, clothing, oil, etc.)	2	_____	
2. Equipment—(mats, watches, whistle or gong, etc.)	2	_____	
3. Timers and scorers—proper instructions	2	_____	
4. Contestants and coaches—check relative to questionable situations	1	_____	
B. During meet			
1. Wrestlers—instructions and final inspection	2	_____	
C. After meet			
1. Coaches (and contestants)—check for clarification of decisions rendered if questioned	1	_____	_____
III. *RULES—KNOWLEDGE, INTERPRETATION, JUDGMENT, ENFORCEMENT:* (40 points)			
A. Off-mat decisions	5	_____	
B. Stalling	5	_____	
C. Illegal holds	5	_____	
D. Falls	5	_____	
E. Near falls	4	_____	

FORM XIV (*Continued*)

OFFICIAL'S CHECK LIST

	Maximum Score	Check*	Total
F. Take-downs, reversals, and escapes	4	-----	
G. Decisions	3	-----	
H. Time advantage	2	-----	
I. Time outs	1	-----	
J. Miscellaneous (injuries, defaults, intermissions)	6	-----	-----
IV. *TECHNIQUE:* (25 points)			
A. Mannerisms on mat	3	-----	-----
B. Use of voice	3	-----	
C. Signals and awarding of points	4	-----	
D. Position and speed			
1. Starting bout	1	-----	
2. Wrestlers in standing position	2	-----	
3. Wrestlers on mat	2	-----	
4. Referee's position	2	-----	
5. Falls	2	-----	
6. Anticipation of wrestlers' movements	2	-----	
7. Near falls	1	-----	
8. Tossing coin and choice of position	1	-----	
9. Off-mat decisions and resuming in neutral position	1	-----	
10. Declaring the winner	1	-----	-----
V. *CONTROL OF MEET:* (10 points)			
A. Commanding respect and co-operation of all concerned			
1. Contestants	4	-----	
2. Coaches	2	-----	
3. Timers and scorers	2	-----	
4. Spectators	2	-----	-----
TOTAL SCORE	100		

Use reverse side for remarks

* Indicate weaknesses in "check" column by W.
Indicate strengths in "check" column by S.
Score value to be recorded also.

21

Hockey

THE RULES COMMITTEE OF THE NCAA URGES THAT OFficials for all collegiate games be selected from the lists approved by the National Collegiate Athletic Association and that they be members of the local Officials' Association. The following list of requirements must be met by a candidate before he can qualify as an NCAA ice hockey referee or assistant referee.

GENERAL QUALIFICATIONS

1. Honesty and fairness of judgment.
2. Ability to make quick decisions.
3. Firmness in abiding by decisions.
4. Agility and speed on ice skates. Must be able to skate well forward or backward and to stop quickly.
5. Good eyesight.
6. Emotional control.
7. Knowledge of the fifteen basic rules of the sport.

The duties of the officials for hockey are comprehensively covered in the officials' rule book.[1] Little can be added to the concise statements found in Rule 15. Likewise, in view of the fast action, the mechanics of working a hockey game are very simple. Diagram 44 represents the complete range of movement except for the mechanics of

[1] *NCAA Official Ice Hockey Rules* (New York: A. S. Barnes and Co., 1949).

Jack be nimble, Jack be quick

putting the puck in play by a face-off. The procedure for the mechanics of the face-off is covered in Rule 10.

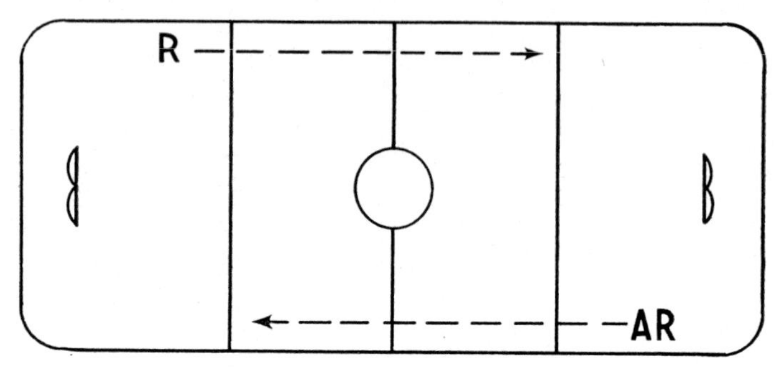

Diagram 44. Movements of referee and assistant referee along boards in a hockey game. One official leads while the other trails. Arrow shows limit of movement of each official in direction as indicated.

GENERAL INFORMATION

All hockey officials should be supplied by the home team. Only the referee need be approved by both teams. Seven officials are needed for a match: referee, assistant referee, two goal umpires, timekeeper, assistant timekeeper, and penalty timekeeper. In an emergency, the timekeeper can do the collateral duties of assistant timekeeper and penalty timekeeper. However, five officials should be the minimum number to insure control of play. In college and secondary school games, the referees are usually the only professional officials. All others are laymen who volunteer their services because of their interest in the sport.

Two important but seldom used rules that the referee should know are:

1. If a team refuses after three minutes to obey a decision of the referee, the latter may award the match on a forfeit to the other team by a score of 1–0.
2. If a team refuses to play an overtime period in the event of a tie game, the referee may award the

There must be a minimum of five hockey officials

match on a forfeit to the other team by a score of 1–0.

Note: This indicates that a referee is complete master of a hockey game and he does not have to tolerate abuse or unsportsmanlike conduct. A hockey match will be clean and fair if a referee is alert and knows his job. A match can be rough-and-tumble if the teams realize the referee is careless and indecisive.

GENERAL DUTIES

The general duties for collegiate hockey officials are indicated in Rule 15 of the official NCAA ice hockey rules as follows:

Rule 15—OFFICIALS AND THEIR DUTIES

Number and Titles—Section 1. The officials of a match shall be: a referee, an assistant referee, two goal umpires, a timekeeper, an assistant timekeeper, and a penalty timekeeper.

Unless otherwise determined, the officials shall toss a coin to determine which shall be the referee in charge.

Note: It is recommended that linesmen be appointed to watch the zone lines and signal or report to the referee or assistant referee, all violations of the antidefense Rule (Rule 11, Sections 2 and 4).

Referee and Assistant Referee—Section 2. The referee and, subject to him, the assistant referee, shall have sole authority and control of the game and they are not required to confer with coaches during a game and its intermission periods. They shall see that the other officials are appointed and in their places, and that markings, cages and goalkeepers' leg pads conform to the rules. They shall start and stop play (except timekeepers' signal always stops play); enforce the rules; settle disputes; decide or interpret cases unprovided for by these rules; appoint, and in their discretion remove the other officials; control the timekeepers; keep the score, announcing each goal as scored; and at the conclusion of the match the referee shall declare the result. If, in the opinion of the referee, the playing conditions become unsatisfactory during the course of the game, he may call the game at any time. It shall be "no game" unless two periods have been completed. The puck shall be considered in play until the referee or assistant referee stops the play, which either may do at any time by sounding a whistle or horn, or by ringing a bell (except timekeepers' signal always stops play). They shall stop the play whenever either observes an infringement of the rules except in the attacking or neutral zones upon commission of a foul to prevent a goal the play shall not be stopped until the particular play or series of plays shall have been completed. The referee or assistant referee shall stop play because of the illness of any player, or for any other cause, which in the judgment of the referees justifies such action. They shall suspend the calling of a foul upon a defending player as provided in Section 6 (a) of Rule 14.

In case a player or players attempt to delay the game as stated in Rule 11, Section 5 (d), the referee shall order play to start and shall immediately resume play by a face-off, even though the offending player or players are not ready.

The decision of the referee on any question whatever shall be final and there shall be no appeal. He may change his own decision, or that of any other official, provided he does so before play is renewed following rendition of the original decision.

Note: The referee should skate along one sideboard and the assistant referee should skate along the opposite side-board. One should watch, primarily, the play of the puck while it is being advanced toward one end of the rink and should follow the play if necessary to a point even with the crease. The other should primarily be concerned with the play not directly connected with the puck and should go as far as the attacking zone line. When the puck is being advanced toward the opposite end of the rink, the special attention of the officials should be reversed. See diagram 44.

However, each official should call any infraction which he sees, regardless of its location or of the location of or direction of movement of the puck. Officials should change ends near the middle of the third

The official rules include the mechanics of officiating

period and at the middle of any overtime period. When play is stopped, the official who is to put the puck into play, should always look toward the players' boxes to see if substitution is to be made, and he should not start the play if more than the proper number of players are on the rink. A signal—horn, or waving of the flag—different from that used by the referees, may be used to call the referee's attention that substitution is to be made, but only when play is stopped.

The referee or assistant referee shall see to it that teams are notified three minutes before play is to start after each intermission.

When an official rules a player off the ice, the official must designate the offense and any special amount of time to the penalty timekeeper and shall announce or have the offense announced.

Play must be stopped whenever a penalty is imposed.

Timekeepers—Section 3. (a) The timekeeper and assistant timekeepers shall use one timer between them. They shall time the actual play, starting when the puck hits the ice on the face-off and stopping whenever the referee or assistant referee signals the play to stop and when a goal is made. They shall ring a gong or shoot a gun at the end of each regular period and of any other period designated by the referee, and this signal shall mark the absolute conclusion of play. They shall time intermissions and shall notify the referee (to inform the teams to be ready to play) three minutes before the expiration of each intermission.

Penalty Timekeeper—Section 3. (b) The penalty timekeeper shall keep a record of the offenses and the players penalized. He shall keep off the rink any player, sent to him by the referee or assistant referee for the full time of the penalty in actual time of play, starting when the puck strikes the ice on the face-off and stopping whenever the referee or the assistant referee signals the play to stop and when a goal is made. He shall notify the referee, when play is stopped, if a penalized player went on the rink before his penalty time was completed. In case of a postponed time penalty, he shall see that no penalized player returns to the ice until there is a stoppage of play or until a substitute has been removed.

Note: If the penalty time is unexpired at the end of a period, the penalty carries over into the next regular or overtime period.

It is recommended that all except the penalty timekeeper and penalized players be excluded from the penalty box. Other officials, coaches and spectators, alike, should be excluded.

Goal Umpires—Section 4. The goal umpire shall signal the referee when the puck enters the cage. The referee shall give the goal umpire an opportunity to inform him as to the manner in which the puck was caused to enter the cage and whether the conditions of the goal crease rule have been complied with. The final decision as to whether or not it shall be scored shall be made by the referee.

The goal umpire shall judge at the same cage during the entire match.

Note: The goal umpire should not talk to the goalkeeper.

BASIC PRINCIPLES FOR HOCKEY OFFICIALS

William J. Stewart [2] has pointed up the duties of the referee in six basic principles which are listed below.

1. Officials should blow whistle loudly and more than once to make sure both teams hear it.

2. When teams are storming around the goal and players are all piled up around the goalkeeper, the official should blow his whistle the instant the puck is out of sight to prevent piling-on, to save injuries, and to protect goalkeepers, of whom most teams have only one.

3. Be very strict on any attempt to injure an opponent. Cross-checking, board-checking, slashing across the hands, etc., should call for instant and full penalties.

---

[2] William J. Stewart, "Hints on Officiating." In the *Official Ice Hockey Guide* (New York: A. S. Barnes and Co., 1948, p. 66.)

When the puck is out of sight—stop the fight

4. Officials should learn to skate backwards with players coming out of their defensive zone, not turning until the player has come out of his defensive zone. In this way the official always has the player in front of him.

5. If an offensive team is fouled, the official must make sure that they have no further opportunity to continue their offensive play before he blows his whistle for a penalty. Similarly the whistle should not be blown when an offensive player is offside in his attacking zone if the defensive team has a good opportunity for an offensive jump out of that zone.

6. To sum it all up: Be an official at all times. You will have to call plays that will hurt teams, but no coach likes a weak-kneed official.

22

Lacrosse[1]

LACROSSE IS ADVERTISED AS THE FASTEST GAME PLAYED on two feet. The very nature of the game requires that the officials be consistent and firm in handling it and that they be quick to penalize infractions of the rules in order to prevent the game from getting out of hand.

The game has an elite following which has worked freely and unselfishly to promote its spread and to keep it on a high and dignified level. In this connection, much has been done to train and develop officials. In order to check on the work of the officials in regular games and in order to get composite ratings of them, each coach reports to the officials' association. A typical rating card for this purpose is shown in Form XV.

The officials for the game consist of a referee, an umpire, a timekeeper and a scorer. The referee and umpire are the professional officials, who are paid for their services. The timer and scorer are appointed by the referee. They are lay officials who are usually obtained from the manager of the home team.

The following procedures are strongly recommended for the lacrosse officials:

---

[1] *Note:* The author is grateful to Nelson N. Cochrane, District Chief Referee of New England, who has generously furnished most of the material for this section of the book.

The nature of the game requires firmness

FORM XV

Rating of Lacrosse Official

UMP. ☐

______________________________ REF. ☐

NAME OF OFFICIAL

Knowledge and Interpretation of Rules	☐ NO ERRORS	☐ FEW ERRORS	☐ MANY ERRORS
Attitude	☐ OVER-OFFICIOUS	☐ FIRM	☐ HESITANT
Coverage of Field	☐ TOO CLOSE	☐ SATISFACTORY	☐ TOO DISTANT
Consistency of Rulings	☐ CONSISTENT	☐ INCONSISTENT	
Over All Rating	☐ ABOVE AV.	☐ AVERAGE (FAIR)	☐ BELOW AV.

Other Comments ______________________________

____

____

____

____

Visiting Team ________________ ________________
SCORE

Home Team ________________ ________________
SCORE

________________________ DATE ________________
SIGNATURE OF COACH

PERSONAL EQUIPMENT

The referee and umpire customarily wear white-and-black-striped shirts, white knickers, black or blue hose, and cap. They should carry a red handkerchief with a weight knotted in it. This is to be used to signal penalties. They both carry the same sounding whistle and a coin to be used for the toss.

PREGAME CONFERENCE

Officials should get together in the dressing room at least a half hour before game time and discuss the important rules and situations that may arise and which will require prompt action on their part. The sides of the field where each is to work, how out-of-bounds balls are to be covered, and the mechanics which will be employed on attacking situations and fast breaks should be worked out at the pregame conference. It is even a good idea to go over the rules together and work for complete harmony during the contest.

CHECKING EQUIPMENT AND FIELD

The officials should be dressed and on the field fifteen minutes before game time. Officials should check goal nets and field markings immediately upon entering the field. If nets are too taut or too loose, the home manager should be notified so that adjustments can be made. All netting should be securely fastened to the ground and posts of the goal. They should arrange with the home team manager to have a spare man at each end of the field with one or two extra balls. When a ball goes over the end line an extra ball should be tossed to the proper player by this spare man who then retrieves the original ball.

The teams should be lined up at the center of the field for inspection of the crosses. The officials should look for small sticks, unlaced heads, anything that may hinder dis-

Inspect the crosses for safety and fair play

lodging the ball by an opponent. This procedure is a safety precaution as well.

INSTRUCTING TIMER AND SCORER

Appoint a timer and be sure he understands rules about intermissions, time outs, and notifications. If there is no pistol, have the timer secure a whistle to signal the end of a period and be sure he uses it only for this purpose. The referee in consultation with the coaches should determine the length of periods before the game.

Appoint a scorer and explain that all substitutes must report to him and that no substitute may run on the field until after he sounds his horn and has received a wave of the hand from an official. Be sure scorer understands how to keep the game record sheet and that a copy is to be furnished the referee at the end of the game. A sample of the Lacrosse Game Record (Form XVI) is shown on page 344.

MEETING OF COACHES AND CAPTAINS

A few minutes before game time the umpire should get the visiting team captain and meet the referee and home team captain on the field. Any local ground rules should be determined. At this time the captains are asked to instruct their squads on the following:

1. After retrieving an out-of-bounds ball, a player must step onto the field before he can expect the official to blow his whistle to resume play.
2. Players for whom substitutes are entering the game should hold up sticks so the new player can find their positions quickly (especially when the entire midfields are substituted).
3. No one but the captains may discuss rulings with the official during the game.

Visiting team captain will call his choice at the toss of the coin. After the toss, the game should be started promptly.

The timer is a volunteer—don't neglect him

277

LACROSSE GAME RECORD SHEET

HOME TEAM ____________ VISITORS ____________

PLAYED AT ________ DATE ________ REFEREE ________ UMPIRE ________

SCORE BY PERIODS		1ST PERIOD	2ND PERIOD	3RD PERIOD	4TH PERIOD	OVERTIME	TOTAL
	HOME TEAM						
	VISITORS						

HOME TEAM LINE-UP

G, PT, CP, 1D, 2D, C, 2A, 1A, OH, IH

VISITORS LINE-UP

G, PT, CP, 1D, 2D, C, 2A, 1A, OH, IH

PENALTIES ON HOME TEAM

NAME	OFFENSE	MIN.	PER.	TIME

PENALTIES ON VISITORS

NAME	OFFENSE	MIN.	PER.	TIME

SCORING BY HOME TEAM

NAME	ASSIST	PER.	TIME

SCORING BY VISITORS

NAME	ASSIST	PER.	TIME

MANAGER'S SIGNATURE ____________ REFEREE'S SIGNATURE ____________

A complete record sheet to be furnished referee at end of each lacrosse game. Referee to forward with comments on reverse side to NELSON N. COCHRANE 138 Grand View Ave., Wollaston, Massachusetts.
DISTRICT CHIEF REFEREE NEW ENGLAND INTERCOLLEGIATE LACROSSE LEAGUE

FORM XVI

POSITIONS OF OFFICIALS AT THE FACE-OFF

Each period starts with a face-off. Likewise, there is a face-off after each goal. The umpire who is on the opposite side of the field from the timer's and scorer's bench handles the ball. He also checks the position of the centers' sticks. To start play, the umpire backs out of the center circle and blows his whistle.

Keep the record complete on the official sheet

The referee, who is on the side of the field nearer the bench, is responsible for fouls and for watching for violations by players who may step into the center circle. The positions of the officials at the face-off are shown in diagram 45.

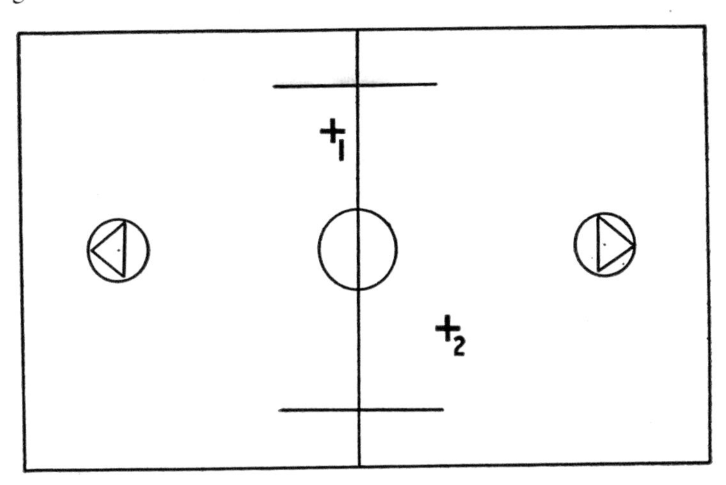

DIAGRAM 45. POSITIONS OF OFFICIALS AT FACE-OFF.

COVERING THE FIELD

After the face-off, the officials assume positions so that one official is in front of the play and one is trailing behind the play. Each covers the end of the field to his right. This direction is determined as the official faces toward the center of the field with his back to the side line.

If the direction of play should change, the trailing official becomes the leading official. Thus, when the attack loses the ball, the official responsible for the other end line must keep ahead of the play as it goes toward the far goal and be ready to call out-of-bounds play at the far end line. The other official should trail the play up the field and at the midfield stripe check for off-side. However, when the play is close to him and near his side line, he should watch the ball and let the other official check the off-side.

Know your duty at the face-off

In general, each official is responsible for play close to the ball in his diagonal half of the field. However, co-operation is important. Neither official should hesitate to call a foul which may appear to be directly in front of the other. The attention of the near official may be turned to note a possible nearby interference, or an illegal check after a pass, or perhaps from his angle of vision he cannot detect the foul.

Diagram 46 shows the area of the field for which each official is generally responsible. The end which each covers is also shown by the direction of the line and arrow.

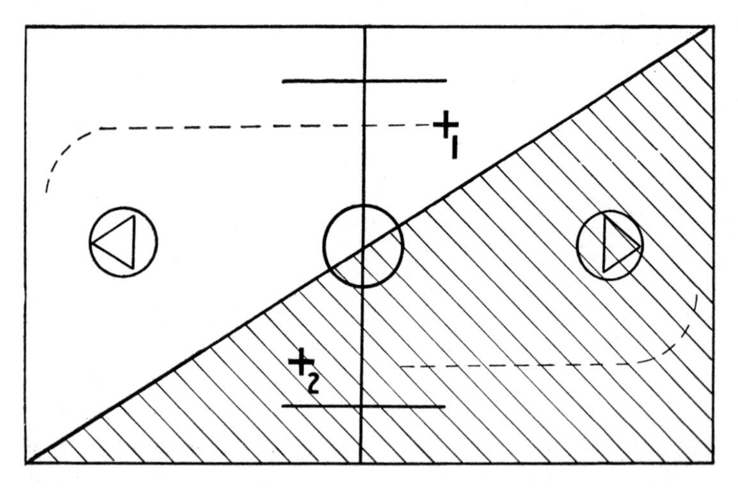

Diagram 46. Positions and movements of officials when ball is in play. One official always leads the play and one trails.

POSITIONS AND DUTIES OF OFFICIALS AT THE GOAL

When play is around the goal, the official responsible for the end line behind the goal should pay strict attention to the player with the ball and all shots. The other official should watch the general play around the goal and be alert for interference, players entering the crease, etc. Dia-

Cover the ball when in your triangle

gram 47 shows the positions of the officials when the ball is in the goal area. Note the end official is back of the goal.

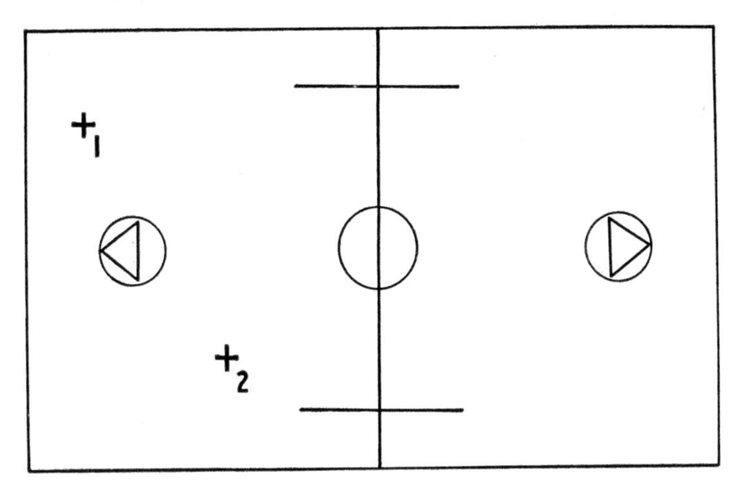

DIAGRAM 47. POSITIONS OF OFFICIALS WHEN THE PLAY IS AROUND THE CREASE.

PROCEDURE IN CALLING FOULS

Except in deliberately slow whistles, fouls should be called promptly by a loud blast. The official should point to the offending player, call his number, and announce clearly and loudly the type of foul and length of penalty. This should be supplemented by giving the proper signal to indicate the foul. The official must rule with firmness as previously stated. He must not, however, be unpleasant, sarcastic, or overofficious. If, in spite of efforts on the part of the official to avoid antagonism, a player argues about his infraction of the rules, he should be given an additional penalty of one minute. Likewise, the official should not tolerate similar unsportsmanlike conduct from other players or from the bench. Penalties of one minute should be assessed without hesitation. If such infractions occur by the coach or players on the bench, the penalty should be assessed on a close attack player.

Call a foul where you see it

It weakens the position of the official and tends to permit the game to get out of hand to give warnings. If it is a foul it deserves a penalty. Therefore, there is no place in lacrosse for such phrases as "If you do that again, I'll put you out" or "Watch that stuff" or "Quit moving after the whistle."

GUIDES TO SPECIFIC PLAY SITUATIONS

The following are guides to actual play situations. They refer to specific rules as indicated. They are so pertinent to the duties and procedures of officials that considerable space is devoted to them on the following pages.

Ball Out-of-Bounds

Unless it is obviously accidental, rule that any ball kicked, batted, thrown, or pushed over the end line is deliberately caused to go over the end line. The ball is given to the opposing team.

Substitutions

If a substitute thinks the whistle has blown and runs on the field while play is still going on, the play is stopped and a technical foul is called for more than ten men on the field. If a player causes confusion by running out on the field before being waved on by an official, the same penalty is inflicted.

Privileges of Goalkeeper

If a goalie stops the ball with the hand and then puts the ball in his stick, this is sufficient evidence that he caught the ball contrary to the rule. A penalty should be inflicted.

Interference

The defense player should be penalized for any shouldering, stick whacking, and shoving about of an attack player (note crease men carefully), except when attack

Don't warn—penalize

man is about to receive an actual pass that has been thrown to him. Careful watch should be made when a goalie yells "Check" to note any defense player who strikes at an attack player's crosse when the latter is not actually about to receive a pass.

Interference should be called on any defense player who hinders an attack player or steps in front of him when the attack player is making a cut toward the goal.

Block plays can be legal but are difficult to execute legitimately. A player may not step in front of a moving opponent who does not have the ball. However, he is entitled to a position on the field and may move or stand anywhere he desires provided that in the process of reaching the desired position he does not hinder an opponent. Once he takes the position he thinks suitable for a block play, he cannot then move again after his opponent has started to move toward him. In other words, after he has assumed his block position, if he takes a step, turns his body, bends over, or does anything else to obstruct the path of his opponent as the latter approaches, he is then guilty of interference.

Holding

An attack player may ward off a blow at his crosse if he keeps his free arm stationary. If he pushes away or bats away a defense man's stick, he must be called for holding. (There should be a better rule to cover this situation, but this rule is the nearest thing to cover an obviously unsuitable act.)

A defense player may reach around the body of an attack player with his stick, or arm on his stick, to thrust at his opponent's crosse provided he does not impede the forward movement of the attack player. However, the instant the attack player's forward movement is checked, even momentarily, by the arm or stick across his body, this becomes holding and should be called promptly.

Develop a clear image for a legal block

Tripping and Pushing

Most trips are probably accidental, but even if a player trips another by falling down in front of him, accidentally getting his foot in the way or unintentionally dangling his stick in the wrong place, the official must call this tripping and inflict a penalty.

When a player is legitimately reaching for a loose ball, and an opponent falls over his stick, this obviously is not a trip.

A defense player may hold off an opponent with his hand closed over the butt end of his stick, but if he punches or pushes the attack player around with this hand, he must be penalized for pushing.

Leaving Position

When the whistle has blown, a player may not toss his stick to a more favorable position and then move to where his stick has fallen.

When the ball goes out-of-bounds, the official should blow his whistle promptly as the ball touches the line. Any player who moves after the whistle is blown should be penalized. When a player is all alone, and there is no decision to make regarding who gets the ball, the player may continue running to retrieve the ball.

General Conduct

The officials should not tolerate any jeers, loud criticism, or other unsportsmanlike conduct from the bench. A penalty may be inflicted on a close attack player when that happens or the coach may be warned to keep his squad under control. On the second offense, penalty should be made on the offending team. It is more important that players learn self-control than that they score a number of goals.

Striking with Crosse (Slashing)

If a player strikes an opponent anywhere except on his stick (or on gloved hand on the stick), it is a slash. If the stick and player are struck at the same time, it is still a slash. All jabs at the stomach, hip, and elbow are called slashes. All follow-through swings that catch a man across the legs and feet are called slashes. Pushing at a man with the end of the stick should be called under this rule. The Rules Committee, the New England Association, and the chief referee have all ordered that officials adhere strictly to this rule. Therefore, all slashes must be called if they are illegal.

A player who just touches an opponent with his stick, or whose stick slides with no force along a helmet, arm, or shoulder is not committing a slash.

If a player, in order to protect his crosse, interposes his arm or shoulder in front of a blow which would not otherwise have struck him, this is not a slash.

If a player runs into a stick, the opponent may not be called for slashing (although in some such situations he may be called for holding).

Every one-handed blow at a crosse is not necessarily a slash if done expertly and with adequate control, but some one-handed swings may be slashes, just as some "wood chopper" two-handed swings may be slashes even though no one is hit.

Penalties

Personal Fouls

Most fouls are accidental and should receive only one-minute penalties. However, when a player deliberately trips an opponent, checks viciously from the rear, or otherwise flagrantly violates a rule in an intentional manner, two- or three-minute penalties should be inflicted.

When the whistle blows, see that the players freeze

Expulsion Fouls

Whenever a player deliberately strikes, kicks, or knees an opponent with intent to injure, an expulsion foul should be called. Whenever a player drops his crosse and starts swinging his fists, an expulsion foul must be called. Whether or not the offender fancies he has just been too roughly handled is insufficient excuse to void expulsion. Sometimes the offender has just been the victim of unnecessary roughness, and an alert official will have noted and should call this foul in addition.

Execution of Penalties

The red handkerchief should always be carried so it will be easily accessible without fumbling. In slow-whistle situations the handkerchief should be tossed promptly and then the whistle blown after play is completed. Generally such situations occur when attack player is within 20 yards of goal and driving in for a shot, but sometimes, for example, when a man is free in front of the goal, the whistle should be held on plays further out until the opportunity for a pass to the free man has occurred. Penalty should be inflicted after the play is completed, whether or not there was a goal.

POSTGAME DUTIES

The following postgame procedures are those which are in vogue in New England. They are recommended for all sections and particularly for college games.

A copy of the game record sheets should be secured from the official scorer. Before signing the sheet, it should be read over to be sure it is filled out completely and correctly. This should be mailed to the District Chief Referee, after writing comments on the reverse side. Comments are desired on the following topics:

Use the flag when there's need for a lag

FIGURE 46. LACROSSE SIGNALS.

1. Efficiency of manager in preparing field and handling game.

2. Attitude of players and coaches during game as judged by behavior.

3. Names of standout players.

4. Salient points of contest, type of play, and unusual occurrences.

After all college varsity games, the referee should send a collect wire, press rates, to the Associated Press, Boston, Mass., announcing place of lacrosse game and scores of each team.

SIGNALS

Lacrosse like other sports has its system of signals to convey to those watching the game the actions taken by the officials. These are reproduced here for the convenience of the reader. No official is fully equipped to officiate a game unless he has a ready knowledge of these signals. (See figure 46.)

23

Organization of Ski Meets

ORGANIZATION OF OFFICIALS

THERE ARE REALLY TWO PHASES TO THE ADMINISTRATION of ski competition: the organization for the meet, and the job of actually running off the meet. Because all preliminary work in preparation for a meet must be done away from the scene of competition, it seems pertinent to include a list of the duties of the officials who arrange for all the details of a ski meet. These officials include the following:

1. A director-in-chief
2. A director of officials
3. A secretary, or clerk of office
4. The clerks of the various courses
5. An equipment director
6. A first-aid director
7. A transportation director

The Director-in-Chief

He shall be the chairman of the committee and shall be responsible for the co-ordination and satisfactory conduct of the program. The director must keep constant check on the members of his committee to make sure that the work is functioning as smoothly as possible.

Make preparations away from the scene of action

His duties begin long in advance of the actual running of the race. His first important consideration must be that of the members of his committee and he must choose them in light of their ability, responsibility, and willingness to do the work and make necessary sacrifices entailed in putting across a successful ski meet.

He must prepare all budgets, and handle all financial matters connected with the meet.

If it is within the province of the tournament committee to take care of such arrangements as housing and entertainment of the competitors, then this also should be listed as among the duties of the director-in-chief. However, it is advisable that this be left to separate committees, or at least to men subordinate to the director of the committee.

He should keep himself free from any particular job during the running of the races, so that he may be ready to apply himself to the ever-present, last-minute needs that will always crop up, no matter how well a race may be organized.

The Director of Officials

It shall be his duty to secure all the officials necessary for the proper running of each event. A list of these officials, which will include such men as referee, judges, timers, starters, recorders, course setters, forerunners, and checkers, will be included in the detailed account of each event. However, a reminder is necessary, that the more respected the name of an official in the ski world, the more respected his word becomes, so that any decision he makes will be beyond question. Therefore the utmost care must be used in choosing officials.

The Secretary or Clerk of Office

His duties are mainly those of secretary and general office worker on the committee. He shall be responsible for mailing entry blanks to the competitors, for publishing lists

Two sets of officials are necessary

of entries, distributing programs, compiling lists of officials, instructions sheets to competitors, etc. It should be his duty to see that all scoring cards for the various events be in the hands of the proper officials at the proper time, and that following the race they be brought to the scorer as soon as possible. He should also be responsible for posting the official results just as soon as possible after the finish of the race, and for publishing, in printed form, the final results of the race. These should be mailed immediately to all contestants.

He should also be responsible for all dealings with the press, all advance publicity, etc. In case of a large important tournament, however, it would be wiser to appoint another man to handle publicity alone, for the job would become too large a one if much publicity work is entailed.

The Clerks of the Courses

The duties of these men will be discussed in detail under the headings of the various races that they will run. It is necessary that there be a separate clerk of course for each event, because his duties are so numerous it would be almost impossible to be in charge of more than one race. It shall be his duty to be responsible for the satisfactory conduct of the event to which he is assigned, and he is subordinate to no one but the director-in-chief. He should organize a subcommittee, and assign to them the various jobs necessary for the running of his event.

Equipment Director

It shall be the duty of the equipment director to collect and distribute to the various clerks of courses the equipment that they will need for the running of their events. Such articles as shovels, rakes, axes, ropes, slalom flags, cross-country flags, finish flags, communications equipment, timing and checking boards, pencils, watches, and

Officials on arrangements organize the meet

number bibs are all necessary for the running of a ski meet.

First-aid Director

He shall be responsible for organizing and equipping a ski patrol competent enough to handle any possible accident that might occur during the conduct of events.

(Literature concerning the organization, equipment, and work of the ski patrol may be obtained by writing to the National Ski Patrol System, Eastern Division, 1416 Massachusetts Ave., Cambridge 36, Mass.)

Transportation Director

In a large tournament, and in a meet where not all of the courses are centrally located, it is advisable to have a director of transportation, who shall be responsible for the transportation of competitors, officials, workers, patrolmen, and all equipment to and from the race courses.

MEET OFFICIALS

The events which may be included in a ski meet are (a) jumping, (b) langlauf, (c) slalom races, (d) downhill races, (e) combined scoring in either jumping and langlauf or downhill and slalom to count the combination as one event.

The officials needed for three events include: a referee, a scorer, a clerk of course, race committee, timing officials, communication officials, course police, first-aid patrol, forerunners, flag keepers, checkers and course patrol, judges, measurers, recorders. The duties of each and the techniques which each should acquire will be discussed in the order named and as they are required for each event. The nature of the ski meets requires quite different conditions for each. As a consequence, each event necessitates a separate course. While the various courses should be conveniently adjacent, it is obvious that in order to provide

Meet officials supervise and run off the events

suitable terrain for each, there will be some distance from one to the other. This fact and the extent of a course will obviously separate the officials.

All of these factors practically demand that only those with skiing experience and with an understanding of the characteristics of competition in an event should be appointed to officiate. In many respects, skiing is a specialized competition and requires officials who are expert in the activity. It is axiomatic that the extent to which a decision of an official is accepted, is dependent upon his standing and recognition in skiing society.

GENERAL MEET OFFICIALS

There are certain officials who serve in official capacity for the meet as a whole, instead of for individual events and for that reason their duties are brought up now.

Referee

He is the general rule-maker or arbitrator of the tournament. He alone must decide upon all disputes arising before and during the race that must be decided at once on the spot. He should be present at the finish of each race course, and receive reports of the officials concerning offenses to the rules. He should make a list of all disqualifications and post it immediately following the completion of the race.

The Scorer

This official is responsible for the computation of the results of each event, and the combined scoring, both team and individual. He must be something close to a mathematical genius, for this work is extremely complicated at times, and often a mistake in the computation of the results will cast a black shadow over an otherwise perfect race. It is obvious that he must be completely familiar with the methods of scoring. An adding machine and an assistant will be of invaluable aid in his work.

The methods of scoring a meet are complicated and detailed and will not be taken up here. There are specific instructions for the scorer in another section of this chapter.

Race Committee

It will be necessary at this time to distinguish between the race committee and the tournament committee, for that question is sure to come up. As has been outlined, the tournament committee is in charge of the management of the meet. The race committee, on the other hand, finds its greatest use in settling disputes that arise during the running of a specific event. Officially, a race committee shall consist of "a chairman and at least two other members of the organizing club." The referee and the clerk of course shall also be members. It shall deal with changes in the location of the course, and matters involving protests, rules, and penalties arising out of the race. Thus, under the system outlined above, the race committee need not function at all except under these specific conditions, and when it is needed, its personnel can be drawn directly from that of the tournament committee.

In a single event meet, the names "tournament committee" and "race committee" are synonymous, but in a large four- or five-event meet the job of the tournament committee is that of several race committees combined, and thus it must be given a separate title.

THE DOWNHILL RACE

In commercial ski areas, where most meets are run, there is little need to worry over the conditions of trails and slopes as they are kept in the best of shape. There might be some corrections made in the various state ski areas that haven't been opened to commercial concerns.

Scoring is complicated and detailed

Selection

Long before the race takes place, the clerk of course must make his selection of the proper course and alternate course that he intends to use for the competition. The degree of drop is a very important consideration, and usually the axiom that the more important the race, and the better the competitors, the steeper the course should be, can be followed. The race should be long for first-class competition, but in the East, with our limited altitude, "long" must necessarily be limited. A race should never be less than one mile in length, and anything over that is desirable. It is obvious that there should be no uphill stretches in any downhill race course. Usually a north or northwest or northeast slope is the one most suitable for a race course, for the sun has less of an opportunity to get at the snow, and the conditions will remain much more favorable, especially at low altitudes. If the race course is cut through the forests, as are most of the New England trails, then a few hints toward preservation of the trail might be found useful. Planting of any type of a tough grass along the trail will prevent some of the damaging erosion that is so prevalent on ski trails, and will also serve the double purpose of holding the early snows. The trail should be cut wide (30–50 feet, or more) to allow for sufficient checking space, alternate ways of running the course, and safety.

Preparations

As soon as the first heavy snow has covered the trail, it should be tramped, and this snow should be allowed to settle so that a good solid base will be covering the entire trail. At least two days before the race, the downhill course should be opened to competitors for practice, so the final tramping should be completed before that time. The course should be tramped to its maximum width, to allow plenty of room for checking, and to minimize the

Selection and preparation of the course must match the class of the competition

accidents that will occur when a racer gets off in the soft snow at the side of the trail. If at any time before the race itself the race committee should decide that further practice would spoil the condition of the trail they may close the race course to further practice.

Care During the Race

There is little that must be done during the race other than that of tramping out the ruts that form on the corners. Rakes, and even gardeners' hoes, have been found very valuable in this task.

Officials

1. Referee: His duties have already been discussed, for he serves in this capacity for all the events of the tournament.

2. Clerk of the Course: He shall have charge of all persons connected with the course, such as course police and flag keepers. He shall have charge of all preliminary preparations and selection of the race course already described. His duties may include those of course setter, but it is advisable to have this job handled by an expert skier, one who is held in respect as a skier by the competitors. As it is a rare occurrence when you can get so expert a skier to accept the other responsibilities of clerk of course, the two jobs are separated.

3. Course Setter: Prior to the race he shall set control gates (blue flags) at such points as he feels necessary for safety, or he may warn competitors by the use of flags of hidden rocks, stumps, etc. (yellow flags). He shall be responsible for setting direction flags (red flags). If in his opinion the course is unsafe to run, he shall have the authority to postpone the race.

4. Timing Officials: Enumeration of the necessary officials (Duties explained on page 373):

Mark the course

At least two timers. One to be known as the chief timer.

The starter and assistant.

Recorders for each timer and starter.

5. *Communication Officials:* There should be, whenever possible, some method of communication between the start and the finish of the race course. Telephones, either field sets or regularly installed phones in little wooden shelters, have been found to be the most satisfactory. Radio is almost as good but is not quite so dependable. The men who take care of this apparatus should be dependable, intelligent workers, able to make repairs to any part of their equipment at a moment's notice.

6. *Course Police:* It is their duty to keep the course in shape during the race, as has already been described. They can also serve to keep the spectators off the course, and as flag keepers at the control gates.

7. *The First-aid Patrol:* In a case where there is little manpower available this usually becomes another of the duties of the course police, but it is much wiser to have a well-trained first-aid group, acting independently.

8. *Forerunners:* Before the start of the first contestant in a downhill race, there shall be at least one forerunner who must run down the course in such time as to finish in front of the first contestant and his time relayed back to starting point as soon as possible. If on the day of the race there is a new fall of snow, there shall be at least three forerunners.

THE SLALOM RACE

The general organization of a slalom race is very similar to that of the downhill. The position of the race course must be selected long before the time of the race. Preferably, it should be on an open slope, although several excellent slalom races have been held on trails, including the

1938 Nationals held on the Nose Dive trail on Mount Mansfield, Stowe, Vt. However, an open slope allows the course setter a great deal more freedom. The hill should have a *minimum vertical drop of 500 feet* for an important race. During the race the course police should be even more diligent than they are in the downhill, and no ruts or grooves surrounding the flags should be allowed to form.

Officials

The officials necessary for the slalom are almost identical to those of the downhill, with slight changes in their duties.

1. Referee: His duties shall remain the same.

2. The Clerk of Course: His duties remain the same.

3. Course Setter: Prior to the race he should set the flag combinations that make up the modern slalom. Large poles (preferably bamboo or tonkin reed) with red, yellow, and blue flags should be used. Each gate through which the competitors must pass should consist of a pair of these flags identical in color. There are all sorts of flag combinations (too varied to discuss here) open to the course setter. However, the importance of securing a capable, reliable, and respected course setter cannot be overlooked, for he plays a major part in the success or failure of any slalom race.

4. Timing Officials: The same. Duties will be explained on page 373.

5. Communications Officials: Their duties remain the same.

6. Course Police: Their duties remain the same, except that in the slalom a separate official serves as flag keeper.

7. The Flag Keepers:

a. *Flags:* Every flag keeper is responsible for the section of the course between his flag and the flag immediately above him.

The course setter may determine the success of the race

The flags must be taken in their proper order. A competitor who has overshot a flag is not deemed to have passed through a lower pair of flags until he has reascended to the upper pair and until some part of his ski has crossed the upper pair of flags.

A flag keeper may direct the attention of a competitor to a pair of flags which he is in danger of missing altogether, but he may give no other information to competitors.

A flag keeper has the choice of two, and of only two answers, in reply to any question which a competitor may ask. He may reply "Right" or "Back." He should reply "Right" to a competitor if any part of the competitors, ski has crossed the line between the flags which he is keeping, even if a competitor has rendered himself liable to a single or double penalty. He should reply "Back" if, and only if, the competitor has rendered himself liable to complete disqualification.

b. *Penalties:* On a record card each flagkeeper shall indicate in the proper place on this card any penalties incurred by a competitor. Symbols for penalties shall be: the figure 1 for a single penalty, the figure 2 for a double penalty, and the letter X for disqualification. To avoid confusion no other marks should be made on the card.

Single Penalty. A single penalty shall be incurred if only one of the competitor's feet crosses the line between the control flags.

Double Penalty. A double penalty shall be imposed if neither of the competitor's feet crosses the line between the control flags, provided that some part of his ski crosses the line.

Disqualification. If neither of the competitor's feet and no part of either of his skis cross the line between the control flag, the competitor shall be disqualified.

At the end of each race the flag keepers will be notified by the starter when the last man has gone through. Flag-

Flag keeper answers only "Right" or "Back"

keepers should then immediately surrender their records to the proper official who shall carry them to the chief timer.

c. *The Penalty Time* in a slalom race shall be reckoned according to the following table:

If the shortest, penalty free time is
40 secs. or less, the single penalty shall be 4 secs.
40.1 secs. to 45 secs., the single penalty shall be 4.5 secs.
45.1 secs. to 50 secs., the single penalty shall be 5 secs.
50.1 secs. to 55 secs., the single penalty shall be 5.5 secs.
55.1 secs. or more, the single penalty shall be 6 secs.

The penalty shall be added to the contestant's time, to give his corrected time.

The basis for reckoning penalties shall be arrived at separately for each part of the slalom.

A double penalty shall be the equivalent of twice a single penalty.

8. *The First-aid Patrol:* Rarely are there any serious accidents incurred in a slalom race. However, it is advisable to have some first-aid equipment and men on hand throughout the event.

9. *Forerunners:* In a slalom race there should be at least two forerunners.

General Remarks

No competitor shall be allowed to run any part of the course after the course setter has placed the flags in position.

A competitor may enter a gate or pair of flags from either side.

The slalom shall always be run on hard packed snow.

There shall be two runs to every slalom, but if necessary, in order to save time, only the best men in the first run may be allowed to enter the second.

Some sort of mark, preferably blueing or ink, should be used in placing the poles in the snow, so that when a flag is removed by a competitor's fall it may be replaced in exactly the same position.

When the flags are set, no practice is let

The course setter has the option of altering the course for a second run.

THE LANGLAUF OR CROSS-COUNTRY RACE

Here again a great deal of the preparation must be done ahead of time. A trail must be chosen that can be divided into approximate thirds—uphill, downhill, and flat—so that as varied terrain as possible be given to test the competitors. The distance of the race must be determined only after careful consideration of the age of the competitors who will run it, their experience, the amount of training they have had, and the time of year.

Officials

The officials necessary for a cross-country race are very similar to those used in the slalom and downhill.

1. The Referee: His duties have already been covered.

2. The Clerk of Course: His duties shall be those of general supervision and management of the race. He should see that a warm room is provided for the competitors at the finish of the race, and that such refreshments as tea, oranges, and sugar are served. In the cross-country race there is a better opportunity for the jobs of the clerk of course and the course setter to be combined into one. The same differentiation that existed in the slalom and downhill race does not exist here. The course setter in the cross-country race must select his own course, and mark it, which is a long and tedious job, and cannot be done just the morning of the race, as the course setter of a slalom would do. The duties of the course setter will be discussed below, but when planning a race it would not be a bad policy to combine both of the jobs into one.

3. The Course Setter: It shall be his duty to put the desired course of the race in shape several days before the actual running of the race, although no competitor shall be allowed to go over the course. All competitors shall be

The job of the clerk and course setter can be combined

provided with a map. He should have a crew of experienced skiers who are willing and able to cover the entire race course several times in order to prepare the snow. Wide downhill skis should be used in this preliminary tramping, and the track should be at least three ski widths wide. Once again flags of three colors should be used: red for direction, yellow for warning, and blue for control, if, for instance, an open slope were encountered. Over a distance of 11 kilometers as many as 200 flags may be used. It is important that the trail be absolutely certain without forcing the skier to stop and look for directions, for a fatigued racer is likely to lose his way even on a trail that looks quite obvious to the course setter. This is extremely important, for even in major races contestants will frequently lose their way. If a trail should overlap itself in a loop, it would be advisable to have large direction signs posted. There should not be too many obstacles such as fences and logs on the course, nor should the trail cross roads frequently used.

4. *Timing Officials:* The same. Their duties shall be explained on page 373.

In a cross-country race, if a competitor arrives at the start after his original starting time is past, he may enter the race at the discretion of the starter, but his time will be recorded as if he had started in his original position.

5. *The Checkers and Course Patrol:* The checkers should be placed at their stations by the clerk of course after consultation with the course setter, and after careful study of the course has been made. The purpose of the checker in the cross-country race is to make sure that each competitor covers the entire distance of the course; therefore the checkers should be placed so that it would be impossible for a racer to cut off any portion of the course and still pass each of the checkers. It shall be their duty to write down the number of each competitor as he passes the position, and to return that record to the clerk of course after

the last contestant has passed him. They should try to prevent the course from becoming rutted, but this is rarely the case in a cross-country race, except in the downhill portion.

6. *Forerunners:* There should be at least one forerunner, though more men are preferred. This is important, for the first man is extremely handicapped if he has no one ahead of him upon whom he can pace his own gait.

THE JUMP

The selection and building of a jump hill, its degree of drop in the inrun and outrun, the position of the take-off, etc., are all technical questions and seldom, if ever, are the concern of any athletic director or ski coach.

Officials

1. *The Judges:* The judges are the men that do the actual scoring of the contestants' jumps on a point basis for form, distance, take-off, etc. This is a job that can only be handled by experienced men who know jumping, and who have worked as judges before. The United States Eastern Amateur Ski Association has a list of accredited jump judges that is worth consulting before making out the judge personnel. There should be at least two, preferably three, judges for a jumping competition.

2. *Measurers:* Four or more measurers are usually necessary to take care of a forty-meter hill. The measuring is done with long poles (bamboo) from the side of the hill. A metal measuring chain marked in meters should extend down the side of the hill, and the measurers merely place their poles perpendicular to this chain, and read off the distances from it. Measuring is done from the outermost point of the lip of the jump to that point where the feet of the contestant touch the outrun slope. Measuring shall be done to the closest half meter.

Preparing a jump hill is the job of a professional

3. *Director of Tournament:* He is actually in charge of running the competition itself. He is usually placed on the judges' stand. He instructs skiers when to start down the inrun, calls out their names, announces distances, etc. It is advisable, especially in a large tournament to have a loudspeaker system for this man, so that he can be heard from all parts of the hill.

4. *Clerk of Course* (also known as the Chief of Hill): He is the man responsible for the condition of the hill at all times. He and his assistants must do the original tramping of the hill and must have it ready two days before the scheduled competition for practice purposes.

5. *Flagman:* A man should be placed under the lip of the jump with a long flag that will extend over the tip of the take-off, and can be seen from the start of the incline. He shall raise the flag as a danger signal to those above, and lower it only after the hill is absolutely clear, and ready for the next jumper.

6. *First Aid:* First-aid men should be present at all times during the jumping competition. They should be stationed at the bottom of the hill, and if any accidents do occur, the casualties will literally slide right into the arms of the waiting patrolmen.

General Remarks

1. It might be advisable to split the job of clerk of course into two parts: that of the chief of hill (to take charge of the tramping and conditioning of the hill during the competition) and that of the clerk of course (to do all the preliminary work, and then to hold himself in readiness to do any one of the last-minute details that spring up during a jumping competition).

2. In case the hill is very icy, it should be broken up to a very rough surface with picks or axes or rakes or anything at all, and then new snow placed on it, and allowed to settle. Even very hard granular snow, or fine ice particles,

if placed on the steep outrun of a jump and then allowed to settle for twenty-four hours, will congeal sufficiently to allow tramping and jumping thereafter.

3. A man should be stationed at the top of the inrun with a list of the correct jumping order of the contestants, so that he can get them in their proper order, and facilitate the job of the director of the tournament.

4. If the outrun of the jump is icy, crampons should be provided for the measurers.

5. The way the snow is tramped at the very edge of the take-off is of utmost importance. A slightly bad angle here may throw the jumpers entirely off. This is a job for some experienced impartial jumper to decide upon. A jumper is the *only one* who can tell if there is too much lift to the take-off.

6. If the snow is very fast and a jumper starting from the top is in danger of landing in the transition, or even out in the flat, the inrun must be shortened. Once again this can only be determined by an experienced jumper—a non-competitor—and so it is advisable to have one or two "exhibition" jumpers who will determine points 5 and 6.

Order of Running of Contestants and Teams

In an individual race there are two methods of selection. The first is that of a simple lot draw. All the contestants' names are placed in a hat, and then the order in which their names are drawn determines the order in which they run. The second is that of the selected group draw. The contestants are arranged in groups according to their previous records, the first group being the best, etc. Then the names of the contestants in each group are drawn from a hat, similar to the first method. Thus if there were ten men in each group, the last man drawn in the first group would race tenth, the first man in the second group would race eleventh, and so on.

The team-draw is that which is used in all competitions

Determine the order of competition in advance

in which there is team scoring. The order in which the individual members of each team are to run is determined previously by their coach, manager, or captain. Then only the names of the teams are drawn, and the competitors' names are placed in their proper position. Thus if there are six teams entered, and team "A" is drawn first, then their men run 1st, 7th, 13th, and 19th, and the men on team "B" run 2nd, 8th, 14th, and 20th, etc.

If there is more than one event in the competition, the skiers nevertheless retain their same numbers and racing order throughout the meet. Thus, if in the cross-country event numbers 2 and 3 are not entered, the man wearing number 4 will be racing second.

STARTING AND TIMING

Types of Timing

There are all sorts of methods used in timing a ski race, methods that have been in use since the beginning of racing and methods just recently developed. Some are very accurate, elaborate, and complicated, and others are extremely simple, and usually inadequate. The most simple of these is known as the gun start. The starter fires a gun at the top of the course as the competitor starts his run. This is heard at the bottom of the course and the timers start their watches at the sound of the gun, and then stop them when the competitor passes the finish.

A more accurate method is used when the start of the race is within view of the bottom. The starter uses a flag which he waves or drops when the contestant starts, and this is recorded at the bottom by the timers. They stop their watches when the racer crosses the finish line.

The method most used today, however, in timing a downhill or slalom race, and even cross-country races, is that of the phone start, where radio or telephone communications are available. (Telephone communications are avail-

Use the most accurate timing procedure available

able at most ski areas for the conducting of races.) The starter's assistant is at the top of the course and relays the start by phone to the timers at the bottom of the course.

Methods of electric timing have been developed and they have proved to be excellent, although sometimes quite costly. Western Union seems to be the leader in this field with a "Sports Timer" that clocks the competitors to one one-hundredth of a second. It starts by the opening of a gate by the competitor himself, and stops automatically as the competitor breaks a string stretched across the finish line.

Specific Duties of the Timing Officials

1. The Starter: It is his duty to see that the competitors leave the start of the race at the proper time and in the proper order. He is the man who gives the commands of 10 seconds, 5, 4, 3, 2, 1, Go! (in the same time intervals) that starts the skier off. These commands must simultaneously be given over the phone so they can reach the finish line, timers, and the racer himself. A good, clear, commanding voice is a great asset to the starter. In the case of flag starts he is also the one who drops the flag. If the starter is not present at the start as in the case of phone starts, the assistant starter performs these duties as directed by the starter over the phone.

2. The Timers: It shall be the duty of the timers to get the time of each racer as he crosses the finish line. A racer shall never be considered to have finished a race until both of his feet have crossed the finish line.

3. The Recorders: There shall be a recorder for each timer and for the starter. It shall be the duty of the recorder to write down the time that the timer reads from his watch as the competitor finishes the race.

The distance and terrain recommend the use of electric timing and telephonic communication

Accuracy and Care of Watches

In timing of a ski race it is of the utmost importance that the watches used are accurate. A watch that behaves normally in a heated room may react in all sorts of ways when exposed to the cold for several hours. Thus it is advisable for all those officials handling watches during a race to keep them as warm as possible. This can be accomplished by keeping the watch in a bare hand, in a wide pocket, or against a heating pad that may be kept in a pocket.

The usual care given watches in other athletic events must also be considered in ski meets.

Issuance of Results

No official times should be issued to the public at the race courses, and if any times are issued it should be emphasized that they are unofficial. The official times should only be issued after the complete results have been tabulated indoors, after all the checkers are in, and after all penalties have been applied.

DISQUALIFICATION

The complete list of disqualifications can best be procured from the *F.I.S. (International Ski Federation) Rule Book* and the National Ski Association *Official Rules for Downhill and Slalom Racing*. Enumerated below are some of the more common ones.

A competitor is disqualified if:

1. Both his feet fail to pass through control gates.
2. He runs the course after it has been officially closed.
3. He fails to appear at the start at the designated time.
4. He descends any part of the course without skis.
5. He replaces any of his equipment with things other than that which he carries (for example, borrowing

Protect the watch

from spectators in the case of losing a ski pole).

6. He toboggans down any part of the trail (that is, sitting on the skis).
7. He holds poles so that they will act as a brake, by placing them between his legs and sitting on them.
8. Uses a different pair of skis for the downhill and slalom in a combined downhill and slalom meet.
9. He alters the course.

NOTES ON SCORING SKI MEETS

Langlauf

It should be the duty of the chief timer to come to headquarters with the cards immediately after the race, and it is desirable that the second timer or his recorder should also come.

The chief timer's card should be the master card, the other being used as a check. As soon as the cards have been compared and the elapsed times properly checked and entered on the master card, the timers should be relieved of duty.

Meantime, two other men should be going over the station checkers' cards noting the number of any man missing a station. This can well be done by one man reading the numbers from the checkers' cards, while the other checks them off on a copy of the printed entry list. Any disqualification resulting must be entered on the master card, with a note of which station or stations he missed.

A frequent source of delay in past years has been in getting the checkers' cards to headquarters after the race. Everybody concerned should know where these cards are to go and be impressed with the need of getting them there at the earliest possible moment.

In case a man is scratched or disqualified, draw a line through his name and everything else clear across the card.

Next pick out the place of each man and enter it in the last column on the master card. *Write it plainly.* Two

Bring in the results promptly

men (scorer and assistant) are required for this if the list runs over onto two cards as is usually the case. It is very easy to overlook someone, so time is saved in the end by doing this carefully the first time. When this is finished, check by counting the number of men to whom places have been given to see that it agrees with the highest number assigned.

While this work has been in progress a competent stenographer has loaded his machine with paper and carbons for four copies. He will type, as the scorer reads them to him from the master card, beginning with the winner, each man's place, name, number, college, and time. For example:

Place	*Name*	*Number*	*College*	*Time*
1	W. Smith	14	Boston U.	1-03-20

The reason for entering a man's number is that it saves a lot of time in checking which will be done by the stenographer reading back to the scorer after the list is complete.

While the list is being read to the typist, another man should be taking down the time of each competitor under the name of his college on a "team score sheet." Times need not be entered on this sheet. As soon as this is complete, he should cross off the slowest time under each college wherever one more time appears than the number of men to score for each team in the event.

After checking, team results should be taken down by the typist.

The scorer should keep *on his person* the original team score sheets, and a copy of the complete results for each event until the meet is over.

Downhill and Slalom

The general procedure in scoring downhill and slalom will be essentially the same as for langlauf, the necessary differences being fairly obvious.

The scoring of jumps is specialized—read the rules

In the slalom there will presumably be only one time card for each run. Corrected times, including penalties for the second run, and total times should be entered on the first run card which will serve as the official record or "master card."

Jump and Combined Event

According to F.I.S. procedure it is the duty of the judges to compute scores for the jump and combined event. The scorer, of course, will offer any assistance desired and take over the final checking and recording of results and computation of team scores. Here again the procedure will be essentially the same as outlined for the langlauf.

Scoring Jumping Competition

The scoring of jumping competititon is a complicated and specialized process. The reader is referred to the official rules for further information on scoring jumping.

Index

(Items pertaining to a particular sport will generally be found under the index entry for that sport.)

A

B

T

U

V